CAREERS AND OCCUPATIONS
LOOKING TO THE FUTURE

D1385264

ISSN 1532-1169

CAREERS AND OCCUPATIONS
LOOKING TO THE FUTURE

Melissa J. Doak

INFORMATION PLUS® REFERENCE SERIES
Formerly Published by Information Plus, Wylie, Texas

GALE
CENGAGE Learning™

Detroit • New York • San Francisco • New Haven, Conn • Waterville, Maine • London

Careers and Occupations: Looking
to the Future

Melissa J. Doak
Paula Kepos, Series Editor

Project Editors: Kathleen J. Edgar, Elizabeth
Manar

Rights Acquisition and Management: Qiana
Gaddie, Kelly Quin, Tim Sisler

Composition: Evi Abou-El-Seoud, Mary Beth
Trimper

Manufacturing: Cynde Bishop

Product Management: Carol Nagel

For product information and technology assistance, contact us at
Gale Customer Support, 1-800-877-4253.
For permission to use material from this text or product,
submit all requests online at **www.cengage.com/permissions.**
Further permissions questions can be e-mailed to
permissionrequest@cengage.com

Gale
27500 Drake Rd.
Farmington Hills, MI 48331-3535

ISBN-13: 978-0-7876-5103-9 (set)   ISBN-10: 0-7876-5103-6 (set)
ISBN-13: 978-1-4144-0746-3   ISBN-10: 1-4144-0746-7

ISSN 1532-1169

This title is also available as an e-book.
ISBN-13: 978-1-4144-3819-1 (set)
ISBN-10: 1-4144-3819-2 (set)
Contact your Gale sales representative for ordering information.

Printed in the United States of America
1 2 3 4 5 6 7 12 11 10 09 08

TABLE OF CONTENTS

PREFACE

Careers and Occupations: Looking to the Future is part of the *Information Plus Reference Series*. The purpose of each volume of the series is to present the latest facts on a topic of pressing concern in modern American life. These topics include today's most controversial and most studied social issues: abortion, capital punishment, care for the elderly, crime, health care, the environment, immigration, minorities, social welfare, women, youth, and many more. Although written especially for the high school and undergraduate student, this series is an excellent resource for anyone in need of factual information on current affairs.

By presenting the facts, it is the intention of Gale, a part of Cengage Learning, to provide its readers with everything they need to reach an informed opinion on current issues. To that end, there is a particular emphasis in this series on the presentation of scientific studies, surveys, and statistics. These data are generally presented in the form of tables, charts, and other graphics placed within the text of each book. Every graphic is directly referred to and carefully explained in the text. The source of each graphic is presented within the graphic itself. The data used in these graphics are drawn from the most reputable and reliable sources, in particular from the various branches of the U.S. government and from major independent polling organizations. Every effort has been made to secure the most recent information available. The reader should bear in mind that many major studies take years to conduct, and that additional years often pass before the data from these studies are made available to the public. Therefore, in many cases the most recent information available in 2008 is dated from 2005 or 2006. Older statistics are sometimes presented as well, if they are of particular interest and no more-recent information exists.

Although statistics are a major focus of the *Information Plus Reference Series*, they are by no means its only content. Each book also presents the widely held positions and important ideas that shape how the book's subject is discussed in the United States. These positions are explained in detail and, where possible, in the words of their proponents. Some of the other material to be found in these books includes: historical background; descriptions of major events related to the subject; relevant laws and court cases; and examples of how these issues play out in American life. Some books also feature primary sources, or have pro and con debate sections giving the words and opinions of prominent Americans on both sides of a controversial topic. All material is presented in an even-handed and unbiased manner; the reader will never be encouraged to accept one view of an issue over another.

HOW TO USE THIS BOOK

Work is a huge part of American life, yet the working world is changing, and at a seemingly ever more rapid pace. Technology is changing the way businesses operate, service industries are replacing traditional manufacturing jobs, businesses are moving from downtown skyscrapers to suburban office parks, and more and more Americans are working from home or as temps rather than in more traditional workplace settings or careers. This book examines all of these trends and more, providing the latest information on what Americans do for a living, how much they earn, how they find work, and what factors influence these key issues.

Careers and Occupations: Looking to the Future consists of nine chapters and three appendixes. Each chapter is devoted to a particular aspect of the American workforce. For a summary of the information covered in each chapter, please see the synopses provided in the Table of Contents at the front of the book. Chapters generally begin with an overview of the basic facts and background information on the chapter's topic, then proceed to examine subtopics of particular interest. For example, Chapter 2: The American Workplace discusses where and when Americans work. It begins with an overview of the twentieth-century shift from a goods-producing economy to one dominated by service industries and covers a number of topics related to current trends affecting the location of work and how much time Americans spend on the job. Included are such issues as productivity, mass layoffs, movement of work overseas, and nonstandard work arrangements, including flexible schedules and work at home. Readers can find their way through a chapter by looking for the section and subsection headings, which are clearly set off from the text. Or, they can refer to the book's extensive index if they already know what they are looking for.

Statistical Information

The tables and figures featured throughout *Careers and Occupations: Looking to the Future* will be of particular use to the reader in learning about this issue. These tables and figures represent an extensive collection of the most recent and important statistics on the American workforce, as well as related issues—for example, graphics in the book cover employment status by age and gender; percent of workers in private industry with access to health-care benefits; median weekly earnings of full-time wage and salary workers; public opinion on job satisfaction; the fastest-growing occupations; and the number of businesses started annually. Gale, a part of Cengage Learning, believes that making this information available to readers is the most important way to fulfill the goal of this book: to help readers understand the issues and controversies surrounding the American workforce and reach their own conclusions.

Each table or figure has a unique identifier appearing above it, for ease of identification and reference. Titles for the tables and figures explain their purpose. At the end of each table or figure, the original source of the data is provided.

In order to help readers understand these often complicated statistics, all tables and figures are explained in the text. References in the text direct the reader to the relevant statistics. Furthermore, the contents of all tables and figures are fully indexed. Please see the opening section of the index at the back of this volume for a description of how to find tables and figures within it.

Appendixes

In addition to the main body text and images, *Careers and Occupations: Looking to the Future* has

three appendixes. The first is the Important Names and Addresses directory. Here readers will find contact information for a number of government and private organizations that can provide further information on aspects of careers and occupations. The second appendix is the Resources section, which can also assist readers in conducting their own research. In this section, the author and editors of *Careers and Occupations: Looking to the Future* describe some of the sources that were most useful during the compilation of this book. The final appendix is the detailed index, which facilitates reader access to specific topics in this book.

ADVISORY BOARD CONTRIBUTIONS

The staff of Information Plus would like to extend its heartfelt appreciation to the Information Plus Advisory Board. This dedicated group of media professionals provides feedback on the series on an ongoing basis. Their comments allow the editorial staff who work on the project to continually make the series better and more user-friendly. Our top priorities are to produce the highest-quality and most useful books possible, and the Advisory Board's contributions to this process are invaluable.

The members of the Information Plus Advisory Board are:

- Kathleen R. Bonn, Librarian, Newbury Park High School, Newbury Park, California

- Madelyn Garner, Librarian, San Jacinto College–North Campus, Houston, Texas

- Anne Oxenrider, Media Specialist, Dundee High School, Dundee, Michigan

- Charles R. Rodgers, Director of Libraries, Pasco-Hernando Community College, Dade City, Florida

- James N. Zitzelsberger, Library Media Department Chairman, Oshkosh West High School, Oshkosh, Wisconsin

COMMENTS AND SUGGESTIONS

The editors of the *Information Plus Reference Series* welcome your feedback on *Careers and Occupations: Looking to the Future*. Please direct all correspondence to:

Editors
Information Plus Reference Series
27500 Drake Rd.
Farmington Hills, MI 48331-3535

CHAPTER 1
TODAY'S LABOR FORCE

The American labor force grew rapidly from 1970 to 2007. This period saw the entry of the post–World War II baby-boom generation into the labor force, an increase in the percentage of women working outside the home, and the addition to the labor force of workers gained through immigration. Statistics from the U.S. Department of Labor's Bureau of Labor Statistics (BLS) show that the number of workers in the American civilian noninstitutionalized labor force (workers not in the army, school, jail, or mental health facilities) almost doubled from 82.8 million men and women in 1970 to 153.1 million men and women in 2007. (See Table 1.1.) These statistics include those who are working part or full time and those who are unemployed but actively looking for jobs. Although the number of workers rose by 85%, the proportion of the civilian noninstitutional population in the labor force rose less. In 1970, 60.4% of the civilian noninstitutional population was in the labor force; by 2007, 66% of the civilian noninstitutional population was in the labor force.

GENDER, AGE, RACE, AND ETHNIC ORIGIN
Gender

In 2007 nearly three-quarters of the male population (73.2%) and three-fifths of the female population (59.3%) aged sixteen years and older participated in the labor force. (See Table 1.2.) The number of men increased from 54.6 million in 1973 to 82.1 million in 2007, a 50.4% increase. Among women in the civilian labor force, however, the increase was more dramatic. In 1973, 34.8 million women were employed or seeking employment, compared with 71 million in 2007, a 104% increase. These numbers reveal a shift in the proportions of women and men in the labor force: 78.8% of men were counted among the civilian labor force in 1973, compared with 73.2% by 2007. At the same time, the percentage of women participating in the labor force increased from 44.7% in 1973 to 59.3% in 2007. In 1973 only 34.8 million of 89.4 million people in the labor force, or 38.9%, were women. By 2007, 46.4% of the labor force was female.

Race and Ethnicity

In 2007 Hispanics had the highest labor force participation rate of all races or ethnicities. In that year, 21.6 million Hispanics were in the labor force, for a labor force participation rate of 68.8%. (See Table 1.3.) Asians had the next highest labor force participation rate in 2007; 7.1 million Asians were in the labor force in that year, for a labor force participation rate of 66.5%. (See Table 1.4.) Whites had a very slightly lower labor force participation rate. In 2007, 124.9 million whites were in the labor force, for a labor force participation rate of 66.4%. African-Americans had the lowest labor force participation rate. In 2007, 17.5 million African-Americans were in the labor force, for a labor force participation rate of 63.7%.

African-American women over twenty years of age (64%) were somewhat more likely to be in the labor force than white women (60.1%), Asian women (60.7%), or Hispanic women (58.8%) of the same age. (See Table 1.4 and Table 1.3.) A somewhat higher percentage of white men twenty years and older (76.3%) were in the labor force compared with African-American men (71.2%). Asian-American men and Hispanic men twenty years of age and over participated in the labor force at the highest rates in 2007 (78.5% and 84.7%, respectively).

While Hispanic men had the highest labor participation rates of any group in 2007, that rate varied by country of origin. Hispanic men age twenty and over from Mexico had the highest labor force participation rate, at 86.4%. (See Table 1.3.) Cuban men and Puerto Rican men also had high labor force participation rates, at 74.2% and 73.2%, respectively, but not as high as Mexican men.

TABLE 1.1

Employment status of the civilian noninstitutional population, selected years, 1950–2007

[Numbers in thousands]

Year	Civilian noninstitutional population	Civilian labor force									Not in labor force
					Employed				Unemployed		
		Total	Percent of population	Total	Percent of population	Agriculture	Nonagricultural industries	Number	Percent of labor force		
				Persons 16 years of age and over							
1950	104,995	62,208	59.2	58,918	56.1	7,160	51,758	3,288	5.3		42,787
1955	109,683	65,023	59.3	62,170	56.7	6,450	55,722	2,852	4.4		44,660
1960*	117,245	69,628	59.4	65,778	56.1	5,458	60,318	3,852	5.5		47,617
1965	126,513	74,455	58.9	71,088	56.2	4,361	66,726	3,366	4.5		52,058
1970	137,085	82,771	60.4	78,678	57.4	3,463	75,215	4,093	4.9		54,315
1975	153,153	93,774	61.2	85,846	56.1	3,408	82,438	7,929	8.5		59,377
1980	167,745	106,940	63.8	99,302	59.2	3,364	95,938	7,637	7.1		60,806
1985	178,206	115,461	64.8	107,150	60.1	3,179	103,971	8,312	7.2		62,744
1990*	189,164	125,840	66.5	118,793	62.8	3,223	115,570	7,047	5.6		63,324
1995	198,584	132,304	66.6	124,900	62.9	3,440	121,460	7,404	5.6		66,280
2000*	212,577	142,583	67.1	136,891	64.4	2,464	134,427	5,692	4.0		69,994
2005*	226,082	149,320	66.0	141,730	62.7	2,197	139,532	7,591	5.1		76,762
2006*	228,815	151,428	66.2	144,427	63.1	2,206	142,221	7,001	4.6		77,387
2007*	231,867	153,124	66.0	146,047	63.0	2,095	143,952	7,078	4.6		78,743

*Not strictly comparable with data for prior years.

SOURCE: Adapted from "1. Employment Status of the Civilian Noninstitutional Population, 1942 to Date," in *Employment and Earnings*, U.S. Department of Labor, Bureau of Labor Statistics, January 2008, http://www.bls.gov/cps/cpsaat1.pdf (accessed February 2, 2008)

TABLE 1.2

Employment status of the population 16 years and over, by sex, selected years, 1973–2007

[Numbers in thousands]

Year	Civilian noninstitutional population	Civilian labor force									Not in labor force
					Employed				Unemployed		
		Total	Percent of population	Total	Percent of population	Agriculture	Nonagricultural industries	Number	Percent of labor force		
Men											
1973*	69,292	54,624	78.8	52,349	75.5	2,847	49,502	2,275	4.2		14,667
1975	72,291	56,299	77.9	51,857	71.7	2,824	49,032	4,442	7.9		15,993
1980	79,398	61,453	77.4	57,186	72.0	2,709	54,477	4,267	6.9		17,945
1985	84,469	64,411	76.3	59,891	70.9	2,535	57,356	4,521	7.0		20,058
1990*	90,377	69,011	76.4	65,104	72.0	2,546	62,559	3,906	5.7		21,367
1995	95,178	71,360	75.0	67,377	70.8	2,559	64,818	3,983	5.6		23,818
2000*	101,964	76,280	74.8	73,305	71.9	1,861	71,444	2,975	3.9		25,684
2005*	109,151	80,033	73.3	75,973	69.6	1,654	74,319	4,059	5.1		29,119
2006*	110,605	81,255	73.5	77,502	70.1	1,663	75,838	3,753	4.6		29,350
2007*	112,173	82,136	73.2	78,254	69.8	1,604	76,650	3,882	4.7		30,036
Women											
1973*	77,804	34,804	44.7	32,715	42.0	622	32,093	2,089	6.0		43,000
1975	80,860	37,475	46.3	33,989	42.0	584	33,404	3,486	9.3		43,386
1980	88,348	45,487	51.5	42,117	47.7	656	41,461	3,370	7.4		42,861
1985	93,736	51,050	54.5	47,259	50.4	644	46,615	3,791	7.4		42,686
1990*	98,787	56,829	57.5	53,689	54.3	678	53,011	3,140	5.5		41,957
1995	103,406	60,944	58.9	57,523	55.6	881	56,642	3,421	5.6		42,462
2000*	110,613	66,303	59.9	63,586	57.5	602	62,983	2,717	4.1		44,310
2005*	116,931	69,288	59.3	65,757	56.2	544	65,213	3,531	5.1		47,643
2006*	118,210	70,173	59.4	66,925	56.6	543	66,382	3,247	4.6		48,037
2007*	119,694	70,988	59.3	67,792	56.6	490	67,302	3,196	4.5		48,707

*Not strictly comparable with data for prior years.

SOURCE: Adapted from "2. Employment Status of the Civilian Noninstitutional Population 16 Years and over by Sex, 1973 to Date," in *Employment and Earnings*, U.S. Department of Labor, Bureau of Labor Statistics, January 2008, http://www.bls.gov/cps/cpsaat2.pdf (accessed February 2, 2008)

TABLE 1.3

Employment status of the Hispanic population, by sex, age, and detailed ethnic group, 2006–07

[Numbers in thousands]

Employment status, sex, and age	Hispanic or Latino ethnicity							
	Total[a]		Mexican origin		Puerto Rican origin		Cuban origin	
	2006	2007	2006	2007	2006	2007	2006	2007
Total								
Civilian noninstitutional population	30,103	31,383	19,036	19,770	2,600	2,711	1,326	1,421
Civilian labor force	20,694	21,602	13,158	13,672	1,599	1,684	807	898
Percent of population	68.7	68.8	69.1	69.2	61.5	62.1	60.9	63.2
Employed	19,613	20,382	12,477	12,908	1,484	1,551	778	862
Unemployed	1,081	1,220	681	764	115	133	29	36
Unemployment rate	5.2	5.6	5.2	5.6	7.2	7.9	3.6	4.0
Not in labor force	9,409	9,781	5,877	6,098	1,001	1,027	519	523
Men, 16 years and over								
Civilian noninstitutional population	15,473	16,154	10,037	10,415	1,208	1,252	646	712
Civilian labor force	12,488	13,005	8,251	8,553	842	865	468	511
Percent of population	80.7	80.5	82.2	82.1	69.7	69.1	72.4	71.7
Employed	11,887	12,310	7,863	8,122	782	791	452	490
Unemployed	601	695	388	431	60	74	16	21
Unemployment rate	4.8	5.3	4.7	5.0	7.2	8.5	3.3	4.1
Not in labor force	2,985	3,149	1,787	1,862	366	387	178	201
Men, 20 years and over								
Civilian noninstitutional population	14,046	14,649	9,086	9,420	1,081	1,119	612	670
Civilian labor force	11,888	12,403	7,833	8,134	797	819	458	497
Percent of population	84.6	84.7	86.2	86.4	73.7	73.2	74.8	74.1
Employed	11,391	11,827	7,515	7,779	749	761	445	478
Unemployed	497	576	318	356	48	58	13	18
Unemployment rate	4.2	4.6	4.1	4.4	6.1	7.1	2.9	3.7
Not in labor force	2,157	2,246	1,253	1,285	284	300	154	173
Women, 16 years and over								
Civilian noninstitutional population	14,630	15,229	8,998	9,355	1,392	1,459	680	709
Civilian labor force	8,206	8,597	4,907	5,119	757	819	339	387
Percent of population	56.1	56.5	54.5	54.7	54.4	56.1	49.9	54.6
Employed	7,725	8,072	4,614	4,786	702	760	326	372
Unemployed	480	525	294	333	55	60	13	15
Unemployment rate	5.9	6.1	6.0	6.5	7.2	7.3	3.9	3.9
Not in labor force	6,424	6,632	4,091	4,236	635	640	340	322
Women, 20 years and over								
Civilian noninstitutional population	13,262	13,791	8,097	8,384	1,267	1,325	634	671
Civilian labor force	7,735	8,108	4,596	4,784	714	770	327	380
Percent of population	58.3	58.8	56.8	57.1	56.4	58.1	51.6	56.6
Employed	7,321	7,662	4,351	4,508	666	720	315	366
Unemployed	414	446	246	276	48	50	12	14
Unemployment rate	5.3	5.5	5.3	5.8	6.8	6.5	3.7	3.7
Not in labor force	5,527	5,682	3,501	3,600	553	555	307	291
Both sexes, 16 to 19 years								
Civilian noninstitutional population	2,796	2,944	1,853	1,967	252	267	79	80
Civilian labor force	1,071	1,091	729	753	88	95	21	21
Percent of population	38.3	37.1	39.3	38.3	34.9	35.5	26.7	26.6
Employed	900	894	611	621	70	69	18	18
Unemployed	170	197	118	132	18	25	3	4
Unemployment rate	15.9	18.1	16.2	17.6	20.9	26.8	[b]	[b]
Not in labor force	1,725	1,853	1,124	1,213	164	172	58	59

[a]Includes persons of Central or South American origin and of other Hispanic or Latino ethnicity, not shown separately.
[b]Data not shown where base is less than 35,000.
Note: Persons whose ethnicity is identified as Hispanic or Latino may be of any race. Updated population controls are introduced annually with the release of January data.

SOURCE: "6. Employment Status of the Hispanic or Latino Population by Sex, Age, and Detailed Ethnic Group," in *Employment and Earnings*, U.S. Department of Labor, Bureau of Labor Statistics, January 2008, http://www.bls.gov/cps/cpsaat6.pdf (accessed February 2, 2008).

Age

The BLS reported in *Employment and Earnings* (January 2008, http://www.bls.gov/cps/cpsa2007.pdf) that Americans between the ages of twenty-five and fifty-four were the most likely age group to be working or looking for work in 2007, with 90.9% of men and 75.4% of women in that age group counted among the labor force. As people aged, their labor force participation rates dropped. Among fifty-five- to sixty-four-year-olds, only 69.6% of men and 58.3% of women were in the labor force. Among those age sixty-five and older, only 20.5% of men and 12.6% of women continued to participate in the labor force.

TABLE 1.4

Employment status of the population, by sex, age, and race, 2006–07

[Numbers in thousands]

Employment status, sex, and age	Total		White		Black or African American		Asian	
	2006	2007	2006	2007	2006	2007	2006	2007
Total								
Civilian noninstitutional population	228,815	231,867	186,264	188,253	27,007	27,485	10,155	10,633
Civilian labor force	151,428	153,124	123,834	124,935	17,314	17,496	6,727	7,067
Percent of population	66.2	66.0	66.5	66.4	64.1	63.7	66.2	66.5
Employed	144,427	146,047	118,833	119,792	15,765	16,051	6,522	6,839
Unemployed	7,001	7,078	5,002	5,143	1,549	1,445	205	229
Unemployment rate	4.6	4.6	4.0	4.1	8.9	8.3	3.0	3.2
Not in labor force	77,387	78,743	62,429	63,319	9,693	9,989	3,427	3,566
Men, 16 years and over								
Civilian noninstitutional population	110,605	112,173	91,021	92,073	12,130	12,361	4,827	5,052
Civilian labor force	81,255	82,136	67,613	68,158	8,128	8,252	3,621	3,796
Percent of population	73.5	73.2	74.3	74.0	67.0	66.8	75.0	75.1
Employed	77,502	78,254	64,883	65,289	7,354	7,500	3,511	3,677
Unemployed	3,753	3,882	2,730	2,869	774	752	110	119
Unemployment rate	4.6	4.7	4.0	4.2	9.5	9.1	3.0	3.1
Not in labor force	29,350	30,036	23,408	23,915	4,002	4,110	1,206	1,256
Men, 20 years and over								
Civilian noninstitutional population	102,145	103,555	84,466	85,420	10,864	11,057	4,515	4,737
Civilian labor force	77,562	78,596	64,540	65,214	7,720	7,867	3,535	3,718
Percent of population	75.9	75.9	76.4	76.3	71.1	71.2	78.3	78.5
Employed	74,431	75,337	62,259	62,806	7,079	7,245	3,437	3,608
Unemployed	3,131	3,259	2,281	2,408	640	622	98	110
Unemployment rate	4.0	4.1	3.5	3.7	8.3	7.9	2.8	3.0
Not in labor force	24,584	24,959	19,927	20,206	3,144	3,189	980	1,019
Women, 16 years and over								
Civilian noninstitutional population	118,210	119,694	95,242	96,180	14,877	15,124	5,328	5,581
Civilian labor force	70,173	70,988	56,221	56,777	9,186	9,244	3,106	3,271
Percent of population	59.4	59.3	59.0	59.0	61.7	61.1	58.3	58.6
Employed	66,925	67,792	53,950	54,503	8,410	8,551	3,011	3,162
Unemployed	3,247	3,196	2,271	2,274	775	693	95	110
Unemployment rate	4.6	4.5	4.0	4.0	8.4	7.5	3.1	3.4
Not in labor force	48,037	48,707	39,021	39,403	5,691	5,879	2,222	2,310
Women, 20 years and over								
Civilian noninstitutional population	109,992	111,330	88,942	89,790	13,578	13,788	5,027	5,265
Civilian labor force	66,585	67,516	53,286	53,925	8,723	8,828	3,038	3,194
Percent of population	60.5	60.6	59.9	60.1	64.2	64.0	60.4	60.7
Employed	63,834	64,799	51,359	51,996	8,068	8,240	2,953	3,096
Unemployed	2,751	2,718	1,927	1,930	656	588	85	99
Unemployment rate	4.1	4.0	3.6	3.6	7.5	6.7	2.8	3.1
Not in labor force	43,407	43,814	35,656	35,864	4,854	4,960	1,989	2,071
Both sexes, 16 to 19 years								
Civilian noninstitutional population	16,678	16,982	12,856	13,043	2,565	2,640	613	631
Civilian labor force	7,281	7,012	6,009	5,795	871	801	154	155
Percent of population	43.7	41.3	46.7	44.4	34.0	30.3	25.1	24.5
Employed	6,162	5,911	5,215	4,990	618	566	132	135
Unemployed	1,119	1,101	794	805	253	235	22	20
Unemployment rate	15.4	15.7	13.2	13.9	29.1	29.4	14.0	12.7
Not in labor force	9,397	9,970	6,847	7,248	1,694	1,839	459	476

Note: Estimates for the above race groups will not sum to totals because data are not presented for all races. Updated population controls are introduced annually with the release of January data.

SOURCE: "5. Employment Status of the Civilian Noninstitutional Population by Sex, Age, and Race," in *Employment and Earnings*, U.S. Department of Labor, Bureau of Labor Statistics, January 2008, http://www.bls.gov/cps/cpsaat5.pdf (accessed February 2, 2008)

According to the BLS in *Employment and Earnings*, unemployment in 2007 was highest among the youngest workers, with those aged sixteen to nineteen experiencing an unemployment rate of 15.7%. The low unemployment rate among those aged fifty-five to sixty-four in 2007 (3.1%), compared with the national average of 4.6% for all workers aged sixteen and over, likely indicates that many of the older workers who had lost their jobs had retired and were no longer in the labor force. Historically, the exit of older workers from the workforce is the result of various reasons, ranging from disability to a genuine desire to retire. For some people, however, leaving the workforce is not a voluntary act. Elimination of middle management positions and other cost-cutting efforts can disproportionately affect older workers, who generally earn more than younger workers with less experience.

TABLE 1.5

Labor force status of persons aged 16 to 24 years old by school enrollment, educational attainment, sex, race, and Hispanic ethnicity, October 2006

[Numbers in thousands]

Characteristic	Civilian noninstitutional population	Civilian labor force						Not in labor force
		Total	Percent of population	Employed		Unemployed		
				Total	Percent of population	Number	Rate	
Total, 16 to 24 years	37,047	22,300	60.2	20,016	54.0	2,285	10.2	14,746
Enrolled in school	20,797	9,001	43.3	8,204	39.4	797	8.9	11,796
Enrolled in high school[a]	10,315	3,235	31.4	2,767	26.8	468	14.5	7,080
Men	5,283	1,587	30.0	1,343	25.4	244	15.4	3,696
Women	5,032	1,648	32.7	1,424	28.3	224	13.6	3,384
White	7,807	2,639	33.8	2,318	29.7	321	12.2	5,168
Black or African American	1,724	419	24.3	321	18.6	99	23.5	1,305
Asian	341	55	16.1	48	14.0	7	[b]	286
Hispanic or Latino ethnicity	1,720	342	19.9	276	16.1	66	19.3	1,377
Enrolled in college	10,482	5,766	55.0	5,437	51.9	329	5.7	4,716
Enrolled in 2-year college	2,705	1,753	64.8	1,636	60.5	117	6.7	952
Enrolled in 4-year college	7,777	4,013	51.6	3,801	48.9	212	5.3	3,764
Full-time students	8,869	4,382	49.4	4,129	46.6	253	5.8	4,487
Part-time students	1,613	1,384	85.8	1,308	81.1	75	5.4	230
Men	4,859	2,586	53.2	2,424	49.9	163	6.3	2,273
Women	5,623	3,179	56.5	3,013	53.6	166	5.2	2,444
White	8,190	4,650	56.8	4,405	53.8	245	5.3	3,540
Black or African American	1,303	635	48.7	564	43.2	71	11.2	669
Asian	670	282	42.1	279	41.7	3	0.9	388
Hispanic or Latino ethnicity	1,198	717	59.8	678	56.6	39	5.4	481
Not enrolled in school	16,250	13,299	81.8	11,811	72.7	1,488	11.2	2,950
16 to 19 years	3,074	2,238	72.8	1,798	58.5	440	19.6	836
20 to 24 years	13,176	11,061	84.0	10,013	76.0	1,048	9.5	2,114
Men	8,564	7,530	87.9	6,692	78.1	838	11.1	1,034
Less than a high school diploma	1,925	1,528	79.4	1,335	69.4	193	12.6	397
High school graduates, no college[c]	4,008	3,531	88.1	3,079	76.8	452	12.8	477
Some college or associate degree	1,674	1,567	93.7	1,444	86.3	124	7.9	106
Bachelor's degree and higher[d]	958	903	94.3	834	87.1	69	7.6	55
Women	7,686	5,769	75.1	5,119	66.6	650	11.3	1,916
Less than a high school diploma	1,506	796	52.9	590	39.2	206	25.9	709
High school graduates, no college[c]	3,147	2,295	72.9	2,008	63.8	287	12.5	852
Some college or associate degree	1,903	1,626	85.5	1,522	80.0	105	6.4	276
Bachelor's degree and higher[d]	1,130	1,052	93.0	999	88.4	53	5.0	79
White	12,769	10,636	83.3	9,643	75.5	993	9.3	2,133
Black or African American	2,418	1,866	77.2	1,447	59.9	418	22.4	552
Asian	455	340	74.6	316	69.4	23	6.9	116
Hispanic or Latino ethnicity	3,518	2,742	77.9	2,506	71.2	236	8.6	776

[a]Includes a small number of persons enrolled in grades below high school.
[b]Data not shown where base is less than 75,000.
[c]Includes persons with a high school diploma or equivalent.
[d]Includes persons with a bachelor's, master's, professional, and doctoral degrees.
Note: Detail for the above race groups (white, black or African American, and Asian) do not sum to totals because data are not presented for all races. In addition, persons whose ethnicity is identified as Hispanic or Latino may be of any race and, therefore, are classified by ethnicity as well as by race. Because of rounding, sums of individual items may not equal totals. Data reflect revised population controls for the Current Population Survey introduced in January 2006.

SOURCE: "Table 2. Labor Force Status of Persons 16 to 24 Years Old by School Enrollment, Educational Attainment, Sex, Race, and Hispanic or Latino Ethnicity, October 2006," in *College Enrollment and Work Activity of 2006 High School Graduates*, U.S. Department of Labor, Bureau of Labor Statistics, April 26, 2007, http://www.bls.gov/news.release/pdf/hsgec.pdf (accessed February 2, 2008)

STUDENT WORKERS. In 2006 approximately 43.3% of American students ages sixteen to twenty-four were employed while enrolled in school. (See Table 1.5.) College students had a higher labor force participation rate than did high school students (55% and 31.4%, respectively). Non-Hispanic white students were more likely than any other group to work while enrolled in high school, while Hispanic students were more likely to work than any other group while enrolled in college.

EDUCATION

As educational attainment increases, so does the likelihood that a person will be part of the labor force. The unemployment rate also is lower for more educated individuals. Among people age twenty-five and over in 2007, those with a bachelor's degree or higher had the highest labor force participation (77.8%) and the lowest unemployment rate (2%). (See Table 1.6.) On the other hand, those with less than a high school diploma had a labor

TABLE 1.6

Employment status of the population aged 25 years and over, by educational attainment, sex, race and Hispanic ethnicity, 2006–07

[Numbers in thousands]

Employment status, sex, race, and Hispanic or Latino ethnicity	Less than a high school diploma		High school graduates, no college[a]		Some college or associate degree						Bachelor's degree and higher[b]	
					Total		Some college, no degree		Associate degree			
	2006	2007	2006	2007	2006	2007	2006	2007	2006	2007	2006	2007
Total												
Civilian noninstitutional population	27,541	26,633	60,748	61,373	49,011	49,831	32,069	32,853	16,942	16,978	54,571	56,620
Civilian labor force	12,758	12,408	38,354	38,539	35,410	35,887	22,504	22,958	12,906	12,928	42,512	44,074
Percent of population	46.3	46.6	63.1	62.8	72.2	72.0	70.2	69.9	76.2	76.1	77.9	77.8
Employed	11,892	11,521	36,702	36,857	34,143	34,612	21,630	22,076	12,514	12,535	41,649	43,182
Employment-population ratio	43.2	43.3	60.4	60.1	69.7	69.5	67.4	67.2	73.9	73.8	76.3	76.3
Unemployed	866	886	1,652	1,682	1,267	1,275	874	882	393	393	863	892
Unemployment rate	6.8	7.1	4.3	4.4	3.6	3.6	3.9	3.8	3.0	3.0	2.0	2.0
Men												
Civilian noninstitutional population	13,565	13,249	28,995	29,232	22,137	22,690	14,879	15,337	7,258	7,353	27,258	28,094
Civilian labor force	8,112	7,974	21,260	21,385	17,520	17,853	11,507	11,810	6,013	6,043	22,554	23,289
Percent of population	59.8	60.2	73.3	73.2	79.1	78.7	77.3	77.0	82.8	82.2	82.7	82.9
Employed	7,614	7,450	20,345	20,434	16,945	17,243	11,110	11,382	5,835	5,862	22,114	22,835
Employment-population ratio	56.1	56.2	70.2	69.9	76.5	76.0	74.7	74.2	80.4	79.7	81.1	81.3
Unemployed	498	523	914	951	575	610	397	429	177	181	440	454
Unemployment rate	6.1	6.6	4.3	4.4	3.3	3.4	3.5	3.6	3.0	3.0	1.9	1.9
Women												
Civilian noninstitutional population	13,976	13,385	31,754	32,141	26,874	27,141	17,189	17,516	9,684	9,625	27,314	28,527
Civilian labor force	4,646	4,434	17,094	17,154	17,890	18,034	10,996	11,148	6,893	6,886	19,958	20,784
Percent of population	33.2	33.1	53.8	53.4	66.6	66.4	64.0	63.6	71.2	71.5	73.1	72.9
Employed	4,278	4,071	16,357	16,423	17,198	17,368	10,520	10,695	6,678	6,674	19,535	20,346
Employment-population ratio	30.6	30.4	51.5	51.1	64.0	64.0	61.2	61.1	69.0	69.3	71.5	71.3
Unemployed	368	363	737	731	692	666	477	454	215	212	423	438
Unemployment rate	7.9	8.2	4.3	4.3	3.9	3.7	4.3	4.1	3.1	3.1	2.1	2.1
White												
Civilian noninstitutional population	21,781	21,102	50,171	50,340	40,396	41,007	26,281	26,927	14,115	14,080	45,213	46,815
Civilian labor force	10,331	10,106	31,351	31,354	28,973	29,287	18,254	18,578	10,719	10,709	35,043	36,215
Percent of population	47.4	47.9	62.5	62.3	71.7	71.4	69.5	69.0	75.9	76.1	77.5	77.4
Employed	9,720	9,446	30,188	30,140	28,056	28,355	17,632	17,936	10,424	10,419	34,357	35,535
Employment-population ratio	44.6	44.8	60.2	59.9	69.5	69.1	67.1	66.6	73.9	74.0	76.0	75.9
Unemployed	611	660	1,162	1,214	917	932	622	642	295	290	686	681
Unemployment rate	5.9	6.5	3.7	3.9	3.2	3.2	3.4	3.5	2.8	2.7	2.0	1.9
Black or African American												
Civilian noninstitutional population	3,975	3,761	7,638	7,884	5,889	6,041	4,075	4,160	1,814	1,881	4,089	4,268
Civilian labor force	1,593	1,470	5,105	5,158	4,428	4,552	3,015	3,093	1,413	1,459	3,356	3,540
Percent of population	40.1	39.1	66.8	65.4	75.2	75.3	74.0	74.4	77.9	77.6	82.1	83.0
Employed	1,389	1,293	4,697	4,783	4,154	4,300	2,816	2,912	1,338	1,389	3,263	3,435
Employment-population ratio	34.9	34.4	61.5	60.7	70.5	71.2	69.1	70.0	73.7	73.8	79.8	80.5
Unemployed	204	177	408	375	274	252	199	181	75	70	93	106
Unemployment rate	12.8	12.0	8.0	7.3	6.2	5.5	6.6	5.9	5.3	4.8	2.8	3.0
Asian												
Civilian noninstitutional population	1,026	999	1,718	1,858	1,439	1,502	847	893	592	609	4,496	4,750
Civilian labor force	455	437	1,079	1,174	1,045	1,088	595	647	450	441	3,486	3,679
Percent of population	44.4	43.8	62.8	63.2	72.6	72.5	70.2	72.5	76.0	72.5	77.5	77.5
Employed	438	425	1,046	1,136	1,012	1,048	573	624	439	423	3,414	3,592
Employment-population ratio	42.7	42.5	60.9	61.1	70.3	69.8	67.7	69.9	74.2	69.5	75.9	75.6
Unemployed	17	13	33	38	32	41	22	23	11	18	72	88
Unemployment rate	3.8	2.9	3.1	3.2	3.1	3.7	3.7	3.5	2.4	4.0	2.1	2.4

force participation rate of only 46.6% and an unemployment rate of 7.1%.

The relationship between education and labor force participation held true for men as well as for women. Men age twenty-five and older with a four-year college degree had a labor force participation rate of 82.9%; men with less than a high school diploma had only a 60.2% participation rate. (See Table 1.6.) College-educated women had a labor force participation rate of 72.9%, while women with less than a high school diploma participated in the labor force at a rate of only 33.1%.

TABLE 1.6

Employment status of the population aged 25 years and over, by educational attainment, sex, race and Hispanic ethnicity, 2006–07

[CONTINUED]

[Numbers in thousands]

| Employment status, sex, race, and Hispanic or Latino ethnicity | Less than a high school diploma | | High school graduates, no college[a] | | Some college or associate degree | | | | | | Bachelor's degree and higher[b] | |
| | | | | | Total | | Some college, no degree | | Associate degree | | | |
	2006	2007	2006	2007	2006	2007	2006	2007	2006	2007	2006	2007
Hispanic or Latino ethnicity												
Civilian noninstitutional population	9,519	9,643	6,738	7,191	4,396	4,665	2,998	3,176	1,398	1,489	3,051	3,292
Civilian labor force	5,948	6,040	5,008	5,344	3,502	3,692	2,374	2,490	1,128	1,201	2,484	2,707
Percent of population	62.5	62.6	74.3	74.3	79.7	79.1	79.2	78.4	80.7	80.7	81.4	82.2
Employed	5,620	5,677	4,801	5,110	3,377	3,542	2,282	2,382	1,095	1,160	2,428	2,644
Employment-population ratio	59.0	58.9	71.3	71.1	76.8	75.9	76.1	75.0	78.3	77.9	79.6	80.3
Unemployed	328	363	207	234	125	150	92	108	33	41	56	63
Unemployment rate	5.5	6.0	4.1	4.4	3.6	4.1	3.9	4.4	2.9	3.5	2.2	2.3

[a]Includes persons with a high school diploma or equivalent.
[b]Includes persons with bachelor's, master's, professional, and doctoral degrees.
Note: Estimates for the above race groups (white, black or African American, and Asian) do not sum to totals because data are not presented for all races. Persons whose ethnicity is identified as Hispanic or Latino may be of any race. Updated population controls are introduced annually with the release of January data.

SOURCE: "7. Employment Status of the Civilian Noninstitutional Population 25 Years and over by Educational Attainment, Sex, Race, and Hispanic or Latino Ethnicity," in *Employment and Earnings*, U.S. Department of Labor, Bureau of Labor Statistics, January 2008, http://www.bls.gov/cps/cpsaat7.pdf (accessed February 2, 2008)

The relationship also held true for all races and ethnic groups. Among all adults age twenty-five and older with a bachelor's degree, African-Americans were the most likely to be counted among the civilian labor force (83%), followed by Hispanics (82.2%), Asians (77.5%), and non-Hispanic whites (77.4%). (See Table 1.6.) African-Americans with a college education were, however, more likely to be unemployed (3%) than Asians (2.4%), Hispanics (2.3%) or non-Hispanic whites (1.9%) with comparable education. This discrepancy hints at the subtle racial discrimination that some African-American and Hispanic people face when trying to find employment.

FAMILIES

According to the BLS in *Employment Characteristics of Families in 2006* (May 9, 2007, http://www.bls.gov/news.release/pdf/famee.pdf), 82.4% of the nation's seventy-seven million families had at least one person working in 2006. Asian families were the most likely to include an employed member (89.9%), followed by Hispanic (87.2%), white (82.7%), and African-American families (78.1%). These data include families that may have members who are beyond the generally accepted working age.

Employment Characteristics of Families in 2006 also revealed that about 4.9 million American families (about 6.4% of all families) had at least one person who was unemployed in 2006. Overall, 69.6% of families that included an unemployed person also contained at least one working family member. White and Asian families

were considerably less likely to have an unemployed person (5.6% and 5.2%, respectively) than were African-American (11.4%) or Hispanic (8%) families.

The BLS further reported that both spouses were employed in about half (51.8%) of the nation's 57.5 million married-couple families in 2006. (See Table 1.7.) That year, there were about 11.4 million married-couple families (19.8%) in which only the husband was employed outside the house, a slight decrease from the 11.6 million such families in 2005. In nearly 3.8 million married-couple families (6.5%), only the wife worked in 2006, approximately the same percentage as the previous year. More than 9.3 million married-couple families (16.2%) included no working members, although many in this group were retirees.

Family structure affected employment of family members. In 2006 the likelihood of having an employed family member was greatest for families maintained by men with no spouse present (84.9%). (See Table 1.7.) Married-couple families were almost as likely to have an employed member (83.8%). Families maintained by women were least likely to have an employed family member (76%).

Whether any family members were unemployed also varied by type of household, with married-couple households being least likely to contain an unemployed member. Of 5.3 million families maintained by men in 2006 (shown in Table 1.7), 516,000 contained an unemployed member (9.7%). (See Table 1.8.) Of 14.2 million families maintained by women, 1.4 million contained an

TABLE 1.7

Families by presence and relationship of employed members and family type, 2005–06

[Numbers in thousands]

Characteristic	Number		Percent distribution	
	2005	2006	2005	2006
Married-couple families				
Total	57,167	57,509	100.0	100.0
Member(s) employed, total	47,895	48,196	83.8	83.8
Husband only	11,562	11,399	20.2	19.8
Wife only	3,715	3,754	6.5	6.5
Husband and wife	29,330	29,799	51.3	51.8
Other employment combinations	3,288	3,244	5.8	5.6
No member(s) employed	9,272	9,313	16.2	16.2
Families maintained by women*				
Total	14,035	14,208	100.0	100.0
Member(s) employed, total	10,609	10,796	75.6	76.0
Householder only	6,052	6,103	43.1	43.0
Householder and other member(s)	2,830	2,955	20.2	20.8
Other member(s), not householder	1,727	1,738	12.3	12.2
No member(s) employed	3,426	3,412	24.4	24.0
Families maintained by men*				
Total	5,242	5,300	100.0	100.0
Member(s) employed, total	4,430	4,500	84.5	84.9
Householder only	2,093	2,089	39.9	39.4
Householder and other member(s)	1,639	1,715	31.3	32.4
Other member(s), not householder	698	696	13.3	13.1
No member(s) employed	812	800	15.5	15.1

*No spouse present.
Note: Detail may not sum to totals due to rounding. Data for 2006 reflect revised population controls used in the Current Population Survey.

SOURCE: "Table 2. Families by Presence and Relationship of Employed Members and Family Type, 2005–06 Annual Averages," in *Employment Characteristics of Families in 2006*, U.S. Department of Labor, Bureau of Labor Statistics, May 9, 2007, http://www.bls.gov/news.release/pdf/famee.pdf (accessed February 6, 2008)

unemployed member (10.1%). Of 57.5 million married-couple families, only three million contained an unemployed member (5.2%).

About eight of ten married-couple families (82.3%) with an unemployed member also contained at least one employed family member in 2006. (See Table 1.8.) In contrast, among families experiencing unemployment in 2006, only 58.3% of families that were headed by a single man also included an employed person. Among households with unemployed members headed by single women, only 47.3% also included an employed person. Families maintained by single people experience greater hardship when unemployment hits.

Families with Children

According to the BLS in *Employment Characteristics of Families in 2006*, both parents were employed in 62% of married-couple families with children under eighteen years old in 2006. In 30.5% of married-couple families, the father, but not the mother, was employed; in only 4.8% of married-couple families, the mother, but not the father, was employed. The proportion of married-couple families in which the father, but not the mother, was employed was much higher among families with pre-school children (under six years of age) than it was in families whose youngest child was six to seventeen years old (38% and 24.3%, respectively).

The BLS also reports in *Employment Characteristics of Families in 2006* that in 2006 higher proportions of single mothers worked than married mothers, while slightly lower proportions of single fathers worked than married fathers. In single-mother families, 72% of mothers worked, compared with 66.8% of mothers in married-couple families. In single-father families, 83.5% of fathers worked, compared with 92.5% of married fathers. In single-mother families, higher proportions of mothers without children under age six worked than did mothers of children with preschool-age children. The age of children had little effect, however, on whether or not single fathers worked.

The unemployment rate of mothers varied by age of children and marital status. In 2006 the unemployment rate of married mothers with children under eighteen years old was 3.1%, compared with an 8.5% rate for unmarried mothers. (Table 1.9.) The unemployment rate for mothers with preschool children (6%) was higher than the rate for mothers whose youngest child was of school age (4.1%).

TABLE 1.8

Unemployment in families by presence and relationship of employed members and family type, 2005–06

[Numbers in thousands]

Characteristic	Number		Percent distribution	
	2005	2006	2005	2006
Married-couple families				
With unemployed member(s), total	3,243	2,968	100.0	100.0
No member employed	580	526	17.9	17.7
Some member(s) employed	2,664	2,442	82.1	82.3
Husband unemployed	1,190	1,061	36.7	35.7
Wife employed	753	679	23.2	22.9
Wife unemployed	1,004	898	31.0	30.3
Husband employed	873	772	26.9	26.0
Other family member unemployed	1,049	1,010	32.4	34.0
Families maintained by women*				
With unemployed member(s), total	1,539	1,429	100.0	100.0
No member employed	797	753	51.8	52.7
Some member(s) employed	743	675	48.2	47.3
Householder unemployed	746	688	48.5	48.2
Other member(s) employed	161	132	10.5	9.3
Other member(s) unemployed	793	740	51.5	51.8
Families maintained by men*				
With unemployed member(s), total	536	516	100.0	100.0
No member employed	225	215	42.1	41.7
Some member(s) employed	310	301	57.9	58.3
Householder unemployed	301	284	56.1	55.0
Other member(s) employed	122	118	22.8	22.8
Other member(s) unemployed	235	232	43.9	45.0

*No spouse present.
Note: Detail may not sum to totals due to rounding. Data for 2006 reflect revised population controls used in the Current Population Survey.

SOURCE: "Table 3. Unemployment in Families by Presence and Relationship of Employed Members and Family Type, 2005–06 Annual Averages," in *Employment Characteristics of Families in 2006*, U.S. Department of Labor, Bureau of Labor Statistics, May 9, 2007, http://www.bls.gov/news.release/pdf/famee.pdf (accessed February 6, 2008)

In 2006 more than half (56.1%) of all mothers with a child under one year old were in the labor force. (See Table 1.10.) This proportion rose among mothers with children two years of age (64.5%). Most mothers of children under three years old worked in 2006, but unmarried, divorced, separated, and widowed mothers with young children were more likely to be in the labor force (65.7%) than were married mothers with children the same age (58.2%). This most likely occurs because single women had fewer financial resources that would allow them to remain out of the labor force than did married women.

Unmarried mothers of children under three years old also experienced higher rates of unemployment than their married counterparts. The unemployment rate for single mothers of children under three years old in 2006 was 13.6%, compared with 3.5% among mothers who were married and had children under age three. (See Table 1.10.) The unemployment rate among single mothers of children under one year old was 16.7%, compared with just 3.9% for married mothers with children the same age.

EMPLOYMENT BY INDUSTRY

One way to look at employment figures is by industry. All employees who work in each industry sector are counted. Industry sectors include goods-producing industries—such as natural resources and mining, construction, and manufacturing—and service-providing industries—such as trade, transportation, and utilities (including wholesale and retail trade), information services, financial services, professional and business services, education and health services, leisure and hospitality, other services, and government. People with the same occupation may work in different industries. For example, an accountant may work in a manufacturing plant, be employed in a tax-preparation office, hold a government job, or teach in a university, and therefore be part of the manufacturing industry, the financial services industry, the government, or the education and health services industry. Wages and working conditions are often tied to the industry in which one works.

According to figures released by the BLS in *The Employment Situation: February 2008* (March 7, 2008, http://www.bls.gov/news.release/pdf/empsit.pdf), there were an estimated 138 million Americans working in private, nonfarm industries, including nearly 21.8 million workers in the goods-producing sector, in February 2008. Approximately 13.7 million of those in the goods-producing industry worked in manufacturing. Nearly two-thirds of manufacturing workers (8.7 million; 63.4%) produced durable

TABLE 1.9

Employment status of the population, by sex, marital status, and presence and age of own children under 18 years old, 2006

[Numbers in thousands]

Characteristic	2006		
	Total	Men	Women
With own children under 18 years			
Civilian noninstitutional population	64,680	28,188	36,492
Civilian labor force	52,391	26,530	25,861
Participation rate	81.0	94.1	70.9
Employed	50,388	25,774	24,614
Employment-population ratio	77.9	91.4	67.4
Full-time workers[a]	43,485	24,884	18,601
Part-time workers[b]	6,902	890	6,013
Unemployed	2,004	756	1,247
Unemployment rate	3.8	2.9	4.8
Married, spouse present			
Civilian noninstitutional population	51,670	25,648	26,022
Civilian labor force	42,136	24,295	17,842
Participation rate	81.5	94.7	68.6
Employed	40,960	23,680	17,280
Employment-population ratio	79.3	92.3	66.4
Full-time workers[a]	35,500	22,925	12,575
Part-time workers[b]	5,460	755	4,705
Unemployed	1,176	614	562
Unemployment rate	2.8	2.5	3.1
Other marital status[c]			
Civilian noninstitutional population	13,010	2,541	10,470
Civilian labor force	10,255	2,236	8,019
Participation rate	78.8	88.0	76.6
Employed	9,427	2,094	7,333
Employment-population ratio	72.5	82.4	70.0
Full-time workers[a]	7,985	1,960	6,026
Part-time workers[b]	1,442	134	1,308
Unemployed	827	142	686
Unemployment rate	8.1	6.3	8.5
With own children 6 to 17 years, none younger			
Civilian noninstitutional population	35,912	15,594	20,318
Civilian labor force	30,100	14,515	15,585
Participation rate	83.8	93.1	76.7
Employed	29,076	14,124	14,952
Employment-population ratio	81.0	90.6	73.6
Full-time workers[a]	25,277	13,648	11,629
Part-time workers[b]	3,799	476	3,323
Unemployed	1,024	392	632
Unemployment rate	3.4	2.7	4.1
With own children under 6 years			
Civilian noninstitutional population	28,768	12,594	16,174
Civilian labor force	22,291	12,015	10,276
Participation rate	77.5	95.4	63.5
Employed	21,311	11,650	9,661
Employment-population ratio	74.1	92.5	59.7
Full-time workers[a]	18,208	11,236	6,972
Part-time workers[b]	3,103	414	2,689
Unemployed	980	365	615
Unemployment rate	4.4	3.0	6.0

goods; the rest (8.7 million, or 36.6%) produced nondurable goods.

BLS data also shows that in February 2008 approximately 116.1 million people were employed in service-providing industries, with about 93.7 million of them employed in the private sector. These figures included 15.4 million people who worked in retail trade; 4.5 million people who worked in transportation and warehousing; 556,500 people who worked in utilities; 3 million people who worked in information services; 8.2 million people who worked in

TABLE 1.9

Employment status of the population, by sex, marital status, and presence and age of own children under 18 years old, 2006
[CONTINUED]

[Numbers in thousands]

Characteristic	2006		
	Total	Men	Women
With no own children under 18 years			
Civilian noninstitutional population	162,438	80,719	81,718
Civilian labor force	97,427	53,115	44,312
Participation rate	60.0	65.8	54.2
Employed	92,460	50,148	42,312
Employment-population ratio	56.9	62.1	51.8
Full-time workers[a]	74,638	42,859	31,780
Part-time workers[b]	17,821	7,289	10,532
Uneamployed	4,967	2,967	2,000
Unemployment rate	5.1	5.6	4.5

[a]Usually work 35 hours or more a week at all jobs.
[b]Usually work less than 35 hours a week at all jobs.
[c]Includes never-married, divorced, separated, and widowed persons.
Note: Own children include sons, daughters, step-children, and adopted children. Not included are nieces, nephews, grandchildren, and other related and unrelated children. Detail may not sum to totals due to rounding. Data for 2006 reflect revised population controls used in the Current Population Survey.

SOURCE: Adapted from "Table 5. Employment Status of the Population by Sex, Marital Status, and Presence and Age of Own Children under 18, 2005–06 Annual Averages," in *Employment Characteristics of Families in 2006*, U.S. Department of Labor, Bureau of Labor Statistics, May 9, 2007, http://www.bls.gov/news.release/pdf/famee.pdf (accessed February 6, 2008)

the financial sector; 18.1 million people who worked in professional and business services; 18.7 million people in education and health services; 13.7 million people in leisure and hospitality; and 5.5 million people in other services. In addition, 22.4 million people worked for the federal, state, or local government in the public sector.

EMPLOYMENT BY OCCUPATION

On the other hand, workers may be counted by occupational group. For example, whether nurses work in schools, large manufacturing plants, or in doctors' offices, they need the same training and perform similar work, even though they work in different industries. The BLS breaks down occupations into several broad categories. Management, professional, and related occupations include such jobs as teachers, physicians, managers, and lawyers. Service occupations include jobs such as nurse's aides, police and firefighters, cafeteria workers, and hairdressers. Sales and office occupations include jobs such as retail clerks and secretaries. Natural resources, construction, and maintenance occupations include jobs such as fishermen, foresters, construction workers, and appliance repair people. Production, transportation, and material moving occupations include jobs such as production workers and truck drivers.

A greater proportion of workers were employed in managerial or professional jobs (35.5%) than in service

TABLE 1.10

Employment status of mothers with own children under 3 years old, by age of youngest child and marital status, 2006

[Numbers in thousands]

2006	Civilian noninstitutional population	Civilian labor force							
		Total	Percent of population	Employed				Unemployed	
				Total	Percent of population	Full-time workers[a]	Part-time workers[b]	Number	Percent of labor force
Total mothers									
With own children under 3 years old	9,431	5,675	60.2	5,315	56.4	3,751	1,564	360	6.3
2 years	2,864	1,847	64.5	1,746	61.0	1,280	466	101	5.5
1 year	3,318	2,006	60.5	1,883	56.7	1,305	577	123	6.1
Under 1 year	3,248	1,822	56.1	1,686	51.9	1,166	520	136	7.4
Married, spouse present									
With own children under 3 years old	6,998	4,076	58.2	3,933	56.2	2,756	1,177	143	3.5
2 years	2,114	1,305	61.7	1,265	59.8	910	354	40	3.1
1 year	2,494	1,456	58.4	1,404	56.3	962	442	52	3.6
Under 1 year	2,390	1,315	55.0	1,264	52.9	883	381	51	3.9
Other marital status[c]									
With own children under 3 years old	2,433	1,600	65.7	1,382	56.8	996	386	217	13.6
2 years	750	543	72.3	481	64.2	369	112	61	11.3
1 year	824	550	66.7	479	58.1	344	135	71	13.0
Under 1 year	859	507	59.0	422	49.2	283	139	85	16.7

[a]Usually work 35 hours or more a week at all jobs.
[b]Usually work less than 35 hours a week at all jobs.
[c]Includes never-married, divorced, separated, and widowed persons.
Note: Own children include sons, daughters, step-children, and adopted children. Not included are nieces, nephews, grandchildren, and other related and unrelated children. Detail may not sum to totals due to rounding. Data for 2006 reflect revised population controls used in the Current Population Survey.

SOURCE: Adapted from "Table 6. Employment Status of Mothers with Own Children under 3 Years Old by Single Year of Age of Youngest Child and Marital Status, 2005–06 Annual Averages," in *Employment Characteristics of Families in 2006*, U.S. Department of Labor, Bureau of Labor Statistics, May 9, 2007, http://www.bls.gov/news.release/pdf/famee.pdf (accessed February 6, 2008)

occupations (16.5%), sales and office occupations (24.8%), natural resources, construction, and maintenance occupations (10.8%), or production, transportation, and material moving occupations (12.4%). (See Table 1.11.) According to BLS figures, the percent of American workers employed in management and professional occupations as well as service occupations is steadily increasing, while the percent of American workers employed in production occupations is decreasing.

Women and men were highly concentrated in certain occupations. Women were more likely to work in professional and related occupations, service occupations, and office and administrative support occupations than were men. In 2007, 25.1% of women and only 16.9% of men worked in professional and business occupations, 20.4% of women and 13.2% of men worked in service occupations, and 21.6% of women and only 6.2% of men worked in office and administrative support occupations. (See Table 1.11.) On the other hand, men were much more likely than women to work in natural resources, construction, and maintenance occupations (19.3% of men and 1% of women) and in production, transportation, and material moving occupations (17.9% of men and 6.2% of women).

According to the BLS, African-Americans and Hispanics were less likely than whites and Asians to work in the fairly high-paid managerial and professional specialties;

nearly half of Asians (48.1%) and over a third of whites (36.1%) worked in these occupations, compared with only 27.1% of African-Americans and 17.8% of Hispanics. (See Table 1.11.) On the other hand, African-Americans and Hispanics were disproportionately concentrated in the relatively low-paid service occupations. Only 15.5% of whites and 16% of Asians worked in these occupations, compared with 23.3% of African-Americans and 24.1% of Hispanics. In addition, a disproportionate number of Hispanic workers (19.4%) worked in natural resources, construction, and maintenance occupations compared with whites (11.6%), African-Americans (7%), and Asians (4.4%).

The BLS also reported in *Employment and Earnings* that in 2007 the vast majority of the American workforce were wage or salary earners in nonagricultural industries (134.3 million). Another 9.6 million Americans were self-employed, and 112,000 Americans were unpaid family workers. Only 2.1 million people were employed in agriculture, approximately 58% of them as wage and salary workers and 40.8% of them as self-employed workers. Most people worked full time; 119.7 million people, or 82.9%, did so.

CONTINGENT WORKERS AND ALTERNATIVE WORK ARRANGEMENTS

According to the BLS, even though most formal studies have found no change in workers' overall job tenure, the effects of media reports and personal experience of corporate

TABLE 1.11

Employed persons by occupation, race, Hispanic ethnicity, and sex, 2006–07

[Percent distribution]

Occupation, race, and Hispanic or Latino ethnicity	Total		Men		Women	
	2006	2007	2006	2007	2006	2007
Total						
Total, 16 years and over (thousands)	144,427	146,047	77,502	78,254	66,925	67,792
Percent	100.0	100.0	100.0	100.0	100.0	100.0
Management, professional, and related occupations	34.9	35.5	32.2	32.7	38.1	38.6
Management, business, and financial operations occupations	14.7	14.8	15.9	15.8	13.3	13.6
Professional and related occupations	20.2	20.7	16.2	16.9	24.8	25.1
Service occupations	16.5	16.5	13.1	13.2	20.4	20.4
Sales and office occupations	25.0	24.8	17.1	16.9	34.2	33.8
Sales and related occupations	11.5	11.4	10.9	10.8	12.2	12.2
Office and administrative support occupations	13.5	13.4	6.2	6.2	22.0	21.6
Natural resources, construction, and maintenance occupations	11.0	10.8	19.5	19.3	1.1	1.0
Farming, fishing, and forestry occupations	.7	.7	1.0	1.0	.3	.3
Construction and extraction occupations	6.6	6.5	11.9	11.9	.4	.4
Installation, maintenance, and repair occupations	3.7	3.6	6.6	6.4	.4	.3
Production, transportation, and material moving occupations	12.6	12.4	18.1	17.9	6.2	6.2
Production occupations	6.5	6.4	8.4	8.4	4.3	4.2
Transportation and material moving occupations	6.1	6.0	9.7	9.5	2.0	2.0
White						
Total, 16 years and over (thousands)	118,833	119,792	64,883	65,289	53,950	54,503
Percent	100.0	100.0	100.0	100.0	100.0	100.0
Management, professional, and related occupations	35.5	36.1	32.6	33.2	38.9	39.5
Management, business, and financial operations occupations	15.4	15.5	16.7	16.7	13.8	13.9
Professional and related occupations	20.1	20.6	15.9	16.5	25.2	25.6
Service occupations	15.4	15.5	12.2	12.4	19.3	19.3
Sales and office occupations	25.1	24.8	17.0	16.7	34.8	34.4
Sales and related occupations	11.8	11.6	11.3	11.0	12.4	12.3
Office and administrative support occupations	13.3	13.2	5.7	5.7	22.4	22.1
Natural resources, construction, and maintenance occupations	11.8	11.6	20.7	20.4	1.1	1.0
Farming, fishing, and forestry occupations	.7	.7	1.1	1.1	.3	.3
Construction and extraction occupations	7.1	7.1	12.7	12.7	.5	.4
Installation, maintenance, and repair occupations	3.9	3.8	6.9	6.7	.4	.3
Production, transportation, and material moving occupations	12.2	12.0	17.6	17.3	5.8	5.7
Production occupations	6.4	6.3	8.3	8.4	4.0	3.9
Transportation and material moving occupations	5.9	5.7	9.2	9.0	1.8	1.9
Black or African American						
Total, 16 years and over (thousands)	15,765	16,051	7,354	7,500	8,410	8,551
Percent	100.0	100.0	100.0	100.0	100.0	100.0
Management, professional, and related occupations	27.0	27.1	22.3	22.3	31.1	31.2
Management, business, and financial operations occupations	9.8	10.1	9.7	9.2	10.0	11.0
Professional and related occupations	17.2	16.9	12.6	13.1	21.1	20.3
Service occupations	24.1	23.3	20.4	19.2	27.3	26.8
Sales and office occupations	25.7	26.2	18.1	18.7	32.3	32.7
Sales and related occupations	9.5	10.3	8.0	8.8	10.9	11.7
Office and administrative support occupations	16.2	15.8	10.2	10.0	21.4	21.0
Natural resources, construction, and maintenance occupations	6.8	7.0	13.5	14.0	1.0	.8
Farming, fishing, and forestry occupations	.3	.3	.4	.4	.2	.2
Construction and extraction occupations	4.0	4.0	8.1	8.1	.3	.3
Installation, maintenance, and repair occupations	2.6	2.7	5.0	5.5	.5	.3
Production, transportation, and material moving occupations	16.4	16.5	25.7	25.7	8.3	8.5
Production occupations	7.3	7.4	9.7	9.6	5.2	5.4
Transportation and material moving occupations	9.1	9.2	16.0	16.1	3.1	3.1

downsizing, production streamlining, and the increasing use of temporary workers can cause workers to question employers' commitment to long-term, stable employment relationships. There is also a growing unease that employers, in their attempts to reduce costs, have increased their use of "employment intermediaries," such as temporary help services and contract companies, and are relying more on alternative staffing arrangements, such as on-call workers and independent contractors (also called freelancers).

Workers may take employment in a nonstandard arrangement, such as working for a temporary agency, for a number of reasons, including inability to find a permanent job, a desire to work fewer hours when they have a young child at home, or a desire to experience varied jobs and job sectors. In addition, nonstandard work arrangements such as consulting or contracting can provide a more flexible workday and more lucrative remuneration.

Contingent Worker Characteristics

The BLS defines contingent work as any job situation in which an individual does not have an explicit or implicit contract for long-term employment. This includes

TABLE 1.11

Employed persons by occupation, race, Hispanic ethnicity, and sex, 2006–07 [CONTINUED]

[Percent distribution]

Occupation, race, and Hispanic or Latino ethnicity	Total		Men		Women	
	2006	2007	2006	2007	2006	2007
Asian						
Total, 16 years and over (thousands)	6,522	6,839	3,511	3,677	3,011	3,162
Percent	100.0	100.0	100.0	100.0	100.0	100.0
Management, professional, and related occupations	47.3	48.1	48.7	49.3	45.7	46.8
Management, business, and financial operations occupations	15.8	15.8	16.9	15.8	14.5	15.7
Professional and related occupations	31.6	32.4	31.8	33.5	31.2	31.1
Service occupations	15.8	16.0	13.4	13.5	18.5	18.9
Sales and office occupations	22.4	21.9	18.2	18.4	27.3	26.0
Sales and related occupations	11.8	11.4	11.9	11.5	11.6	11.4
Office and administrative support occupations	10.7	10.5	6.3	6.9	15.7	14.7
Natural resources, construction, and maintenance occupations	4.4	4.4	7.6	7.4	.7	.9
Farming, fishing, and forestry occupations	.2	.2	.3	.2	.2	.3
Construction and extraction occupations	1.7	1.7	3.0	3.1	.3	.1
Installation, maintenance, and repair occupations	2.4	2.4	4.3	4.1	.3	.5
Production, transportation, and material moving occupations	10.1	9.6	12.1	11.4	7.7	7.4
Production occupations	7.0	6.5	7.1	6.7	6.7	6.3
Transportation and material moving occupations	3.1	3.0	4.9	4.7	1.0	1.0
Hispanic or Latino ethnicity						
Total, 16 years and over (thousands)	19,613	20,382	11,887	12,310	7,725	8,072
Percent	100.0	100.0	100.0	100.0	100.0	100.0
Management, professional, and related occupations	17.0	17.8	13.7	14.3	22.1	23.1
Management, business, and financial operations occupations	7.5	7.7	7.1	7.2	8.3	8.6
Professional and related occupations	9.5	10.0	6.6	7.1	13.9	14.5
Service occupations	23.7	24.1	19.2	19.7	30.6	30.7
Sales and office occupations	21.2	21.1	13.7	13.2	32.7	33.1
Sales and related occupations	9.4	9.3	7.3	7.2	12.6	12.4
Office and administrative support occupations	11.8	11.8	6.4	6.0	20.2	20.7
Natural resources, construction, and maintenance occupations	19.8	19.4	31.3	31.0	2.2	1.8
Farming, fishing, and forestry occupations	1.9	1.9	2.6	2.5	1.0	1.0
Construction and extraction occupations	14.2	14.0	22.9	22.8	.9	.6
Installation, maintenance, and repair occupations	3.7	3.6	5.9	5.7	.3	.2
Production, transportation, and material moving occupations	18.3	17.6	22.1	21.7	12.3	11.3
Production occupations	9.9	9.4	10.4	10.4	9.0	8.0
Transportation and material moving occupations	8.4	8.2	11.7	11.3	3.3	3.3

Note: Estimates for the above race groups (white, black or African American, and Asian) do not sum to totals because data are not presented for all races. Persons whose ethnicity is identified as Hispanic or Latino may be of any race. Updated population controls are introduced annually with the release of January data.

SOURCE: "10. Employed Persons by Occupation, Race, Hispanic or Latino Ethnicity, and Sex," in *Employment and Earnings*, U.S. Department of Labor, Bureau of Labor Statistics, January 2008, http://www.bls.gov/cps/cpsaat10.pdf (accessed February 2, 2008)

independent contractors, on-call workers, and those working for temporary help services. In the report *Contingent and Alternative Employment Arrangements, February 2005* (July 27, 2005, http://www.bls.gov/news.release/pdf/conemp.pdf), the BLS estimated that contingent workers accounted for between 1.8% and 4.1% of total employment in the United States. In February 2005, 22.6%–27.2% of all contingent workers in the United States were employed in professional and related occupations. Other high rates of contingency were in the education and health services industries (21.8%–27.1%), sales and office occupations (20.6%–24.3%), office and administrative support occupations (14.8%–19.4%), and service occupations (15.7%–17.6).

The BLS also reported in *Contingent and Alternative Employment Arrangements* that laborers who were between the ages of twenty and thirty-four years were more than twice as likely to be contingent workers as workers who

were younger or older. The trend was evident for both male and female contingent workers. Contingent workers were also more likely to be employed full-time than part-time.

Alternative Work Arrangements

Employees in alternative work arrangements are individuals whose place, time, and quantity of work are potentially unpredictable or individuals whose employment is arranged through an employment intermediary. Examples include independent contractors, on-call workers, workers paid by temporary help firms, and workers whose services are provided through contract firms.

Some of the alternative arrangements have been in existence for decades; there is, however, a lack of data analyzing the number of workers in these arrangements. The ranks of independent contractors include construction workers and farmhands, whose working situations did not change much in the twentieth century. Similarly, on-call workers such as substitute teachers, registered nurses, and performance artists did not see much change in the manner of obtaining work. Temporary help agencies, though, can only trace their widespread existence in the United States to shortly after World War II, and there is evidence that providing employees to fulfill the administrative or business needs of other companies is a spreading phenomenon.

According to the BLS in *Contingent and Alternative Employment Arrangements*, 14.8 million people, or 10.7% of the total workforce of 139 million, could be categorized in four alternative arrangement categories. Independent contractors made up 10.3 million people (7.4% of the total workforce) in February 2005, followed by on-call workers (2.5 million, or 1.8%), temporary help agency workers (1.2 million, or 0.9%), and contract company employees (813,000, or 0.6%).

Workers with alternative arrangements were less likely than workers with traditional arrangements to be enrolled in school in February 2005, the BLS noted in the same report. About one-quarter (26.6%) of independent contractors aged sixteen to twenty-four with alternative work arrangements, 41.4% of on-call workers with alternative work arrangements in that age group, 4.7% of temporary agency workers, and 13% of contract company workers were enrolled in school in February 2005, compared with 44.1% of sixteen- to twenty-four-year-old workers with traditional arrangements.

THE WORKING POOR

In 2005 approximately 7.7 million people who were in the labor force for twenty-seven weeks or more, or 5.4% of the total labor force, lived below the official poverty level, according to data presented by the BLS in *A Profile of the Working Poor, 2005* (September 2007, http://www.bls.gov/cps/cpswp2005.pdf). These people are called the "working poor" because, despite working for at least twenty-seven weeks, their incomes still fell below the official poverty threshold. The poverty rate among families that had at least one member in the labor force for more than half the year was higher, at 6.4%.

The BLS also notes in *A Profile of the Working Poor, 2005* that the poverty rate among those working or looking for work for at least twenty-seven weeks during 2005 was 5.4%. Among individuals who spent fifty to fifty-two weeks in the labor force in that year, the poverty rate was slightly lower, at 4.9%. Among people in the labor force for the full year who usually worked full-time, the poverty rate was 3.5%; among those who usually worked part-time, the poverty rate was 11.4%.

Gender, Race, and Age

Of the 142.8 million people aged sixteen and over who were in the labor force at least twenty-seven weeks during 2005, more women (4 million) than men (3.8 million) were poor. (See Table 1.12.) Because fewer women than men participated in the labor force in 2005 (65.5 million women, compared with 77.3 million men), there was an even greater discrepancy between the percentage of working women living in poverty (6.1%) and the percentage of working men whose earnings fell below the poverty threshold (4.8%).

Seven out of ten (70.7%) of the 7.5 million working poor in 2005 were white workers, yet African-American and Hispanic workers continued to experience poverty rates that were more than twice the rates of whites. (See Table 1.12.) More than one in ten working Hispanics (10.5%) as well as more than one in ten working African-Americans (10.5%) were living in poverty. Only 4.7% of whites and 4.7% of Asians were making wages below the poverty level. The poverty rate among working African-American women was much higher than among working African-American men (13% and 7.7%, respectively), just as the poverty rate was higher among working white women than it was among working white men (5% and 4.4%, respectively). Hispanic men and women had about equal poverty rates, while working Asian women actually had a lower poverty rate than working Asian men (4.4% and 5%, respectively).

Education and Poverty Rate

Among all the people in the labor force at least twenty-seven weeks during 2005, those with less than a high school diploma had a much higher poverty rate (14.1%) than did high school graduates (6.6%). (See Table 1.13.) Workers who had attained at least an associate's degree (4.7%) or who had graduated from college (1.7%) reported the lowest poverty rates. Poverty rates for African-American and Hispanic workers were 1.5 to two times higher than for white workers at many corresponding education levels. Poverty rates for Asian workers were also greater than for white workers, although the differences were less than for African-American or Hispanic workers. For example, the poverty rate of white high school graduates was 5.5% in 2005; in comparison, the poverty rates of African-American graduates (12.7%), Hispanic graduates (9.4%), and Asian graduates (7.3%) were all significantly higher.

Poverty disproportionately affected working women at all education levels. Men without a high school diploma had a poverty rate of 12.6%, while women had a poverty rate of 16.8%. (See Table 1.13.) Male high school graduates had a poverty rate of 5.6%, while female graduates had a rate of 8%. Men with an associate's degree had a poverty rate of 3.7%, while women with comparable education had a rate of 5.6%. Only among college graduates did the rate even out; it was 1.6% among men with bachelor's degrees and 1.7% among women. Poverty rates among working African-American women were particularly high, affecting

TABLE 1.12

Poverty status of people in the labor force for 27 weeks or more, by age, sex, race, and Hispanic ethnicity, 2005

[Numbers in thousands]

Age and sex	Total	White	Black or African American	Asian	Hispanic or Latino ethnicity	Below poverty level Total	White	Black or African American	Asian	Hispanic or Latino ethnicity	Rate[a] Total	White	Black or African American	Asian	Hispanic or Latino ethnicity
Total, 16 years and older	**142,824**	**117,078**	**16,122**	**6,290**	**18,905**	**7,744**	**5,477**	**1,694**	**298**	**1,983**	**5.4**	**4.7**	**10.5**	**4.7**	**10.5**
16 to 19 years	4,192	3,483	511	78	602	438	313	100	8	105	10.5	9.0	19.5	9.7	17.5
20 to 24 years	13,370	10,767	1,704	447	2,347	1,610	1,144	353	50	328	12.0	10.6	20.8	11.1	14.0
25 to 34 years	31,022	24,581	3,914	1,621	5,873	2,138	1,472	516	76	681	6.9	6.0	13.2	4.7	11.6
35 to 44 years	34,779	27,978	4,223	1,782	4,974	1,752	1,268	352	70	557	5.0	4.5	8.3	3.9	11.2
45 to 54 years	34,422	28,688	3,701	1,371	3,311	1,166	804	246	73	196	3.4	2.8	6.6	5.4	5.9
55 to 64 years	19,649	16,851	1,701	787	1,445	532	399	105	13	93	2.7	2.4	6.2	1.7	6.4
65 years and older	5,390	4,730	368	205	353	108	77	22	8	22	2.0	1.6	6.0	4.1	6.3
Men, 16 years and older	**77,329**	**64,603**	**7,482**	**3,396**	**11,557**	**3,750**	**2,846**	**574**	**170**	**1,203**	**4.8**	**4.4**	**7.7**	**5.0**	**10.4**
16 to 19 years	2,082	1,739	246	43	369	182	129	34	7	56	8.8	7.4	13.8	b	15.1
20 to 24 years	7,211	5,897	832	245	1,453	727	536	124	32	194	10.1	9.1	14.9	12.8	13.4
25 to 34 years	17,342	14,076	1,826	887	3,807	1,043	804	141	46	457	6.0	5.7	7.7	5.2	12.0
35 to 44 years	19,104	15,738	1,950	976	3,021	891	705	116	40	323	4.7	4.5	6.0	4.1	10.7
45 to 54 years	18,159	15,362	1,708	729	1,879	603	430	115	37	111	3.3	2.8	6.7	5.0	5.9
55 to 64 years	10,400	9,083	753	412	817	244	195	35	7	51	2.3	2.1	4.6	1.6	6.2
65 years and older	3,030	2,708	166	104	212	59	47	10	2	12	2.0	1.7	5.9	2.2	5.6
Women, 16 years and older	**65,495**	**52,475**	**8,640**	**2,894**	**7,348**	**3,994**	**2,631**	**1,119**	**128**	**780**	**6.1**	**5.0**	**13.0**	**4.4**	**10.6**
16 to 19 years	2,110	1,744	265	35	234	256	184	66	1	50	12.1	10.6	24.9	b	21.3
20 to 24 years	6,159	4,870	872	202	894	882	608	230	18	134	14.3	12.5	26.4	9.0	15.0
25 to 34 years	13,680	10,504	2,088	733	2,066	1,095	668	374	30	223	8.0	6.4	17.9	4.1	10.8
35 to 44 years	15,674	12,240	2,272	806	1,953	861	562	236	30	234	5.5	4.6	10.4	3.7	12.0
45 to 54 years	16,263	13,326	1,993	641	1,432	563	375	131	37	86	3.5	2.8	6.6	5.7	6.0
55 to 64 years	9,249	7,768	948	375	628	288	204	70	6	42	3.1	2.6	7.4	1.7	6.7
65 years and older	2,360	2,022	202	101	141	49	30	12	6	10	2.1	1.5	6.1	b	7.4

[a]Number below the poverty level as a percent of the total in the labor force for 27 weeks or more.
[b]Data not shown where base is less than 80,000.
Note: Estimates for the above race groups (white, black or African American, and Asian) do not sum to totals because data are not presented for all races. In addition, people whose ethnicity is identified as Hispanic or Latino may be of any race and, therefore, are classified by ethnicity as well as by race.

SOURCE: "Table 2. People in the Labor Force for 27 Weeks or More: Poverty Status by Age, Sex, Race, and Hispanic or Latino Ethnicity, 2005," in *A Profile of the Working Poor, 2005*, U.S. Department of Labor, Bureau of Labor Statistics, September 2007, http://www.bls.gov/cps/cpswp2005.pdf (accessed February 8, 2008)

TABLE 1.13

Poverty status of people in the labor force for 27 weeks or more, by educational attainment, race, Hispanic ethnicity, and sex, 2005

[Numbers in thousands]

Educational attainment, race, and Hispanic or Latino ethnicity	Total	Men	Women	Below poverty level			Rate[a]		
				Total	Men	Women	Total	Men	Women
Total, 16 years and older	142,824	77,329	65,495	7,744	3,750	3,994	5.4	4.8	6.1
Less than a high school diploma	15,961	10,136	5,825	2,255	1,277	979	14.1	12.6	16.8
High school graduates, no college[b]	42,947	24,154	18,793	2,844	1,343	1,500	6.6	5.6	8.0
Some college or associate degree	41,514	20,570	20,944	1,937	766	1,170	4.7	3.7	5.6
Bachelor's degree and higher[c]	42,402	22,469	19,933	708	364	345	1.7	1.6	1.7
White, 16 years and older	117,078	64,603	52,475	5,477	2,846	2,631	4.7	4.4	5.0
Less than a high school diploma	12,939	8,495	4,444	1,683	1,023	660	13.0	12.0	14.8
High school graduates, no college[b]	34,885	19,938	14,947	1,917	978	939	5.5	4.9	6.3
Some college or associate degree	34,111	17,221	16,890	1,349	574	775	4.0	3.3	4.6
Bachelor's degree and higher	35,143	18,949	16,194	528	272	257	1.5	1.4	1.6
Black or African American, 16 years and older	16,122	7,482	8,640	1,694	574	1,119	10.5	7.7	13.0
Less than a high school diploma	1,956	1,035	922	434	163	271	22.2	15.8	29.4
High school graduates, no college[b]	5,778	2,898	2,881	736	246	490	12.7	8.5	17.0
Some college or associate degree	5,050	2,151	2,899	435	123	312	8.6	5.7	10.8
Bachelor's degree and higher[c]	3,337	1,398	1,938	89	42	47	2.7	3.0	2.4
Asian, 16 years and older	6,290	3,396	2,894	298	170	128	4.7	5.0	4.4
Less than a high school diploma	568	303	265	57	36	21	10.0	11.9	7.8
High school graduates, no college[b]	1,243	690	552	90	59	31	7.3	8.6	5.6
Some college or associate degree	1,208	618	590	73	33	40	6.1	5.4	6.7
Bachelor's degree and higher[c]	3,271	1,785	1,487	78	41	36	2.4	2.3	2.5
Hispanic or Latino ethnicity, 16 years and older	18,905	11,557	7,348	1,983	1,203	780	10.5	10.4	10.6
Less than a high school diploma	6,651	4,604	2,047	1,099	720	379	16.5	15.6	18.5
High school graduates, no college[b]	5,747	3,524	2,223	542	319	223	9.4	9.1	10.0
Some college or associate degree	4,141	2,207	1,935	280	129	151	6.8	5.9	7.8
Bachelor's degree and higher[c]	2,365	1,222	1,143	62	35	27	2.6	2.9	2.4

[a]Number below the poverty level as a percent of the total in the labor force for 27 weeks or more.
[b]Includes people with a high school diploma or equivalent.
[c]Includes people with bachelor's, master's, professional, and doctoral degrees.
Note: Estimates for the above race groups (white, black or African American, and Asian) do not sum to totals because data are not presented for all races. In addition, people whose ethnicity is identified as Hispanic or Latino may be of any race and, therefore, are classified by ethnicity as well as by race.

SOURCE: Adapted from "Table 3. People in the Labor Force for 27 Weeks or More: Poverty Status by Educational Attainment, Race, Hispanic or Latino Ethnicity, and Sex, 2005," in *A Profile of the Working Poor, 2005*, U.S. Department of Labor, Bureau of Labor Statistics, September 2007, http://www.bls.gov/cps/cpswp2005.pdf (accessed February 8, 2008)

29.4% of those without a high school diploma, 17% of women with a high school diploma, 10.8% of those with an associate's degree, and 2.4% of those with a bachelor's degree.

Occupations

During 2005, people working in managerial and professional specialty occupations had the lowest probability of being poor; only 1.8% of working managers and professionals had incomes below the poverty line. (See Table 1.14.) In contrast, the average poverty rate for workers in service occupations was quite high, at 10.8%. The BLS in *A Profile of the Working Poor, 2005* reports that those working in the farming/fishing/forestry sector also had a high poverty rate, at 13.7%. In addition, construction workers had a higher probability than average (8.1%) of making wages below the poverty line, perhaps in part because of the seasonal nature of much construction work. In general, African-Americans and those of Hispanic/Latino ethnicity were more likely than whites to earn annual wages below the poverty level, regardless of occupation.

In all occupational groups except office and administrative support, women were more likely than men were to be poor. In 2003 men experienced a higher poverty rate in only one occupational group, office and administrative support, with a rate of 4% compared with 3.5% for women, according to *A Profile of the Working Poor, 2005*. In all other occupations, men fared better than women did. The poverty rate for women employed in sales and related occupations (9.2%) was more than two times that of their male counterparts (3.7%).

Poverty Trends by Family Structure

In 2005, of the 4.1 million working families who lived below the poverty level, 1.9 million of them were headed by single women, illustrating the disproportionate poverty suffered by families headed by single mothers. (See Table 1.15.) The poverty rate for families was 6.4%. The poverty rate for families with just one member in the labor force (12.7%) was more than seven times more than that of families with two or more members in the work-

TABLE 1.14

Poverty status of people in the labor force for 27 weeks or more, by occupation of longest job held, race, Hispanic ethnicity, and sex, 2005

[Numbers in thousands]

Occupation, race, and Hispanic or Latino ethnicity	Total	Men	Women	Below poverty level			Rate[a]		
				Total	Men	Women	Total	Men	Women
Total, 16 years and older[b]	**142,824**	**77,329**	**65,495**	**7,744**	**3,750**	**3,994**	**5.4**	**4.8**	**6.1**
Management, professional, and related occupations	48,356	24,167	24,189	868	396	472	1.8	1.6	2.0
Service occupations	22,165	9,751	12,415	2,392	854	1,538	10.8	8.8	12.4
Sales and office occupations	34,467	12,768	21,699	1,672	485	1,186	4.8	3.8	5.5
Natural resources, construction, and maintenance occupations	15,462	14,861	601	1,044	985	59	6.8	6.6	9.8
Production, transportation, and material moving occupations	17,863	13,836	4,027	1,139	766	374	6.4	5.5	9.3
White, 16 years and older[b]	**117,078**	**64,603**	**52,475**	**5,477**	**2,846**	**2,631**	**4.7**	**4.4**	**5.0**
Management, professional, and related occupations	40,540	20,610	19,930	637	290	347	1.6	1.4	1.7
Service occupations	16,738	7,433	9,305	1,585	595	989	9.5	8.0	10.6
Sales and office occupations	28,518	10,761	17,757	1,148	371	778	4.0	3.4	4.4
Natural resources, construction, and maintenance occupations	13,655	13,156	499	885	830	55	6.5	6.3	11.0
Production, transportation, and material moving occupations	14,147	11,155	2,993	821	590	232	5.8	5.3	7.7
Black or African American, 16 years and older[b]	**16,122**	**7,482**	**8,640**	**1,694**	**574**	**1,119**	**10.5**	**7.7**	**13.0**
Management, professional, and related occupations	4,090	1,552	2,538	129	40	89	3.2	2.6	3.5
Service occupations	3,753	1,526	2,227	646	170	476	17.2	11.1	21.4
Sales and office occupations	3,899	1,194	2,705	405	81	324	10.4	6.8	12.0
Natural resources, construction, and maintenance occupations	1,088	1,024	63	97	96	1	8.9	9.4	(c)
Production, transportation, and material moving occupations	2,600	1,894	706	241	120	120	9.2	6.4	17.0
Asian, 16 years and older[b]	**6,290**	**3,396**	**2,894**	**298**	**170**	**128**	**4.7**	**5.0**	**4.4**
Management, professional, and related occupations	2,825	1,565	1,259	63	40	24	2.2	2.5	1.9
Service occupations	1,049	492	557	95	57	38	9.0	11.6	6.8
Sales and office occupations	1,296	546	751	64	22	43	5.0	3.9	5.7
Natural resources, construction, and maintenance occupations	275	252	23	14	14	—	5.2	5.6	—
Production, transportation, and material moving occupations	644	438	206	35	26	9	5.4	5.9	4.3
Hispanic or Latino ethnicity, 16 years and older[b]	**18,905**	**11,557**	**7,348**	**1,983**	**1,203**	**780**	**10.5**	**10.4**	**10.6**
Management, professional, and related occupations	3,078	1,477	1,601	92	54	38	3.0	3.6	2.4
Service occupations	4,371	2,282	2,089	645	313	332	14.7	13.7	15.9
Sales and office occupations	3,835	1,577	2,258	290	95	195	7.6	6.0	8.6
Natural resources, construction, and maintenance occupations	3,698	3,543	156	485	461	24	13.1	13.0	15.4
Production, transportation, and material moving occupations	3,349	2,463	886	355	241	114	10.6	9.8	12.8

[a]Number below the poverty level as a percent of the total in the labor force for 27 weeks or more who worked during the year.
[b]Includes a small number of people whose last job was in the Armed Forces.
[c]Data not shown where base is less than 80,000.
Note: Estimates for the above race groups (white, black or African American, and Asian) do not sum to totals because data are not presented for all races. In addition, people whose ethnicity is identified as Hispanic or Latino may be of any race and, therefore, are classified by ethnicity as well as by race. Dash represents or rounds to zero.

SOURCE: Adapted from "Table 4. People in the Labor Force for 27 Weeks or More Who Worked during the Year: Poverty Status by Occupation of Longest Job Held, Race, Hispanic or Latino Ethnicity, and Sex, 2005," in *A Profile of the Working Poor, 2005*, U.S. Department of Labor, Bureau of Labor Statistics, September 2007, http://www.bls.gov/cps/cpswp2005.pdf (accessed February 8, 2008)

force (1.6%). Families maintained by women with one member in the labor force (with a poverty rate of 22.4%) were significantly more likely to be poor than similar families maintained by men (11.7%). Married-couple families with two or more members in the labor force had the lowest poverty rate (1.2%).

EMPLOYEE TENURE

Information on tenure (how long a person has worked for his or her current employer) is often used to gauge employment security. A trend of increasing tenure in the economy can be interpreted as a sign of improving job security, with the opposite being an indicator of deteriorating security.

TABLE 1.15

Poverty status of families by presence of related children, work experience of family members in the labor force for 27 weeks or more, and type of family, 2005

[Numbers in thousands]

Characteristic	Total families	At or above poverty level	Below poverty level	Rate*
Total primary families	64,360	60,266	4,094	6.4
With related children under 18 years	36,075	32,658	3,417	9.5
Without children	28,285	27,608	676	2.4
With one member in the labor force	27,498	24,003	3,494	12.7
With two or more members in the labor force	36,862	36,263	600	1.6
With two members	31,025	30,481	544	1.8
With three or more members	5,837	5,782	55	1.0
Married-couple families	48,899	47,111	1,787	3.7
With related children under 18 years	26,287	24,846	1,441	5.5
Without children	22,612	22,265	347	1.5
With one member in the labor force	16,772	15,377	1,394	8.3
Husband	12,451	11,372	1,079	8.7
Wife	3,665	3,405	260	7.1
Relative	655	600	55	8.4
With two or more members in the labor force	32,127	31,734	393	1.2
With two members	27,270	26,911	359	1.3
With three or more members	4,857	4,823	34	.7
Families maintained by women	10,966	9,041	1,925	17.6
With related children under 18 years	7,461	5,772	1,689	22.6
Without children	3,505	3,269	236	6.7
With one member in the labor force	7,924	6,151	1,773	22.4
Householder	6,597	5,060	1,537	23.3
Relative	1,326	1,090	236	17.8
With two or more members in the labor force	3,042	2,890	152	5.0
Families maintained by men	4,496	4,114	382	8.5
With related children under 18 years	2,328	2,040	288	12.4
Without children	2,168	2,074	94	4.3
With one member in the labor force	2,802	2,475	327	11.7
Householder	2,287	2,013	274	12.0
Relative	515	462	53	10.3
With two or more members in the labor force	1,693	1,639	55	3.2

*Number below the poverty level as a percent of the total in the labor force for 27 weeks or more.
Note: Data relate to primary families with at least one member in the labor force for 27 weeks or more.

SOURCE: "Table 5. Primary Families: Poverty Status, Presence of Related Children, and Work Experience of Family Members in the Labor Force for 27 Weeks or More, 2005," in *A Profile of the Working Poor, 2005*, U.S. Department of Labor, Bureau of Labor Statistics, September 2007, http://www.bls.gov/cps/cpswp 2005.pdf (accessed February 8, 2008).

However, job security trends are not necessarily that simple. During recessions or other periods of declining job security, the proportion of median-tenure and long-tenure workers could rise because workers with less seniority are more likely to lose their jobs than are workers with longer tenure. During periods of economic growth, the proportion of median-tenure and long-tenure workers could fall, because more job opportunities are available for new job entrants, and experienced workers have more opportunities to change employers and take better jobs. However, tenure can also rise under improving economic conditions, as fewer layoffs occur and good job matches develop between workers and employers.

As shown in Table 1.16, median tenure (the point at which half the workers had more tenure and half had less) in January 2006 was four years, the same as in January 2004 but higher than figures obtained in 2002, 2000, 1998, or 1996. Between 1996 and 2006 the median tenure with

current employer for male workers held fairly steady, at four years in 1996 and 4.1 years in 2006. Job tenure for male workers age twenty-five and over, though, actually declined during the decade, from 5.3 years in 1996 to 5 years in 2006. Overall median tenure with current employer among women rose somewhat between 1996 and 2006, from 3.5 in 1996 to 3.9 in 2006. This can be explained by fewer women taking time out of the labor force to care for small children. However, the median employee tenure was still half a year longer among men than among women.

In addition to tracking trends in median tenure, the BLS, in *Employee Tenure in 2006* (September 8, 2006, http://www.bls.gov/news.release/pdf/tenure.pdf), charts trends in the proportion of workers with relatively long tenures of ten years or more. Among workers age twenty-five and over, the percent of workers with these long tenures dropped slightly from 30.5% in February 1996 to 30% in 2006. The percent of women with tenures of ten years or more with current

TABLE 1.16

Median years of tenure with current employer for employed wage and salary workers, by age and sex, selected years, 1996–2006

Age and sex	February 1996	February 1998	February 2000	January 2002	January 2004	January 2006
Total						
16 years and over	3.8	3.6	3.5	3.7	4.0	4.0
16 to 17 years	.7	.6	.6	.7	.7	.6
18 to 19 years	.7	.7	.7	.8	.8	.7
20 to 24 years	1.2	1.1	1.1	1.2	1.3	1.3
25 years and over	5.0	4.7	4.7	4.7	4.9	4.9
25 to 34 years	2.8	2.7	2.6	2.7	2.9	2.9
35 to 44 years	5.3	5.0	4.8	4.6	4.9	4.9
45 to 54 years	8.3	8.1	8.2	7.6	7.7	7.3
55 to 64 years	10.2	10.1	10.0	9.9	9.6	9.3
65 years and over	8.4	7.8	9.4	8.6	9.0	8.8
Men						
16 years and over	4.0	3.8	3.8	3.9	4.1	4.1
16 to 17 years	.6	.6	.6	.8	.7	.7
18 to 19 years	.7	.7	.7	.8	.8	.7
20 to 24 years	1.2	1.2	1.2	1.4	1.3	1.4
25 years and over	5.3	4.9	4.9	4.9	5.1	5.0
25 to 34 years	3.0	2.8	2.7	2.8	3.0	2.9
35 to 44 years	6.1	5.5	5.3	5.0	5.2	5.1
45 to 54 years	10.1	9.4	9.5	9.1	9.6	8.1
55 to 64 years	10.5	11.2	10.2	10.2	9.8	9.5
65 years and over	8.3	7.1	9.0	8.1	8.2	8.3
Women						
16 years and over	3.5	3.4	3.3	3.4	3.8	3.9
16 to 17 years	.7	.6	.6	.7	.6	.6
18 to 19 years	.7	.7	.7	.8	.8	.7
20 to 24 years	1.2	1.1	1.0	1.1	1.3	1.2
25 years and over	4.7	4.4	4.4	4.4	4.7	4.8
25 to 34 years	2.7	2.5	2.5	2.5	2.8	2.8
35 to 44 years	4.8	4.5	4.3	4.2	4.5	4.6
45 to 54 years	7.0	7.2	7.3	6.5	6.4	6.7
55 to 64 years	10.0	9.6	9.9	9.6	9.2	9.2
65 years and over	8.4	8.7	9.7	9.4	9.6	9.5

Note: Data for 1996 and 1998 are based on population controls from the 1990 census. Data beginning in 2000 reflect the introduction of census 2000 population controls and are not strictly comparable with data for prior years. In addition, data for January 2004 reflect the introduction of revisions to population controls in January 2003 and 2004, and data for January 2006 reflect the introduction of revisions to population controls in January 2005 and 2006.

SOURCE: "Table 1. Median Years of Tenure with Current Employer for Employed Wage and Salary Workers by Age and Sex, Selected Years, 1996–2006," in *Employee Tenure in 2006*, U.S. Department of Labor, Bureau of Labor Statistics, September 8, 2006, http://www.bls.gov/news.release/pdf/tenure.pdf (accessed February 3, 2008)

employer, however, actually rose during that decade, from 27.6% in 1996 to 28.8% in 2006. The proportion of men who had worked for their current employer ten years or longer fell from 33.1% in 1996 to 31.1% in 2006.

In January 2006, about one-quarter (24.4%) of workers aged sixteen and over had worked for their current employer for twelve months or less, the BLS notes in *Employee Tenure in 2006*. These included workers who had recently entered the workforce, as well as workers who had changed employers in the previous year. Another 29.1% of the workforce had worked for their current employer for one to five years. One-fifth (20.9%) had worked for their current employer for five to nine years, 9.5% had worked for ten to fourteen years, 6.7% had worked for fifteen to nineteen years, and almost one in ten (9.4%) had worked for their current employer for twenty years or more.

Industry

Employee Tenure in 2006 also reports that in January 2006 workers in utilities had the highest median tenure (10.4 years) of the major industries identified by the BLS. (See Table 1.17.) Government employees tended to have above average median employee tenures; the median tenure for federal government employees was 9.9 years, for local government employees it was 6.6 years, and for state government employees it was 6.3 years. Employee tenure was fairly short in leisure and hospitality, with a median tenure of only 1.9 years.

Number of Jobs Held

The more jobs a person holds in their working years, the shorter their employee tenures. From 1978 to 2004 Americans held an average of 10.5 different jobs when they were between the ages of eighteen and forty. Men had held 10.7 jobs on average, and women had held 10.3 jobs. People with associate's or bachelor's degrees had a higher average number of jobs, at 10.9 and 10.7, respectively, perhaps because students tend to hold part-time jobs during the school year or summers that may change frequently. (See Table 1.18.)

TABLE 1.17

Median years of tenure with current employer for employed wage and salary workers, by industry, selected years, 2000–06

Industry	February 2000	January 2002	January 2004	January 2006
Total, 16 years and over	**3.5**	**3.7**	**4.0**	**4.0**
Private sector	3.2	3.3	3.5	3.6
Agriculture and related industries	3.7	4.2	3.7	3.8
Nonagricultural industries	3.2	3.3	3.5	3.6
Mining	4.8	4.5	5.2	3.8
Construction	2.7	3.0	3.0	3.0
Manufacturing	4.9	5.4	5.8	5.5
Durable goods manufacturing	4.8	5.5	6.0	5.6
Nonmetallic mineral products	5.5	5.3	4.8	5.0
Primary metals and fabricated metal products	5.0	6.3	6.4	6.2
Machinery manufacturing	5.3	6.8	6.4	6.6
Computers and electronic products	3.9	4.7	5.2	5.9
Electrical equipment and appliances	5.0	5.5	9.8	6.2
Transportation equipment	6.4	7.0	7.7	7.2
Wood products	3.7	4.3	5.0	4.7
Furniture and fixtures	4.4	4.7	4.7	4.2
Miscellaneous manufacturing	3.7	4.5	4.6	3.9
Nondurable goods manufacturing	5.0	5.3	5.5	5.4
Food manufacturing	4.6	5.0	4.9	5.2
Beverage and tobacco products	5.5	4.6	8.0	5.4
Textiles, apparel, and leather	4.7	5.0	5.0	4.4
Paper and printing	5.1	6.2	6.9	6.3
Petroleum and coal products	9.5	9.8	11.4	5.0
Chemicals	6.0	5.7	5.3	6.1
Plastics and rubber products	4.6	5.3	5.7	5.0
Wholesale and retail trade	2.7	2.8	3.1	3.1
Wholesale trade	3.9	3.9	4.3	4.6
Retail trade	2.5	2.6	2.8	2.8
Transportation and utilities	4.7	4.9	5.3	4.9
Transportation and warehousing	4.0	4.3	4.7	4.3
Utilities	11.5	13.4	13.3	10.4
Information*	3.4	3.3	4.3	4.8
Publishing, except Internet	4.2	4.8	4.7	5.3
Motion picture and sound recording industries	1.6	2.3	2.2	1.9
Broadcasting, except Internet	3.6	3.1	4.0	4.6
Telecommunications	4.3	3.4	4.6	5.3
Financial activities	3.5	3.6	3.9	4.0
Finance and insurance	3.6	3.9	4.1	4.1
Finance	3.3	3.6	4.0	3.9
Insurance	4.4	4.5	4.4	4.7
Real estate and rental and leasing	3.1	3.0	3.3	3.4
Real estate	3.1	3.2	3.5	3.5
Rental and leasing services	3.0	2.2	2.9	3.1
Professional and business services	2.4	2.7	3.2	3.2
Professional and technical services	2.6	3.1	3.6	3.8
Management, administrative, and waste services*	2.0	2.1	2.6	2.5
Administrative and support services	1.8	1.9	2.4	2.4
Waste management and remediation services	3.6	4.3	3.4	4.1
Education and health services	3.4	3.5	3.6	4.0
Educational services	3.2	3.6	3.8	4.0
Health care and social assistance	3.5	3.5	3.6	4.1
Hospitals	5.1	4.9	4.7	5.2
Health services, except hospitals	3.2	3.1	3.3	3.6
Social assistance	2.4	2.5	2.8	3.1
Leisure and hospitality	1.7	1.8	2.0	1.9
Arts, entertainment, and recreation	2.6	2.3	2.8	3.1
Accommodation and food services	1.5	1.6	1.9	1.6
Accommodation	2.8	2.7	3.1	2.5
Food services and drinking places	1.4	1.4	1.6	1.4

Among non-Hispanic whites, average number of jobs held did not vary between men and women—each had an average of 10.6 jobs. (See Table 1.18.) However, African-American and Hispanic men and women differed markedly in average number of jobs held. African-American men held an average of 10.8 jobs between the ages of eighteen and forty, while African-American women of the same age held an average of only 9.3 jobs. Hispanic men held an average of 11.2 jobs between the ages of eighteen and forty, while Hispanic women held an average of only 8.7.

UNION MEMBERSHIP

In 2007, 12.1% of American workers were union members. (See Table 1.19.) This figure represented a

TABLE 1.17

Median years of tenure with current employer for employed wage and salary workers, by industry, selected years, 2000–06 [CONTINUED]

Industry	February 2000	January 2002	January 2004	January 2006
Other services	3.1	3.3	3.3	3.2
Other services, except private households	3.2	3.3	3.5	3.3
Repair and maintenance	3.0	3.0	3.2	2.9
Personal and laundry services	2.7	2.8	3.4	2.8
Membership associations and organizations	4.0	4.1	3.9	4.2
Other services, private households	3.0	2.7	2.3	2.8
Public sector	7.1	6.7	6.9	6.9
Federal government	11.5	11.3	10.4	9.9
State government	5.5	5.4	6.4	6.3
Local government	6.7	6.2	6.4	6.6

*Includes other industries, not shown separately.

Note: Data for January 2004 reflect the introduction of revisions to population controls in January 2003 and 2004. Data for January 2006 reflect the introduction of revisions to population controls in January 2005 and 2006.

SOURCE: "Table 5. Median Years of Tenure with Current Employer for Employed Wage and Salary Workers by Industry, Selected Years, 2000–06," in *Employee Tenure in 2006*, U.S. Department of Labor, Bureau of Labor Statistics, September 8, 2006, http://www.bls.gov/news.release/pdf/tenure.pdf (accessed February 3, 2008)

dramatic decline from 1973, when nearly one-quarter (24%) of wage and salary workers in the United States belonged to a union. According to Barry T. Hirsch and David A. Macpherson in the *Union Membership and Coverage Database* ("Union Membership, Coverage, Density, and Employment among All Wage and Salary Workers, 1973–2007," February 8, 2008, http://wwww.unionstats.com/), union membership declined rapidly during the 1980s to 16.1% by 1990, and the downward trend has continued into the twenty-first century, hitting a low of 12% in 2006.

It should be noted that a worker might be represented by a union in contract negotiations but not be a dues-paying member. In a "right-to-work" state a worker is allowed to join a unionized company and not be forced to join the union. By law, the nonunion worker, working in a unionized company, must benefit from any union contract. Unions represented 13.3% of wage and salary employees in 2007; that is, 13.3% of workers held jobs that were covered by a union contract whether or not they were affiliated with the union personally. (See Table 1.19.)

Studies, such as that by Solomon W. Polachek of the State University of New York at Binghamton ("What Can We Learn about the Decline in U.S. Union Membership from International Data?" September 2002, http://www.middlebury.edu/NR/rdonlyres/0A720CA0-1033-4ACC-917D-746553305EBF/0/Polachek_final_paper.pdf), have explored why union membership has dwindled. It has been established that the recession of the early 1980s, the movement of jobs overseas, the decline in traditionally unionized heavy industry, as well as the expansion of traditionally nonunionized sectors of the economy (such as management and business services and other service occupations) contributed to a general decline in union membership that has been documented in data comparable from year to year since 1983. Auburn University's Anju Mehta, in "Is Outsourcing the End of Unionism? Exploring the Impact of

Outsourcing on Labor Unions in the U.S." (July 2007, http://www.globalwork.in/GDW07/pdf/25-317-324.pdf), notes that in a strategy that was counter to past contract negotiations, many unions in the 1980s agreed to "give backs" (surrendering existing benefits) and lower salaries in exchange for job guarantees. Nonetheless, movement of jobs from the United States to other countries continued, which resulted in fewer jobs for American workers and more plant closings, and prompted more aggressive recruitments of members by unions during the 1990s.

As of 2008, leading labor unions in the United States included:

- *AFL-CIO*—Formed in 1955 by the merger of the American Federation of Labor and the Congress of Industrial Organizations, the AFL-CIO, according to its Web site (http://www.aflcio.org/aboutus/), by 2008 represented about 10.5 million American workers in fifty-six affiliated unions, ranging from the Air Line Pilots Association (ALPA) and the Screen Actors Guild (SAG) to the International Union of Bricklayers and Allied Craftworkers (BAC) and the National Association of Letter Carriers (NALC).

- *American Federation of State, County, and Municipal Employees (AFSCME)*—Boasting membership of 1.4 million in 2008 (http://www.afscme.org/about/aboutindex.cfm), the nation's largest union of public service employees was founded during the Great Depression of the 1930s to protect the rights of state and local government employees.

- *American Federation of Teachers (AFT)*—Representing the economic, social, and professional interests of classroom teachers since 1916, the AFT included more than three thousand local affiliates and over 1.4 million members in 2008 (http://www.aft.org/about/index.htm).

- *Communications Workers of America*—Growing out of the telephone industry in the early part of the

TABLE 1.18

Number of jobs held by individuals from age 18 to age 40, by demographic characteristics, 1978–2004

Characteristic	Total	Percent distribution by number of jobs held						Mean number of jobs held
		0 or 1 job	2 to 4 jobs	5 to 7 jobs	8 to 10 jobs	11 to 14 jobs	15 or more jobs	
Total	100.0	1.4	13.4	20.2	23.1	20.8	21.2	10.5
Less than a high school diploma	100.0	4.3	16.8	17.5	18.5	18.1	24.8	10.6
High school graduates, no college[a]	100.0	1.3	16.0	22.2	20.9	19.6	20.0	10.2
Some college or associate degree	100.0	1.0	11.9	20.1	23.9	21.0	22.1	10.9
Bachelor's degree and higher[b]	100.0	0.9	9.0	18.1	27.9	23.4	20.7	10.7
Men	100.0	1.0	14.2	19.8	22.1	20.2	22.7	10.7
Less than a high school diploma	100.0	0.7	13.8	17.1	17.9	18.2	32.3	12.0
High school graduates, no college[a]	100.0	1.5	16.3	20.3	20.9	18.2	22.8	10.5
Some college or associate degree	100.0	0.4	13.2	22.6	19.2	19.4	25.3	11.1
Bachelor's degree and higher[b]	100.0	0.7	11.6	18.2	28.3	25.3	15.8	10.4
Women	100.0	1.9	12.6	20.5	24.1	21.3	19.6	10.3
Less than a high school diploma	100.0	9.3	21.0	18.1	19.2	18.0	14.4	8.6
High school graduates, no college[a]	100.0	1.0	15.8	24.3	20.8	21.3	16.9	9.8
Some college or associate degree	100.0	1.5	10.9	18.2	27.6	22.3	19.5	10.7
Bachelor's degree and higher[b]	100.0	1.0	6.4	18.0	27.5	21.5	25.7	11.2
White non-Hispanic	100.0	1.2	13.5	19.7	23.3	20.9	21.6	10.6
Less than a high school diploma	100.0	4.0	13.6	17.6	18.5	17.8	28.5	11.3
High school graduates, no college[a]	100.0	1.1	17.1	22.1	20.6	19.4	19.7	10.1
Some college or associate degree	100.0	0.4	12.4	19.1	23.2	21.0	23.8	11.1
Bachelor's degree and higher[b]	100.0	1.0	9.1	17.4	28.5	23.7	20.3	10.7
White non-Hispanic men	100.0	0.9	15.0	20.2	22.0	19.7	22.1	10.6
Less than a high school diploma	100.0	0.0	12.4	16.9	17.7	15.0	38.1	12.8
High school graduates, no college[a]	100.0	1.6	18.4	21.1	20.4	17.4	21.2	10.2
Some college or associate degree	100.0	0.0	14.3	24.1	17.2	17.8	26.6	11.1
Bachelor's degree and higher[b]	100.0	0.8	11.5	17.6	29.1	26.0	14.9	10.1
White non-Hispanic women	100.0	1.5	11.9	19.1	24.5	22.1	21.0	10.6
Less than a high school diploma	100.0	9.2	15.3	18.6	19.4	21.6	15.8	9.3
High school graduates, no college[a]	100.0	0.5	15.7	23.2	20.8	21.7	18.1	10.1
Some college or associate degree	100.0	0.8	10.9	15.1	28.1	23.6	21.5	11.2
Bachelor's degree and higher[b]	100.0	1.1	6.6	17.2	27.8	21.4	25.8	11.2
Black non-Hispanic	100.0	2.3	13.0	21.2	22.8	21.0	19.6	10.1
Less than a high school diploma	100.0	3.5	24.5	17.1	18.7	18.3	17.9	9.2
High school graduates, no college[a]	100.0	2.0	12.1	20.7	22.5	22.2	20.5	10.3
Some college or associate degree	100.0	3.0	9.9	23.4	25.9	21.0	16.7	10.0
Bachelor's degree and higher[b]	100.0	0.0	9.2	23.4	21.9	20.4	25.1	10.5
Black non-Hispanic men	100.0	1.5	11.6	17.0	23.8	22.9	23.2	10.8
Less than a high school diploma	100.0	2.8	19.4	16.5	17.4	24.7	19.1	10.0
High school graduates, no college[a]	100.0	1.0	9.1	15.6	24.7	21.7	28.0	11.4
Some college or associate degree	100.0	2.3	9.1	18.5	28.2	24.3	17.6	10.6
Bachelor's degree and higher[b]	100.0	—	14.8	21.1	21.2	22.9	19.9	9.9
Black non-Hispanic women	100.0	3.1	14.6	25.8	21.8	18.9	15.8	9.3
Less than a high school diploma	100.0	4.6	32.5	18.0	20.8	8.2	15.9	7.9
High school graduates, no college[a]	100.0	3.4	16.3	27.9	19.5	22.9	10.1	8.8
Some college or associate degree	100.0	3.6	10.5	26.7	24.4	18.7	16.1	9.7
Bachelor's degree and higher[b]	100.0	—	4.8	25.2	22.4	18.5	29.0	11.1
Hispanic or Latino	100.0	2.1	15.0	24.0	20.2	19.0	19.7	10.0
Less than a high school diploma	100.0	3.6	21.9	15.8	19.4	20.5	18.7	9.8
High school graduates, no college[a]	100.0	2.2	13.7	28.6	17.5	16.3	21.7	10.0
Some college or associate degree	100.0	1.5	13.3	22.8	25.0	20.2	17.2	10.1
Bachelor's degree and higher[b]	100.0	—	8.5	26.7	20.7	23.5	20.6	10.4
Hispanic or Latino men	100.0	1.2	11.5	20.7	21.1	19.3	26.2	11.2
Less than a high school diploma	100.0	0.8	12.3	14.8	20.5	24.2	27.4	11.9
High school graduates, no college[a]	100.0	2.5	10.4	24.2	19.2	16.8	26.9	10.8
Some college or associate degree	100.0	0.0	12.7	19.5	22.5	19.6	25.7	11.5
Bachelor's degree and higher[b]	100.0	c	c	c	c	c	c	c

twentieth century, the CWA is the nation's largest communications and media union with, according to its Web site (http://www.cwa-union.org/about/profile.html), more than seven hundred thousand members in such sectors as telecommunications, broadcasting, cable TV, journalism, publishing, and electronics.

- *The International Union, United Automobile, Aerospace, and Agricultural Implement Workers of America (UAW)*—With 640,000 active and over 500,000 retired members in more than 800 local unions in 2008 (http://www.uaw.org/about/uawmembership.html), the UAW protects the rights of automobile and aeronautics

TABLE 1.18

Characteristic	Total	Percent distribution by number of jobs held						Mean number of jobs held
		0 or 1 job	2 to 4 jobs	5 to 7 jobs	8 to 10 jobs	11 to 14 jobs	15 or more jobs	
Hispanic or Latino women	100.0	3.1	18.8	27.6	19.3	18.7	12.5	8.7
Less than a high school diploma	100.0	7.3	34.9	17.2	17.9	15.6	6.9	7.0
High school graduates, no college[a]	100.0	1.8	17.2	33.2	15.7	15.7	16.3	10.0
Some college or associate degree	100.0	3.1	13.9	26.0	27.4	20.8	8.8	10.1
Bachelor's degree and higher[b]	100.0	c	c	c	c	c	c	c

[a]Includes persons with a high school diploma or equivalent.
[b]Includes persons with a bachelor's, master's, professional, and doctoral degrees.
[c]Data not shown where cell size is less than 50.

Notes: This table excludes individuals who turned age 18 before Jan. 1, 1978, or who had not yet turned age 41 when interviewed in 2004/05. The National Longitudinal Survey of Youth 1979 consists of men and women who were born in the years 1957–64 and were ages 14 to 22 when first interviewed in 1979. These individuals were ages 39 to 48 in 2004–05. Educational attainment is defined as of the 2004 survey. Race and Hispanic or Latino ethnicity groups are mutually exclusive but not exhaustive. Other race groups, which are included in the overall totals, are not shown separately because their representation in the survey sample is not sufficiently large to provide statistically reliable estimates.

SOURCE: "Number of Jobs Held by Individuals from Age 18 to Age 40 in 1978 to 2004 by Education Attainment, Sex, Race, Hispanic or Latino Ethnicity, and Age," in *National Longitudinal Surveys*, U.S. Department of Labor, Bureau of Labor Statistics, Undated, http://www.bls.gov/nls/y79r21jobsbyedu.pdf (accessed February 3, 2008)

workers, and since 1935 has won such landmark concessions as employer-paid health care and cost-of-living allowances.

- *United Mine Workers of America*—The United Mine Workers, an AFL-CIO affiliated union, has won several hard-fought battles to ensure fair compensation, health care, and safety standards in the mining industry since the union's inception in 1890 (http://www.umwa.org/who/).

Industry and Occupation

According to the BLS in *Union Members in 2007* (January 25, 2008, http://www.bls.gov/news.release/pdf/union2.pdf), in 2007 public sector workers had a much higher rate of union membership than did private sector employees (35.9% and 7.5%, respectively). Among the private nonagricultural industries, transportation and utilities had the highest unionization rate (22.1%) in 2007; 28.4% of workers in the utilities sub-sector belonged to unions and 20.9% of workers in the transportation and warehousing sub-sector belonged to unions. Although about an average number of workers in information services were unionized in 2007, almost one in five (19.7%) telecommunications workers were.

People in certain occupations were more likely to be unionized than others. In 2007, as noted by the BLS in *Union Members in 2007*, professionals had a high unionization rate of 18.2%, fueled largely by the very high unionization rate among people working in education, training, and library services (37.2%). People in protective service occupations, which include many government workers (such as police, prison guards, and firefighters), also had a high percentage of union members, at 35.2%.

Characteristics of Union Members

A greater proportion of African-Americans were union members in 2007 than any other group. Among

working African-Americans, 14.3% were union members in 2007, compared with 11.8% of whites, 10.9% of Asians, and 9.8% of Hispanics. (See Table 1.19.) Among whites, African-Americans, and to a lesser degree Hispanics, union membership was lower for women than for men. Although 15.8% of employed African-American men were union members in 2007, only 13% of African-American women were. White men had higher union membership (12.8%) than white women (10.8%); Hispanic men (9.9%) had higher union membership than Hispanic women (9.6%). Conversely, among Asians, women had the higher rate of union membership, at 11.6%, compared with a rate of 10.2% for Asian men.

Earnings

In 2007 union members garnered a median weekly salary ($863) that was $200 higher than the median weekly salary of those not represented by unions ($663). (See Table 1.20.) Unionized women earned a median weekly paycheck of $790, compared with $592 for women not belonging to or represented by a union, a difference of $198 per week. Men who belonged to a union had median weekly earnings of $913, compared with $738 for nonunion men, a difference of $175 per week. The disparity in earnings was greatest for Hispanic workers in 2007. The median weekly earnings of unionized Hispanic workers was $736, compared with just $487 for nonunionized Hispanic employees, a difference of $249 per week. These differences are in part due to a union's ability to win higher wages for its members, and in part due to the fact that unionized employees are often working in relatively higher-paid industries than nonunionized employees.

According to the BLS in *Union Members in 2007*, in nearly all occupations, with the exception of people in management, professional, and related occupations,

TABLE 1.19

Union affiliation of employed wage and salary workers, by selected characteristics, 2006–07

[Numbers in thousands]

	2006					2007				
		Members of unions[a]		Represented by unions[b]			Members of unions[a]		Represented by unions[b]	
Characteristic	Total employed	Total	Percent of employed	Total	Percent of employed	Total employed	Total	Percent of employed	Total	Percent of employed
Age and sex										
Total, 16 years and over	**128,237**	**15,359**	**12.0**	**16,860**	**13.1**	**129,767**	**15,670**	**12.1**	**17,243**	**13.3**
16 to 24 years	19,538	857	4.4	978	5.0	19,395	939	4.8	1,068	5.5
25 years and over	108,699	14,502	13.3	15,883	14.6	110,372	14,731	13.3	16,176	14.7
25 to 34 years	28,805	2,899	10.1	3,195	11.1	29,409	3,050	10.4	3,358	11.4
35 to 44 years	30,526	3,997	13.1	4,356	14.3	30,296	3,972	13.1	4,362	14.4
45 to 54 years	29,401	4,710	16.0	5,131	17.5	29,731	4,664	15.7	5,087	17.1
55 to 64 years	16,095	2,568	16.0	2,832	17.6	16,752	2,691	16.1	2,967	17.7
65 years and over	3,872	328	8.5	370	9.5	4,183	355	8.5	402	9.6
Men, 16 years and over	**66,811**	**8,657**	**13.0**	**9,360**	**14.0**	**67,468**	**8,767**	**13.0**	**9,494**	**14.1**
16 to 24 years	10,130	543	5.4	608	6.0	9,959	551	5.5	627	6.3
25 years and over	56,682	8,114	14.3	8,752	15.4	57,509	8,217	14.3	8,867	15.4
25 to 34 years	15,677	1,650	10.5	1,793	11.4	15,994	1,736	10.9	1,884	11.8
35 to 44 years	16,159	2,309	14.3	2,488	15.4	16,070	2,318	14.4	2,501	15.6
45 to 54 years	14,867	2,617	17.6	2,807	18.9	15,040	2,578	17.1	2,745	18.3
55 to 64 years	7,990	1,370	17.1	1,474	18.4	8,286	1,403	16.9	1,532	18.5
65 years and over	1,989	167	8.4	190	9.6	2,119	181	8.5	205	9.7
Women, 16 years and over	**61,426**	**6,702**	**10.9**	**7,501**	**12.2**	**62,299**	**6,903**	**11.1**	**7,749**	**12.4**
16 to 24 years	9,408	315	3.3	370	3.9	9,436	388	4.1	441	4.7
25 years and over	52,018	6,388	12.3	7,131	13.7	52,863	6,514	12.3	7,308	13.8
25 to 34 years	13,127	1,249	9.5	1,401	10.7	13,416	1,313	9.8	1,474	11.0
35 to 44 years	14,368	1,687	11.7	1,867	13.0	14,226	1,653	11.6	1,861	13.1
45 to 54 years	14,534	2,093	14.4	2,325	16.0	14,691	2,086	14.2	2,341	15.9
55 to 64 years	8,106	1,198	14.8	1,358	16.8	8,466	1,288	15.2	1,435	17.0
65 years and over	1,883	160	8.5	180	9.5	2,065	174	8.4	197	9.5
Race, Hispanic or Latino ethnicity, and sex										
White, 16 years and over	104,668	12,259	11.7	13,424	12.8	105,515	12,487	11.8	13,715	13.0
Men	55,459	7,115	12.8	7,668	13.8	55,771	7,134	12.8	7,708	13.8
Women	49,209	5,144	10.5	5,756	11.7	49,743	5,352	10.8	6,007	12.1
Black or African American, 16 years and over	14,878	2,163	14.5	2,391	16.1	15,177	2,165	14.3	2,403	15.8
Men	6,788	1,056	15.6	1,158	17.1	6,945	1,097	15.8	1,205	17.3
Women	8,090	1,107	13.7	1,233	15.2	8,232	1,067	13.0	1,198	14.6
Asian, 16 years and over	5,703	592	10.4	657	11.5	6,016	654	10.9	720	12.0
Men	3,015	286	9.5	316	10.5	3,168	324	10.2	348	11.0
Women	2,688	306	11.4	340	12.7	2,849	330	11.6	372	13.1
Hispanic or Latino ethnicity, 16 years and over	18,121	1,770	9.8	1,935	10.7	18,778	1,837	9.8	2,026	10.8
Men	10,842	1,064	9.8	1,144	10.6	11,163	1,108	9.9	1,208	10.8
Women	7,279	706	9.7	791	10.9	7,615	728	9.6	818	10.7
Full- or part-time status[c]										
Full-time workers	106,106	13,938	13.1	15,244	14.4	107,339	14,201	13.2	15,570	14.5
Part-time workers	21,863	1,382	6.3	1,573	7.2	22,172	1,437	6.5	1,635	7.4

[a]Data refer to members of a labor union or an employee association similar to a union.

[b]Data refer to members of a labor union or an employee association similar to a union as well as workers who report no union affiliation but whose jobs are covered by a union or an employee association contract.

[c]The distinction between full- and part-time workers is based on hours usually worked. These data will not sum to totals because full- or part-time status on the principal job is not identifiable for a small number of multiple jobholders.

Note: Estimates for the above race groups (white, black or African American, and Asian) do not sum to totals because data are not presented for all races. Persons whose ethnicity is identified as Hispanic or Latino may be of any race. Data refer to the sole or principal job of full- and part-time wage and salary workers. Excluded are all self-employed workers regardless of whether or not their businesses are incorporated. Updated population controls are introduced annually with the release of January data.

SOURCE: "Table 1. Union Affiliation of Employed Wage and Salary Workers by Selected Characteristics," in *Union Members in 2007*, U.S. Department of Labor, Bureau of Labor Statistics, January 25, 2008, http://www.bls.gov/news.release/pdf/union2.pdf (accessed February 3, 2008)

people represented by unions earned more than those who were not in 2007. The better wages among unionized employees also held true in all private sector industries except in financial activities and professional and technical services, where nonunionized employees earned slightly more than unionized ones. In the public sector, nonunionized federal employees made slightly more than unionized federal employees, although at the state and local levels, unionized employees had the wage advantage.

TABLE 1.20

Median weekly earnings of full-time wage and salary workers, by union affiliation and selected characteristics, 2006–07

Characteristic	2006				2007			
	Total	Members of unions[a]	Represented by unions[b]	Nonunion	Total	Members of unions[a]	Represented by unions[b]	Nonunion
Age and sex								
Total, 16 years and over	$671	$833	$827	$642	$695	$863	$857	$663
16 to 24 years	409	526	523	404	424	566	551	418
25 years and over	718	850	845	691	738	880	876	712
25 to 34 years	621	773	766	606	643	789	781	622
35 to 44 years	748	853	849	728	769	910	907	745
45 to 54 years	773	888	884	750	790	900	899	763
55 to 64 years	765	882	883	741	803	925	921	766
65 years and over	583	675	667	573	605	634	682	597
Men, 16 years and over	743	887	885	717	766	913	910	738
16 to 24 years	418	526	521	413	443	567	557	432
25 years and over	797	904	902	771	823	930	928	796
25 to 34 years	661	831	822	640	687	823	819	664
35 to 44 years	836	918	914	816	873	971	969	847
45 to 54 years	897	936	939	883	909	958	961	892
55 to 64 years	902	928	930	893	933	954	952	926
65 years and over	658	650	653	659	686	732	776	672
Women, 16 years and over	600	758	753	579	614	790	784	592
16 to 24 years	395	527	529	391	409	564	540	403
25 years and over	627	768	763	607	646	805	800	620
25 to 34 years	583	727	716	565	597	753	745	580
35 to 44 years	645	759	755	626	668	826	820	640
45 to 54 years	659	807	798	628	677	813	810	650
55 to 64 years	658	819	822	627	679	886	881	641
65 years and over	510	690	678	495	534	582	608	520
Race, Hispanic or Latino ethnicity, and sex								
White, 16 years and over	690	859	854	659	716	889	884	684
Men	761	909	907	735	788	937	934	757
Women	609	777	772	588	626	814	807	603
Black or African American, 16 years and over	554	707	694	520	569	732	727	533
Men	591	745	734	557	600	768	763	573
Women	519	665	656	502	533	697	691	513
Asian, 16 years and over	784	834	840	774	830	853	881	823
Men	882	838	852	888	936	867	898	940
Women	699	828	824	681	731	842	871	712
Hispanic or Latino ethnicity, 16 years and over	486	686	681	469	503	736	729	487
Men	505	732	724	490	520	793	782	505
Women	440	607	614	420	473	675	672	446

[a]Data refer to members of a labor union or an employee association similar to a union.
[b]Data refer to members of a labor union or an employee association similar to a union as well as workers who report no union affiliation but whose jobs are covered by a union or an employee association contract.
Note: Estimates for the above race groups (white, black or African American, and Asian) do not sum to totals because data are not presented for all races. Persons whose ethnicity is identified as Hispanic or Latino may be of any race. Data refer to the sole or principal job of full-time wage and salary workers. Excluded are all self-employed workers regardless of whether or not their businesses are incorporated. Updated population controls are introduced annually with the release of January data.

SOURCE: "Table 2. Median Weekly Earnings of Full-Time Wage and Salary Workers by Union Affiliation and Selected Characteristics," in *Union Members in 2007*, U.S. Department of Labor, Bureau of Labor Statistics, January 25, 2008, http://www.bls.gov/news.release/pdf/union2.pdf (accessed February 3, 2008)

CHAPTER 2
THE AMERICAN WORKPLACE

WHERE AMERICANS WORK
The Shift to a Service Economy

The American economy has undergone a fundamental shift since the conclusion of World War II (1939–1945) from primarily a goods-producing nation to one that is increasingly service-oriented. According to Joseph R. Meisenheimer II of the Bureau of Labor Statistics (BLS) in "The Services Industry in the 'Good' versus 'Bad' Jobs Debate" (*Monthly Labor Review*, February 1998, http://www.bls.gov/opub/mlr/1998/02/art3full.pdf), service industries accounted for just 10% of nonfarm employment in 1945 compared with 38% in goods-producing industries. Since the 1970s the American economy has moved increasingly away from producing goods to providing services, and the service-producing sector has accounted for a growing proportion of workers. In 1970, for example, there were 48.8 million service-providing workers, and 22.2 million people in the goods-producing sector (see Table 2.1), representing a service-to-goods ratio of 2.2 to one. By 2000 the number of workers in the service-providing sector was 107.1 million, compared with 24.6 million in the goods-producing sector, representing a service-to-goods ratio of 4.4 to one. In 2007, according to preliminary statistics compiled by the BLS, workers who provided services (115.4 million) outnumbered workers who produced goods (22.2 million) by a ratio of 5.2 to one.

Service-producing industries include eight subsectors:

- Transportation and utilities
- Information services
- Financial activities
- Professional and business services
- Education and health services
- Leisure and hospitality services

- Other services (ranging from automobile repair shops to religious and political organizations)
- Government

Jobs in the service industry are incredibly diverse, including occupations such as teaching, social work, nursing, food service, retail sales, accounting, data entry, truck driving, and many more. Goods-producing industries include agriculture and related industries, mining, construction, and manufacturing. Jobs in the goods-producing industry include mining, forestry, farm work, construction, assembly-line work, and other manufacturing jobs. However, workers in different industries may have similar occupations, that is, they do similar kinds of work. For example, a buildings and grounds maintenance worker might work at a large manufacturing plant, and therefore be employed in the goods-producing industry, or at a hospital, and therefore be employed in the service-producing industry.

Table 2.1 shows that the number of goods-producing workers in 2007 at 22.2 million was virtually the same as in 1970, whereas the number of workers in the service sector had more than doubled from 48.8 million to 115.4 million. From 1995 to 2006 construction was the only industry in the goods-producing area that consistently employed more workers each year, employing 5.3 million workers in 1995 and 7.7 million workers in 2006. That year, however, was a peak for the construction industry; the BLS reports in *Current Employment Statistics Highlights April 2008* (May 2008, http://www.bls.gov/web/ceshighlights.pdf) that between September 2006 and April 2008 construction jobs fell by 457,000 due to the downturn in the housing market. The number of employees working in natural resources and mining fell from a fifty-year industry high of 1.2 million workers in 1981 to 723,000 in 2007. The number of workers in manufacturing remained roughly the same from 1970 (17.8 million workers) through 2000 (17.3 million workers). Since then,

TABLE 2.1

Employees on nonfarm payrolls by major industry sector, selected years, 1970–2007

[In thousands]

Year	Total	Total private	Total goods-producing	Goods-producing Natural resources and mining	Construction	Manufacturing
				Annual averages		
1970	71,006	58,318	22,179	677	3,654	17,848
1975	77,069	62,250	21,318	802	3,608	16,909
1980	90,528	74,154	24,263	1,077	4,454	18,733
1985	97,511	80,978	23,585	974	4,793	17,819
1990	109,487	91,072	23,723	765	5,263	17,695
1995	117,298	97,865	23,156	641	5,274	17,241
2000	131,785	110,995	24,649	599	6,787	17,263
2005	133,703	111,899	22,190	628	7,336	14,226
2006	136,086	114,113	22,531	684	7,691	14,155
2007	137,623	115,420	22,221	723	7,614	13,884

Year	Total service-providing	Service-providing Trade, transportation and utilities	Information	Financial activities	Professional and business services	Education and health services	Leisure and hospitality	Other services	Government
					Annual averages				
1970	48,827	14,144	2,041	3,532	5,267	4,577	4,789	1,789	12,687
1975	55,751	15,606	2,061	4,047	6,034	5,497	5,544	2,144	14,820
1980	66,265	18,413	2,361	5,025	7,544	7,072	6,721	2,755	16,375
1985	73,926	20,379	2,437	5,815	8,871	8,657	7,869	3,366	16,533
1990	85,764	22,666	2,688	6,614	10,848	10,984	9,288	4,261	18,415
1995	94,142	23,834	2,843	6,827	12,844	13,289	10,501	4,572	19,432
2000	107,136	26,225	3,630	7,687	16,666	15,109	11,862	5,168	20,790
2005	111,513	25,959	3,061	8,153	16,954	17,372	12,816	5,395	21,804
2006	113,556	26,276	3,038	8,328	17,566	17,826	13,110	5,438	21,974
2007	115,402	26,608	3,029	8,308	17,962	18,327	13,474	5,491	22,203

Note: Data are currently projected from March 2007 benchmark levels. When more recent benchmark data are introduced with the release of January 2009 estimates, all unadjusted data from April 2007 forward and all seasonally adjusted data from January 2004 forward are subject to revision. Data reflect the conversion to the 2007 version of the North American Industry Classification System (NAICS) as the basis for the assignment and tabulation of economic data by industry, replacing NAICS 2002.

SOURCE: Adapted from "B-1. Employees on Nonfarm Payrolls by Major Industry Sector, 1958 to Date," in *Establishment Data: Historical Employment*, U.S. Department of Labor, Bureau of Labor Statistics, 2008, ftp://ftp.bls.gov/pub/suppl/empsit.ceseeb1.txt (accessed February 4, 2008)

however, this sector has experienced a steady decline in workers. In 2007 only 13.9 million people worked in manufacturing. (See Table 2.1.) The proportion of manufacturing jobs has fallen from 25.1% of all nonfarm jobs in 1970 to 10.1% in 2007.

In 2007 government provided the largest number of jobs in the service sector (22.2 million), followed closely by education and health services (18.3 million jobs) and professional and business services (18 million jobs). The smallest number of jobs in the service sector was provided by the information subsector (3 million jobs). Manufacturing still provided the most jobs in the goods-producing sector (13.9 million jobs), although the number of manufacturing jobs was shrinking while the number of construction jobs was rising. (See Table 2.1.)

In *Employer Costs for Employee Compensation— December 2007* (March 12, 2008, http://www.bls.gov/news .release/pdf/ecec.pdf), the BLS reported that average wages in goods-producing industries in December 2007 were $20.62 per hour, and the average wages in service indus-

tries were $18.18 per hour. The difference is even more pronounced when factoring in the cost of benefits such as paid leave, insurance, and retirement. The average cost per hour worked to employers in goods-producing industries when taking benefits into account was $30.94; the average cost per hour to employers in service industries was $25.30.

Because average wages, including benefits provided, are higher in manufacturing than in services, some observers view the shift in employment from goods-producing to service-providing as a change from "good" to "bad" jobs. Meisenheimer, however, found that many service industries equal or exceed manufacturing and other industries on measures of job quality, while some service industries could be viewed as less desirable by these measures.

Meisenheimer stressed the importance of examining more than just average pay when assessing the quality of jobs in each industry. Within each industry, there are jobs at a variety of different quality levels. The quality of service-industry jobs is especially diverse, encompassing many of the "best" jobs in the economy along with a substantial share of the "worst." Thus, employment shifts away from manufacturing and toward services can, but do not necessarily, signal deterioration in overall domestic job quality.

Movement of Work

Whereas a generation ago many of the goods sold in the United States had been produced by American workers, the labor market in the early twenty-first century presents a different picture. In an effort to maximize profits, many companies now "outsource" production (pay another company to manufacture something that its workers once made) or move work "offshore" (relocate the manufacture of an item from the United States to an overseas location where labor and material costs are cheaper).

According to Sharon P. Brown of the Bureau of Labor Statistics in "Mass Layoff Statistics Data in the United States and Domestic and Overseas Relocation" (December 2004, http://www.bls.gov/mls/mlsrelocation.pdf), 6,181 layoff events occurred during 2003, affecting approximately 1.2 million workers. Fifteen percent of these layoff events were permanent, due mainly to company restructuring. These closures affected 210,903 workers. The industries that were most affected were those involved in the manufacture of computer and electronic products, machinery, textiles, and clothing. In addition, overseas relocation of business affected 13,000 workers in manufacturing industries in 2003 (representing 9% of all layoffs). More than 40% of these relocations were to Mexico.

Two years later, in *Extended Mass Layoffs in 2005* (September 2006, http://www.bls.gov/mls/mlsreport997 .pdf), the Bureau of Labor Statistics reported that there were 277 mass layoff events involving movement of work resulting in the layoffs of 53,628 workers in 2005. These numbers represented a drop of about 25% from 2004, when there were 366 mass layoff events involving 73,217 workers .The location where the work was moved in 2005 was identified in 259 cases. Out-of-country moves accounted for about 35% of these 259 mass layoff events and resulted in the layoff of 12,030 workers. Two-thirds of the time the work had moved to either Mexico or China.

At-Home Work

Between 1960 and 1980 the number of Americans working at home steadily declined, largely reflecting a drop in the number of family farmers as many gave up farming in the face of dropping profitability. In addition, many professionals, such as doctors and lawyers, left their home offices and joined group practices or larger firms in office buildings. This trend was reversed by 1990, according to the U.S. Census Bureau ("Increase in At-Home Workers Reverses Earlier Trend," March 1998, http://www.census.gov/prod/3/98pubs/cenbr982.pdf), which reported a 56% increase over 1980 (to 3.4 million) in the number of people who worked at home most of the time.

Data from the BLS in *Work at Home in 2004* (September 22, 2005, http://www.bls.gov/news.release/ pdf/homey.pdf) indicated that in 2004, 15.1% of employed workers worked at home at least once per week, up from 14.9% in 2001. (These figures are not comparable to the earlier Census figures, which counted only people who worked at home most of the time). Nearly half (49.3%) of these people were not paid for their work at home; 16.2% of them were paid. A third (33.7%) were self-employed and worked at home in a home-based business. More than 4.6 million Americans conducted a home-based business as their primary occupation and worked exclusively at home, according to the BLS.

In *Work at Home in 2004*, the BLS also reported that in May 2004 women (15.4%) were more likely than men (14.9%) to do work related to their primary employment at home each week. However, a larger percentage of all men who did work at home were self-employed (37.6% of men and 29.4% of women), while a larger percentage of female wage and salary workers did paid work at home (17.8% of women and 14.7% of men) and unpaid work at home (51.4% of women and 47.3% of men).

White people were more likely than any other group to work at home as part of their primary job, according to the BLS in *Work at Home in 2004*. Over 16% of white workers usually worked at home, compared with 12.7% of Asian workers, 7.9% of African-American workers, and 7.1% of Hispanic workers. This difference may be partly due to the fact that the more educated a worker was, the more likely he or she was to do work at home. African-American and Hispanic workers were less likely than whites or Asians in 2004 to have attained a bachelor's degree or higher.

The BLS also reported in *Work at Home in 2004* that people in management, professional, and related occupations were more likely to work at home as part of their primary occupation than were people in other occupations. Nearly three out of ten (29.2%) people who worked in management, business, and financial operations occupations usually did work at home each week, and 27.4% of people in professional occupations did so. On the other hand, people working in service occupations (6.2%), sales and office occupations (12.2%), natural resources, construction, and maintenance occupations (7.9%), and production, transportation, and material moving occupations (2.7%) were much less likely to work at home as part of their primary employment.

WHEN AMERICANS WORK
How Much Time Do Americans Spend at Work?

Compared with other countries with advanced economies, workers in the United States have a long work year, due in part to a lack of legally mandated, employer-paid vacation time. Such paid vacation time is common in many countries in Europe. In 2006, according to the U.S. Department of Labor in *A Chartbook of International Labor Comparisons: The Americas, Asia-Pacific, Europe* (January 2008 http://www.dol.gov/asp/media/reports/chartbook/2008-01/chartbook.pdf), only South Koreans (2,305 hours per year) and Mexicans (1,883 hours per year) averaged more hours worked per year than Americans (1,804). These figures contrasted sharply with such European countries as the Netherlands (1,391 hours), Norway (1,407), France (1,564), and Germany (1,436). (See Figure 2.1.)

In 2007, as the BLS reported in *Employment and Earnings* (January 2008, http://www.bls.gov/cps/cpsaat23.pdf), 107.9 million Americans out of the total nonfarm laborer population of 140.3 million (76.9%) were working full-time (defined as thirty-five hours or more), while the remaining 32.4 million workers (23.1%) were working fewer than thirty-five hours per workweek (defined as part-time). The average part- and full-time workweek in 2007 was 39.2 hours per week, while the average full-time employee worked 42.8 hours per week. (See Table 2.2.) In that year, according to the BLS in *Employment and Earnings*, 27.3% of all nonfarm workers spent 41 hours per week or more on the job, and 41.9% of agricultural workers labored more than 41 hours per week.

Men tended to work longer hours than women. In 2007 men averaged 41.7 hours per workweek, while women averaged 36.1 hours. Of persons who worked full-time, men averaged 44.1 hours per workweek, and women averaged 41 hours. (See Table 2.2.)

People in some occupations worked longer than people in others. For example, in 2007 transportation and material-moving workers labored an average of 40.6 hours per week; the average number of hours among those who usually worked full-time was 44 hours. Workers in management, business, and financial occupations also worked fairly long hours. They averaged 43.5 hours per week in 2007, and 45.3 hours if they usually worked full time. People in construction and extraction occupations, however, worked shorter hours. They averaged 40.2 hours per week, up to 41.5 hours if they usually worked full-time. (See Table 2.2.)

As reported by the BLS in *American Time Use Survey—2006 Results* (June 28, 2007, http://www.bls.gov/news.release/pdf/atus.pdf), the majority of full- and part-time employees (83.5%) worked on an average weekday in 2006. (See Table 2.3.) On those days, they worked an average of 7.99 hours. About a third of all full- and part-time employees (34.8%) worked on an average Saturday, Sunday, or holiday. Those who worked on these days tended to average shorter hours of work (5.43 hours). The more educated a worker, the more likely he or she was to work on weekends or holidays (38.9% of them did), reflecting the tendency of workers in high-responsibility positions to work longer hours and do work at home. In fact, 21.1% of employed persons in that year worked at home on an average

FIGURE 2.1

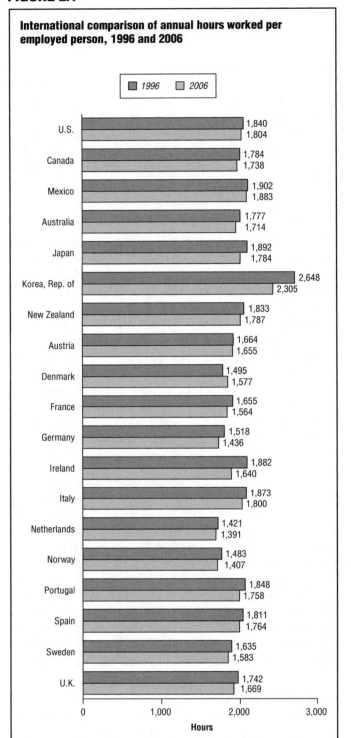

International comparison of annual hours worked per employed person, 1996 and 2006

Note: In both years, Koreans worked the most hours annually. The Republic of Korea and Ireland experienced the largest reductions in annual hours worked per employed person.

SOURCE: "Chart 2.9. Annual Hours Worked per Employed Person, 1996 and 2006," in *A Chartbook of International Labor Comparisons: The Americas, Asia-Pacific, Europe*, U.S. Department of Labor, January 2008, http://www.dol.gov/asp/media/reports/chartbook/2008-01/chartbook.pdf (accessed February 4, 2008). Data from Organisation for Economic Co-operation and Development.

TABLE 2.2

Persons at work by occupation, sex, and usual full- or part-time status, 2007

[Numbers in thousands]

Occupation and sex	Total at work	2007 Worked 1 to 34 hours — Total	For economic reasons	For noneconomic reasons — Usually work full time	For noneconomic reasons — Usually work part time	Worked 35 hours or more	Average hours — Total at work	Average hours — Persons who usually work full time
Total, 16 years and over	**140,328**	**32,435**	**4,401**	**8,278**	**19,756**	**107,892**	**39.2**	**42.8**
Management, professional, and related occupations	49,322	9,252	734	3,242	5,275	40,070	41.0	43.8
Management, business, and financial operations occupations	20,874	2,866	244	1,214	1,409	18,007	43.5	45.3
Professional and related occupations	28,448	6,385	490	2,028	3,867	22,063	39.2	42.6
Service occupations	23,221	8,375	1,300	1,164	5,912	14,846	35.3	41.7
Sales and office occupations	34,997	9,453	988	2,001	6,464	25,543	37.4	41.9
Sales and related occupations	16,108	4,565	570	725	3,270	11,543	38.2	43.7
Office and administrative support occupations	18,888	4,888	418	1,276	3,194	14,000	36.8	40.5
Natural resources, construction, and maintenance occupations*	15,225	2,393	759	957	678	12,832	40.9	42.3
Construction and extraction occupations	9,196	1,606	603	635	368	7,590	40.2	41.5
Installation, maintenance, and repair occupations	5,100	567	106	271	190	4,532	42.1	43.2
Production, transportation, and material moving occupations	17,563	2,962	621	915	1,427	14,601	40.9	43.2
Production occupations	9,118	1,191	244	501	446	7,927	41.2	42.5
Transportation and material moving occupations	8,446	1,772	377	414	981	6,674	40.6	44.0
Men, 16 years and over	**75,803**	**12,510**	**2,322**	**4,022**	**6,166**	**63,293**	**41.7**	**44.1**
Management, professional, and related occupations	24,733	3,224	328	1,418	1,477	21,510	43.9	45.6
Management, business, and financial operations occupations	12,034	1,278	149	608	521	10,756	45.7	47.0
Professional and related occupations	12,700	1,945	179	810	956	10,754	42.2	44.3
Service occupations	10,026	2,639	498	469	1,672	7,387	38.3	43.0
Sales and office occupations	12,904	2,429	333	572	1,524	10,474	41.0	44.2
Sales and related occupations	8,192	1,445	200	322	923	6,746	42.2	45.4
Office and administrative support occupations	4,712	984	134	249	601	3,728	38.9	42.2
Natural resources, construction, and maintenance occupations*	14,590	2,222	725	909	588	12,367	41.0	42.3
Construction and extraction occupations	8,951	1,533	586	615	332	7,418	40.3	41.5
Installation, maintenance, and repair occupations	4,905	534	103	254	176	4,371	42.2	43.2
Production, transportation, and material moving occupations	13,550	1,995	438	654	904	11,554	41.9	43.9
Production occupations	6,393	667	142	317	209	5,726	42.3	43.2
Transportation and material moving occupations	7,157	1,328	297	337	695	5,829	41.6	44.5
Women, 16 years and over	**64,525**	**19,926**	**2,079**	**4,257**	**13,590**	**44,599**	**36.1**	**41.0**
Management, professional, and related occupations	24,588	6,028	406	1,824	3,798	18,560	38.2	41.7
Management, business, and financial operations occupations	8,840	1,588	95	606	888	7,252	40.5	42.9
Professional and related occupations	15,748	4,440	311	1,218	2,911	11,309	36.9	41.0
Service occupations	13,195	5,736	802	694	4,240	7,459	33.0	40.5
Sales and office occupations	22,093	7,024	655	1,429	4,940	15,069	35.4	40.3
Sales and related occupations	7,917	3,120	370	403	2,347	4,796	34.2	41.3
Office and administrative support occupations	14,176	3,904	285	1,026	2,593	10,273	36.1	39.9
Natural resources, construction, and maintenance occupations*	635	171	33	48	90	464	37.7	41.5
Construction and extraction occupations	245	73	17	20	36	172	37.1	41.4
Installation, maintenance, and repair occupations	195	34	3	17	14	161	39.7	41.4
Production, transportation, and material moving occupations	4,013	967	182	261	523	3,047	37.7	40.7
Production occupations	2,725	524	102	184	237	2,201	38.8	40.8
Transportation and material moving occupations	1,289	443	80	77	286	845	35.3	40.5

*Includes farming, fishing, and forestry occupations, not shown separately.
Note: Updated population controls are introduced annually with the release of January data.

SOURCE: "23. Persons at Work by Occupation, Sex, and Usual Full- or Part-Time Status," in *Employment and Earnings*, U.S. Department of Labor, Bureau of Labor Statistics, January 2008, http://www.bls.gov/cps/cpsaat23.pdf (accessed February 2, 2008)

day, averaging 2.64 hours per day. While only 5.5% of employees without a high school diploma worked at home on an average day, 37% of those with a bachelor's degree or higher did. (See Table 2.4.)

Many employees are working longer hours by skipping or shortening their lunch breaks. The National Restaurant Association reported (in "What's for Lunch? A Survey of Full-Time Employees," 2002) that 40.6% of the surveyed

TABLE 2.3

Employed persons working and time spent working on days worked, by selected characteristics, 2006

[Numbers in thousands. Unless otherwise specified, data refer to persons 15 years and over.]

Characteristic	Total employed	Employed persons who worked on an average day			Employed persons who worked on an average weekday			Employed persons who worked on an average Saturday, Sunday, and holiday[a]		
		Number	Percent of employed	Average hours of work[b]	Number[c]	Percent of employed	Average hours of work[b]	Number[d]	Percent of employed	Average hours of work[b]
Full- and part-time status and sex										
Total, 15 years and over[e]	151,175	104,048	68.8	7.60	126,176	83.5	7.99	52,673	34.8	5.43
Full-time workers	117,880	85,035	72.1	8.12	104,111	88.3	8.54	40,760	34.6	5.59
Part-time workers	33,295	19,012	57.1	5.30	22,067	66.3	5.40	11,914	35.8	4.87
Men[e]	80,637	57,426	71.2	8.04	69,041	85.6	8.47	30,198	37.4	5.75
Full-time workers	68,954	50,722	73.6	8.44	61,214	88.8	8.89	25,697	37.3	5.82
Part-time workers	11,684	6,704	57.4	5.08	7,747	66.3	5.01	4,491	38.4	5.34
Women[e]	70,538	46,622	66.1	7.06	57,124	81.0	7.41	22,506	31.9	5.00
Full-time workers	48,926	34,314	70.1	7.65	42,891	87.7	8.03	15,146	31.0	5.21
Part-time workers	21,611	12,308	57.0	5.42	14,320	66.3	5.60	7,390	34.2	4.55
Jobholding status										
Single jobholders	135,379	91,292	67.4	7.53	112,022	82.7	7.90	43,576	32.2	5.40
Multiple jobholders	15,795	12,756	80.8	8.08	14,130	89.5	8.75	9,317	59.0	5.55
Educational attainment, 25 years and over										
Less than a high school diploma	11,035	7,301	66.2	7.87	9,279	84.1	7.96	2,713	24.6	7.12
High school graduates, no college[f]	36,699	24,815	67.6	8.05	30,589	83.4	8.28	11,539	31.4	6.67
Some college or associate degree	34,941	24,388	69.8	7.74	29,668	84.9	8.13	11,780	33.7	5.38
Bachelor's degree and higher[g]	44,584	32,735	73.4	7.38	39,511	88.6	8.06	17,335	38.9	3.87

[a]Holidays are New Year's Day, Easter, Memorial Day, the Fourth of July, Labor Day, Thanksgiving Day, and Christmas Day.
[b]Includes work at main and other job(s), and excludes travel related to work.
[c]Number was derived by multiplying the "total employed" by the percent of employed persons who worked on an average weekday.
[d]Number was derived by multiplying the "total employed" by the percent of employed persons who worked on an average Saturday, Sunday, and holiday.
[e]Includes workers whose hours vary.
[f]Includes persons with a high school diploma or equivalent.
[g]Includes persons with bachelor's, master's, professional, and doctoral degrees.

SOURCE: "Table 4. Employed Persons Working and Time Spent Working on Days Worked by Full- and Part-Time Status and Sex, Jobholding Status, Educational Attainment, and Day of Week, 2006 Annual Averages," in *American Time Use Survey—2006 Results*, U.S. Department of Labor, Bureau of Labor Statistics, June 28, 2007, http://www.bls.gov/news.release/pdf/atus.pdf (accessed February 28, 2008)

workers reported they did not leave the office for a lunch break. Forty-five percent reported they had less time for lunch than they ever had. A frequently expressed motivation for staying on the job was a fear of being downsized.

An earlier study by BLS economists Philip L. Rones, Randy E. Ilg, and Jennifer M. Gardner ("Trends in the Hours of Work since the Mid-1970s" *Monthly Labor Review*, April 1997) attributed growth in the share of workers reporting very long workweeks to a shift in employment toward high-hour, increased responsibility occupations such as managers, professionals, and certain sales workers. Robert Whaples of Wake Forest University reported in "Hours of Work in U.S. History" (EH.Net, August 15, 2001, http://eh.net/encyclopedia/article/whaples.work .hours.us) that while hours of work fell over the course of the twentieth century, well-educated men and women, who theoretically are in higher-responsibility positions and paid by salary, not by the hour, are working longer hours than other workers.

There are some indications that as work hours decrease, the amount of time spent in leisure and recreation is increasing.

The BLS reported in *American Time Use Survey—2006 Results* that people aged fifteen and older spent, on average, about 4.77 hours per weekday and 1.36 hours per weekend day and holiday on working and work-related activities in 2006. The amount of time spent on leisure approached the amount of time spent on work each weekday. The average American spent 4.54 hours per weekday on leisure and sports, including socializing, watching television, or participating in exercise or sports. Although about 56.2% of Americans aged fifteen and older did work-related activities each weekday, almost everyone (95.9%) took part in some kind of leisure or sports activity. This discrepancy is partly due to the inclusion of students and retirees in these counts. (See Table 2.5.)

Survey of Workers' Hours

Of the respondents to an August 2005 Gallup Poll, 45% reported that they worked between 35 and 44 hours per week; 30% worked between 45 and 59 hours per week; and 9% worked more than 60 hours each week (Joseph Carroll, "Workers Describe Jobs, Pay, and Hours," September 13, 2005, http://www.gallup.com/poll/18499/ Workers-Describe-Jobs-Pay-Hours.aspx). These numbers

TABLE 2.4

Employed persons working at home and at their workplace and time spent working at each location, by selected characteristics, 2006

[Numbers in thousands. Data refer to persons 15 years and over. Includes work at main and other job(s) and at locations other than home or workplace. Excludes travel related to work.]

Characteristic	Total employed	Employed persons who worked on an average day			Employed persons who worked at their workplace on an average day[a]			Employed persons who worked at home on an average day[a, b]		
		Number	Percent of employed	Average hours of work	Number	Percent of those who worked	Average hours of work at workplace	Number	Percent of those who worked	Average hours of work at home
Full- and part-time status and sex										
Total, 15 years and over[c]	**151,175**	**104,048**	**68.8**	**7.60**	**89,664**	**86.2**	**7.87**	**21,980**	**21.1**	**2.64**
Full-time workers	117,880	85,035	72.1	8.12	74,487	87.6	8.31	17,729	20.8	2.76
Part-time workers	33,295	19,012	57.1	5.30	15,177	79.8	5.74	4,251	22.4	2.17
Men[c]	80,637	57,426	71.2	8.04	49,741	86.6	8.28	12,386	21.6	2.60
Full-time workers	68,954	50,722	73.6	8.44	44,428	87.6	8.61	10,828	21.3	2.69
Part-time workers	11,684	6,704	57.4	5.08	5,313	79.2	5.59	1,558	23.2	2.01
Women[c]	70,538	46,622	66.1	7.06	39,923	85.6	7.36	9,594	20.6	2.70
Full-time workers	48,926	34,314	70.1	7.65	30,059	87.6	7.87	6,901	20.1	2.87
Part-time workers	21,611	12,308	57.0	5.42	9,865	80.1	5.82	2,693	21.9	2.27
Jobholding status										
Single jobholders	135,379	91,292	67.4	7.53	79,351	86.9	7.85	17,054	18.7	2.47
Multiple jobholders	15,795	12,756	80.8	8.08	10,313	80.8	8.05	4,926	38.6	3.24
Educational attainment, 25 years and over										
Less than a high school diploma	11,035	7,301	66.2	7.87	6,869	94.1	7.92	402	5.5	(f)
High school graduates, no college[d]	36,699	24,815	67.6	8.05	22,402	90.3	8.15	3,227	13.0	2.94
Some college or associate degree	34,941	24,388	69.8	7.74	21,212	87.0	8.04	4,983	20.4	2.39
Bachelor's degree and higher[e]	44,584	32,735	73.4	7.38	25,496	77.9	7.88	12,104	37.0	2.71

[a]Individuals may have worked at more than one location.
[b]"Working at home" includes any time persons did work at home and it is not restricted to persons whose usual workplace is their home.
[c]Includes workers whose hours vary.
[d]Includes persons with a high school diploma or equivalent.
[e]Includes persons with bachelor's, master's, professional, and doctoral degrees.
[f]Data not shown where base is less than 1.2 million.

SOURCE: "Table 6. Employed Persons Working at Home and at Their Workplace and Time Spent Working at Each Location by Full- and Part-Time Status and Sex, Jobholding Status, and Educational Attainment, 2006 Annual Averages," in *American Time Use Survey—2006 Results*, U.S. Department of Labor, Bureau of Labor Statistics, June 28, 2007, http://www.bls.gov/news.release/pdf/atus.pdf (accessed February 28, 2008)

had fluctuated somewhat over the previous fifteen years but had not changed significantly in a manner that indicated a decided trend except at the high end, where fewer workers were reporting that they worked 60 hours or more. In a poll conducted during July 1991, for example, 44% of workers said that their typical workweek was between 35 and 44 hours; 27% worked between 45 and 59 hours per week; and 13% worked more than 60 hours per week. In 1991 the median workweek (half of respondents said they worked more, and half said they worked less) was 43.4 hours and the average workweek was 40 hours. In 2005 the median workweek of those surveyed was 41.9 hours, and the average workweek was 40 hours.

As to the flexibility of their work schedule, respondents to an August 2007 Gallup Poll were generally satisfied. Sixty-eight percent of respondents indicated that they were completely satisfied with the flexibility of their hours. (See Figure 2.2.) Another 22% indicated they were at least somewhat satisfied; and only 9% were dissatisfied with the flexibility of their hours. The percentage of those who were completely satisfied had increased markedly from those surveyed in July 1991.

At that time only 39% of respondents reported that they were completely satisfied with the flexibility of their work schedule.

Flexible Schedules

An increase in flexible work schedules was widespread across demographic groups, occupations, and industries in 2004, according to the BLS in *Workers on Flexible and Shift Schedules in May 2004* (July 1, 2005, http://www.bls.gov/news.release/pdf/flex.pdf). In May 2004, 28.7% of white workers had flexible work schedules that included at-home work, compared with 19.7% of African-Americans and 18.4% of Hispanics.

The BLS also reported in *Workers on Flexible and Shift Schedules in May 2004* that about 44.7% of executives, administrators, and managers, 52.4% of workers in computer and mathematical occupations, 47.5% of workers in life, physical, and social science occupations, and 38.1% of sales workers were able to vary their work hours. However, only 21.2% of those employed as service workers, 13.1% of workers in education, training, and library occupations, and 12.4% of production workers

TABLE 2.5

Time spent in primary activities and percent of civilian population engaging in each activity, averages per day on weekdays and weekends, 2006

[Data refer to persons 15 years and over]

Activity[a]	Average hours per day, civilian population		Average percent engaged in the activity per day		Average hours per day for persons who engaged in the activity	
	Weekdays	Weekends and holidays[b]	Weekdays	Weekends and holidays[b]	Weekdays	Weekends and holidays[b]
Total, all activities[c]	24.00	24.00	—	—	—	—
Personal care activities	9.12	10.08	100.0	100.0	9.12	10.08
Sleeping	8.33	9.32	100.0	99.9	8.33	9.33
Eating and drinking	1.18	1.37	96.1	95.7	1.22	1.43
Household activities	1.66	2.11	73.3	75.5	2.26	2.79
Housework	.57	.70	35.1	38.5	1.62	1.82
Food preparation and cleanup	.51	.57	52.1	50.5	.98	1.13
Lawn and garden care	.16	.27	9.6	11.9	1.72	2.30
Household management	.12	.15	18.7	18.0	.62	.83
Purchasing goods and services	.76	.93	44.8	46.9	1.69	1.98
Consumer goods purchases	.34	.55	39.3	45.2	.87	1.22
Professional and personal care services	.10	.04	10.7	4.2	.98	1.02
Caring for and helping household members	.56	.45	26.6	21.8	2.10	2.04
Caring for and helping household children	.43	.37	22.8	18.8	1.87	1.99
Caring for and helping nonhousehold members	.19	.26	12.5	14.5	1.53	1.81
Caring for and helping nonhousehold adults	.06	.11	7.6	9.5	.80	1.14
Working and work-related activities	4.77	1.36	56.2	23.9	8.48	5.70
Working	4.33	1.23	54.2	22.8	7.98	5.42
Educational activities	.63	.16	10.7	6.4	5.90	2.49
Attending class	.42	.04	8.5	2.7	4.90	1.63
Homework and research	.16	.10	6.9	4.0	2.38	2.54
Organizational, civic, and religious activities	.20	.53	10.4	20.0	1.95	2.63
Religious and spiritual activities	.04	.30	4.1	16.0	1.06	1.88
Volunteering (organizational and civic activities)	.13	.15	6.7	6.7	1.89	2.25
Leisure and sports	4.54	6.37	95.9	97.6	4.73	6.52
Socializing and communicating	.60	1.11	37.9	46.1	1.59	2.41
Watching television	2.35	3.10	78.6	81.6	2.99	3.80
Participating in sports, exercise, and recreation	.26	.33	17.5	16.3	1.48	2.03
Telephone calls, mail, and e-mail	.20	.17	27.9	21.3	.71	.81
Other activities, not elsewhere classified	.20	.22	13.9	13.8	1.45	1.62

[a]A primary activity refers to an individual's main activity. Other activities done simultaneously are not included.
[b]Holidays are New Year's Day, Easter, Memorial Day, the Fourth of July, Labor Day, Thanksgiving Day, and Christmas Day.
[c]All major activity categories include related travel time.
—Not applicable.

SOURCE: "Table 2. Time Spent in Primary Activities and Percent of the Civilian Population Engaging in Each Activity, Averages per Day on Weekdays and Weekends, 2006 Annual Averages," in *American Time Use Survey—2006 Results*, U.S. Department of Labor, Bureau of Labor Statistics, June 28, 2007, http://www.bls.gov/news.release/pdf/atus.pdf (accessed February 28, 2008)

had such flexibility. Among private-sector employees, the proportion of workers with flexible schedules was much higher in such service-producing industries as financial activities (37.7%) and professional and business services (37.6%) than in goods-producing industries (24%). In the public sector, flexible schedules were more common among federal and state government employees (28.8% and 28.4%, respectively) than workers in local government (13.7%), which includes public elementary and secondary schools.

Shift Schedules

According to 2004 BLS data in *Workers on Flexible and Shift Schedules in May 2004*, 84.6% of full-time wage and salary workers had regular daytime schedules; 14.8% worked on alternative schedules, including evening shifts, employer-arranged irregular schedules, night shifts, and rotating shifts. According to the BLS, 4.7% of those who worked alternative shifts worked evening shifts, 3.2% worked night shifts, 3.1% worked employer-arranged irregular schedules, and 2.5% worked rotating shifts.

As indicated by the May 2004 data, shift work was most common among workers in service-oriented occupations, such as food preparation and serving (40.4%) and protective services (50.6%; police, firefighters, and guards), and among those employed in production, transportation, and material moving occupations (26.2%). Shift work in 2004 tended to be lowest for managers and professionals (7.6%) and those in natural resources, construction, and maintenance occupations (7.5%).

Women (87%) were more likely than men (82.7%) to work regular daytime shifts in 2004, and men (16.7%) were more likely than women (12.4%) to work alternative shifts, such as evening or night shifts, according to the BLS research. African-American shift workers (20.8%) were

FIGURE 2.2

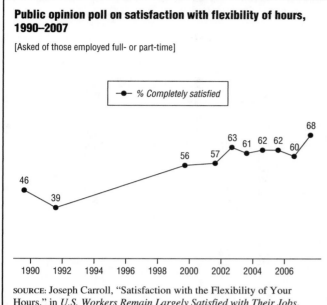

Public opinion poll on satisfaction with flexibility of hours, 1990–2007

[Asked of those employed full- or part-time]

— ● — % Completely satisfied

SOURCE: Joseph Carroll, "Satisfaction with the Flexibility of Your Hours," in *U.S. Workers Remain Largely Satisfied with Their Jobs*, The Gallup Organization, November 27, 2007, http://www.gallup.com/poll/102898/US-Workers-Remain-Largely-Satisfied-Their-Jobs.aspx (accessed February 18, 2008). Copyright © 2008 by The Gallup Organization. Reproduced by permission of The Gallup Organization.

more likely to work an alternative shift than shift workers who were white (13.7%), Asian (15.7%), or Hispanic (16%).

Multiple Jobs

In 2007, 5.2% of workers aged sixteen and older held multiple jobs, according to the Bureau of Labor Statistics in *Employment and Earnings*. The proportion of women holding more than one job (5.6%) was higher than that of men (4.9%). Of women, those who were single (6.3%) and widowed, divorced, or separated (6.5%) were more likely than married women (5%) to have more than one job in 2005. Among men, however, those who were single (4.3%), or divorced, widowed, or separated (4.6%), were less likely than married men (5.3%) to have multiple jobs. (See Table 2.6.) This difference may have to do with the traditional view that upon marriage, men's primary responsibility is to take financial responsibility for the family, while women's primary responsibility is to do the work in the home.

Part-Time Work

People work part-time for various reasons. The BLS reported in *Employment and Earnings* that in 2007, 4.4 million of the total 32.4 million part-time workers (13.6%) took part-time work due to economic conditions. The most common economic reasons cited by workers were slack work or business conditions (2.9 million workers, or 8.9% of all part-time workers) and the ability to find only part-time work (1.2 million workers, or 3.7% of all part-time workers). Most workers, however, cited noneco-

nomic reasons. More than 6.2 million (19.2% of all part-time workers) worked part-time because they were in school or vocational training; 5.7 million (17.7% of all part-time workers) cited family or personal obligations, other than child-care; and 2.2 million workers (6.8% of all part-time workers) said that retirement or a limit on earnings required by social security led them to work part time. Other noneconomic reasons cited were child-care problems and health problems. (See Table 2.7.)

PRODUCTIVITY

Measured

Productivity, measured in output per worker hour, increased every year between 1998 and 2007, according to the Bureau of Labor Statistics in *Productivity and Costs* (February 6, 2008, http://www.bls.gov/news.release/archives/prod2_02062008.pdf). In 2007 productivity had increased 1.6% over the previous year. (See Table 2.8.) Productivity growth had reached a high in 2002 of 4.1% growth over the previous year. It hit a low point of growth in 2006, when it had grown only 1% over the previous year. Changes in productivity do not reflect an increase in labor per hour, however. Jerome A. Mark of the BLS explained in "Problems Encountered in Measuring Single- and Multifactor Productivity" (*Monthly Labor Review,* December 1986, http://www.bls.gov/opub/mlr/1986/12/art1exc.htm) that these changes reflect the interrelationship of factors such as technological changes, capital investment, utilization of capacity, economies of scale, new ways of organizing production, changes in management practices, as well as changes in efforts of the workforce.

Perceived

In fact, some measures show that workers are spending less time actually working while at work. The widespread use of the Internet and e-mail at work provides employees with ample opportunities to waste time on the job. An August 2007 Gallup Poll reported by Joseph Carroll (September 6, 2007, http://www.gallup.com/poll/28618/US-Workers-Say-They-Waste-About-Hour-Work-Each-Day.aspx) found that the average American worker reported wasting about an hour at work each day. Only one in four (26%) said they waste no time at work each day; another quarter (25%) said they waste less than an hour. A slightly larger proportion (29%) said they waste an hour each day, 11% admitted to wasting two hours each day, 3% said they waste three hours each day, and 4% confessed that they waste at least half their workday, four hours or more.

The same workers stated that their coworkers, on average, waste more time than they do—about an hour and a half—each day. Only 31% of workers surveyed said that their coworkers waste no time or less than an hour each day. A quarter (25%) reported their coworkers waste an hour, one in five (20%) believe their coworkers waste two hours, and 12% said their coworkers waste three hours or more at work each day.

TABLE 2.6

Multiple jobholders by selected demographic and economic characteristics, 2006–07

[Numbers in thousands]

Characteristic	Both sexes				Men				Women			
	Number		Rate[a]		Number		Rate[a]		Number		Rate[a]	
	2006	2007	2006	2007	2006	2007	2006	2007	2006	2007	2006	2007
Age												
Total, 16 years and over[b]	7,576	7,655	5.2	5.2	3,822	3,833	4.9	4.9	3,753	3,822	5.6	5.6
16 to 19 years	270	249	4.4	4.2	103	96	3.4	3.3	167	153	5.4	5.1
20 years and over	7,306	7,406	5.3	5.3	3,719	3,737	5.0	5.0	3,586	3,669	5.6	5.7
20 to 24 years	774	738	5.6	5.3	341	309	4.6	4.2	432	429	6.7	6.5
25 years and over	6,532	6,668	5.3	5.3	3,378	3,427	5.0	5.0	3,154	3,241	5.5	5.6
25 to 54 years	5,368	5,432	5.4	5.4	2,760	2,783	5.1	5.1	2,608	2,649	5.7	5.7
55 years and over	1,164	1,236	4.7	4.8	618	645	4.7	4.7	546	592	4.7	4.9
55 to 64 years	988	1,022	5.1	5.1	517	522	5.1	4.9	471	501	5.1	5.2
65 years and over	176	214	3.3	3.8	101	123	3.4	4.0	75	91	3.2	3.6
Race and Hispanic or Latino ethnicity												
White	6,321	6,467	5.3	5.4	3,199	3,250	4.9	5.0	3,122	3,217	5.8	5.9
Black or African American	818	753	5.2	4.7	404	375	5.5	5.0	415	379	4.9	4.4
Asian	249	249	3.8	3.6	127	119	3.6	3.2	122	130	4.1	4.1
Hispanic or Latino ethnicity	598	638	3.0	3.1	337	353	2.8	2.9	261	284	3.4	3.5
Marital status												
Married, spouse present	4,136	4,215	5.1	5.1	2,420	2,435	5.3	5.3	1,716	1,780	4.9	5.0
Widowed, divorced, or separated	1,308	1,339	5.6	5.7	440	446	4.4	4.6	868	893	6.3	6.5
Single (never married)	2,131	2,101	5.3	5.2	962	952	4.4	4.3	1,169	1,149	6.5	6.3
Full- or part-time status												
Primary job full time, secondary job part time	3,981	4,174	—	—	2,233	2,320	—	—	1,748	1,854	—	—
Primary and secondary jobs both part time	1,676	1,764	—	—	508	531	—	—	1,168	1,233	—	—
Primary and secondary jobs both full time	310	288	—	—	208	193	—	—	102	95	—	—
Hours vary on primary or secondary job	1,564	1,383	—	—	849	765	—	—	715	618	—	—

[a]Multiple jobholders as a percent of all employed persons in specified group.
[b]Includes a small number of persons who work part time on their primary job and full time on their secondary jobs(s), not shown separately.
Note: Estimates for the above race groups (white, black or African American, and Asian) do not sum to totals because data are not presented for all races. Persons whose ethnicity is identified as Hispanic or Latino may be of any race. Updated population controls are introduced annually with the release of January data. Dash indicates no data or data that do not meet publication criteria.

SOURCE: "36. Multiple Jobholders by Selected Demographic and Economic Characteristics," in *Employment and Earnings*, U.S. Department of Labor, Bureau of Labor Statistics, January 2008, http://www.bls.gov/cps/cpsaat36.pdf (accessed February 2, 2008).

WORK STOPPAGES

Following the terrorist attacks on New York City and Washington, D.C., on September 11, 2001, the BLS reported significant disruptions to local economies and an increase in layoffs, particularly in the last quarter of that year. The rate of layoffs tapered off by the first quarter of 2002 to lower than 2001 levels. This trend continued through the third quarter of 2006, although layoffs were up slightly in 2007. In that year, there were a total of 5,170 layoff events with a total of 931,053 "separations" (workers who were laid off), up from 4,885 layoff events and 935,969 separations the year before. However, in 2006, there were a higher number of initial claims for unemployment insurance than in the following year (951,102 in 2006 and 865,227 in 2007). (See Table 2.9.)

Displaced Workers

Displaced workers are defined as people twenty years and older who lost or left jobs because their plant or company closed or moved, because there was insufficient work for them to do, or because their position or shift was abolished. According to the BLS in *Worker Displacement, 2003–2005* (August 17, 2006, http://www.bls.gov/news.release/pdf/disp.pdf), 3.8 million workers aged twenty and over had been displaced between January 2003 and December 2005. Of these, 69.9% had found other employment, 13.4% had remained unemployed, and 16.7% had left the labor force (leaving the workforce means that a worker is no longer actively seeking work or receiving unemployment benefits). These figures differed by gender. Women were less likely to be employed (65.6%) than men (73.5%), were less likely to be unemployed (13.1%) than men (13.6%), and more likely to have left the labor force (21.3%) than men (12.9%). (See Table 2.10.)

Manufacturing, with 1.1 million worker displacements, accounted for the largest proportion of displacements in January 2004 (28.4%), as reported in *Worker Displacement, 2003–2005*. Workers in some occupations were more likely to have found work than in others. Although 76.9% of people in installation, maintenance, and repair occupations and 76.8% of people in professional occupations had found new work, only 59.4% of people in production occupations had found new work. These figures represent the general decline of the manufacturing sector and the rise of certain service occupations, such as those in management and the professions.

TABLE 2.7

Persons at work 1 to 34 hours per week, by reason for working less than 35 hours and usual full- or part-time status, 2007

[Numbers in thousands]

	2007					
	All industries			Nonagricultural industries		
Reason for working less than 35 hours	Total	Usually work full time	Usually work part time	Total	Usually work full time	Usually work part time
Total, 16 years and over	**32,435**	**9,976**	**22,460**	**31,902**	**9,813**	**22,089**
Economic reasons	4,401	1,697	2,704	4,317	1,647	2,670
Slack work or business conditions	2,877	1,436	1,441	2,827	1,403	1,423
Could only find part-time work	1,210	—	1,210	1,199	—	1,199
Seasonal work	175	122	53	154	106	48
Job started or ended during week	139	139	—	137	137	—
Noneconomic reasons	28,034	8,278	19,756	27,585	8,166	19,419
Child-care problems	728	72	656	723	72	651
Other family or personal obligations	5,739	799	4,940	5,657	787	4,870
Health or medical limitations	853	—	853	830	—	830
In school or training	6,239	89	6,150	6,165	87	6,079
Retired or Social Security limit on earnings	2,200	—	2,200	2,106	—	2,106
Vacation or personal day	3,579	3,579	—	3,539	3,539	—
Holiday, legal or religious	582	582	—	579	579	—
Weather-related curtailment	669	669	—	645	645	—
All other reasons	7,443	2,488	4,956	7,340	2,457	4,883
Average hours:						
Economic reasons	23.1	23.8	22.6	23.1	23.8	22.7
Other reasons	21.3	25.0	19.8	21.4	25.0	19.8

Note: Updated population controls are introduced annually with the release of January data. Dash indicates no data or data that do not meet publication criteria.

SOURCE: "20. Persons at Work 1 to 34 Hours in All and in Nonagricultural Industries by Reason for Working Less Than 35 Hours and Usual Full- or Part-Time Status," in *Employment and Earnings*, U.S. Department of Labor, Bureau of Labor Statistics, January 2008, http://www.bls.gov/cps/cpsaat20.pdf (accessed February 2, 2008)

TABLE 2.8

Annual average changes in productivity and related measures, 1998–2007

Measure	1998	1999	2000	2001	2002	2003	2004	2005	2006	2007
Business										
Productivity	2.8	3.1	2.9	2.6	4.1	3.8	2.9	2.0	1.0	1.6
Output	4.8	5.1	3.9	0.3	1.5	3.1	4.2	3.6	3.1	2.3
Hours	2.0	2.0	1.0	−2.2	−2.5	−0.7	1.3	1.6	2.1	0.7
Hourly compensation	6.1	4.9	7.1	4.2	3.5	4.1	3.7	4.0	3.9	4.8
Real hourly compensation	4.6	2.7	3.7	1.4	1.9	1.7	1.1	0.6	0.6	1.9
Unit labor costs	3.2	1.8	4.1	1.6	−0.5	0.2	0.9	2.0	2.9	3.1
Nonfarm business										
Productivity	2.8	2.9	2.8	2.5	4.1	3.7	2.7	1.9	1.0	1.6
Output	5.0	5.2	3.8	0.4	1.5	3.1	4.1	3.6	3.2	2.3
Hours	2.1	2.2	1.0	−2.0	−2.6	−0.6	1.4	1.6	2.2	0.7
Hourly compensation	6.0	4.7	7.2	4.0	3.6	4.0	3.6	4.0	3.9	4.8
Real hourly compensation	4.5	2.5	3.7	1.2	2.0	1.7	0.9	0.7	0.6	1.8
Unit labor costs	3.1	1.8	4.2	1.5	−0.5	0.3	0.9	2.0	2.9	3.1
Manufacturing										
Productivity	5.4	4.4	4.1	1.6	6.9	6.2	2.1	4.8	4.0	2.9
Output	5.2	3.8	2.7	−5.1	−0.7	1.0	1.8	3.5	4.9	2.0
Hours	−0.2	−0.6	−1.3	−6.5	−7.1	−4.9	−0.3	−1.2	0.9	−1.0
Hourly compensation	5.8	3.9	9.2	2.3	7.3	7.0	2.0	4.2	2.5	4.6
Real hourly compensation	4.4	1.8	5.7	−0.5	5.6	4.7	−0.6	0.8	−0.8	1.7
Unit labor costs	0.4	−0.5	4.9	0.7	0.3	0.8	−0.1	−0.6	−1.5	1.6

SOURCE: "Table B. Annual Average Changes in Productivity and Related Measures, 1998–2007," in *Productivity and Costs*, U.S. Department of Labor, Bureau of Labor Statistics, February 6, 2008, http://www.bls.gov/news.release/archives/prod2_02062008.pdf (accessed February 6, 2008)

TABLE 2.9

Selected measures of extended mass layoff activity, 2003–07

Period	Layoff events	Separations	Initial claimants
2003			
January–March	1,502	286,947	297,608
April–June	1,799	368,273	348,966
July–September	1,190	236,333	227,909
October–December	1,690	325,333	326,328
2004			
January–March	1,339	276,503	238,392
April–June	1,358	278,831	254,063
July–September	886	164,608	148,575
October–December	1,427	273,967	262,049
2005			
January–March	1,142	186,506	185,486
April–June	1,203	246,099	212,673
July–September	1,136	201,878	190,186
October–December	1,400	250,178	246,188
2006			
January–March	963	183,089	193,510
April–June	1,353	295,964	264,927
July–September	929	160,254	161,764
October–December[a]	1,640	296,662	330,901
2007			
January–March[a]	1,111	226,074	199,295
April–June[a]	1,421	278,719	258,812
July–September[a]	1,019	160,806	172,508
October–December[a]	1,619	265,454	234,612

[a]Revised.
[b]Preliminary.

SOURCE: "Table A. Selected Measures of Extended Mass Layoff Activity," in *Extended Mass Layoffs in the Fourth Quarter of 2007 and Annual Totals for 2007*, U.S. Department of Labor, Bureau of Labor Statistics, February 14, 2008, http://www.bls.gov/news.release/pdf/mslo.pdf (accessed February 15, 2008)

TABLE 2.10

Displaced workers by age, sex, race, Hispanic ethnicity, and employment status, January 2006

Age, sex, race, and Hispanic or Latino ethnicity	Total (thousands)	Percent distribution by employment status			
		Total	Employed	Unemployed	Not in the labor force
Total					
Total, 20 years and over	3,815	100.0	69.9	13.4	16.7
20 to 24 years	111	100.0	66.4	21.4	12.2
25 to 54 years	2,841	100.0	74.5	13.4	12.0
55 to 64 years	728	100.0	60.6	12.3	27.0
65 years and over	135	100.0	25.4	10.8	63.8
Men					
Total, 20 years and over	2,076	100.0	73.5	13.6	12.9
20 to 24 years	67	100.0	77.4	21.4	1.2
25 to 54 years	1,552	100.0	78.6	12.8	8.5
55 to 64 years	378	100.0	61.5	14.5	24.0
65 years and over	80	100.0	27.5	18.3	54.2
Women					
Total, 20 years and over	1,739	100.0	65.6	13.1	21.3
20 to 24 years	44	100.0	*	*	*
25 to 54 years	1,289	100.0	69.6	14.2	16.2
55 to 64 years	350	100.0	59.7	10.0	30.3
65 years and over	55	100.0	*	*	*
White					
Total, 20 years and over	3,169	100.0	70.0	13.2	16.8
Men	1,784	100.0	74.1	13.1	12.8
Women	1,386	100.0	64.8	13.3	22.0
Black or African American					
Total, 20 years and over	452	100.0	71.2	13.4	15.4
Men	181	100.0	72.1	16.3	11.6
Women	271	100.0	70.7	11.5	17.9
Asian					
Total, 20 years and over	113	100.0	72.0	12.3	15.7
Men	65	100.0	*	*	*
Women	48	100.0	*	*	*
Hispanic or Latino ethnicity					
Total, 20 years and over	416	100.0	60.2	22.9	16.9
Men	230	100.0	63.5	25.0	11.5
Women	187	100.0	56.2	20.3	23.5

*Data not shown where base is less than 75,000.
Notes: Data refer to persons who had 3 or more years of tenure on a job they had lost or left between January 2003 and December 2005 because of plant or company closings or moves, insufficient work, or the abolishment of their positions or shifts. Estimates for the above race groups (white, black or African American, and Asian) do not sum to totals because data are not presented for all races. In addition, persons whose ethnicity is identified as Hispanic or Latino may be of any race and, therefore, are classified by ethnicity as well as by race.

SOURCE: "Table 1. Displaced Workers by Age, Sex, Race, Hispanic or Latino Ethnicity, and Employment Status in January 2006," in *Worker Displacement, 2003–2005*, U.S. Department of Labor, Bureau of Labor Statistics, August 17, 2006, http://www.bls.gov/news.release/pdf/disp.pdf (accessed February 4, 2008)

CHAPTER 3
UNEMPLOYMENT

The U.S. unemployment rate reached a post–World War II high of 9.7% in 1982. The U.S. Department of Labor's Bureau of Labor Statistics (BLS), which tracks such data in *Employment and Earnings* (January 2008, http://www.bls.gov/cps/cpsa2007.pdf), further notes that unemployment remained high at 9.6% in 1983 as a result of the most severe economic recession since the Great Depression of the 1930s. The unemployment rate then dropped, approaching 5% in 1989, but again began increasing, reaching 6.8% in 1991 and rising to 7.5% in 1992. As the economy began to improve, the rate fell to 6.9% in 1993. By 1998 the U.S. unemployment rate had dropped to 4.5% and in 2000 dropped to 4%, the lowest level in three decades.

With a creeping recession, unemployment once again began to rise in early 2001 and rose significantly following the terrorist attacks on the United States on September 11, 2001. In June 2003, 9.4 million people were out of work, and the national unemployment rate spiked to 6%. Between 2003 and early 2007 the unemployment rate generally declined. It then began to rise again in 2007. In January 2008 the unemployment rate was 4.9%. (See Figure 3.1.) The unemployment rate measures people without jobs who are looking for work and thus does not count workers who have lost their jobs and eventually stopped looking for work, such as those who have become discouraged or decided to retire.

FACTORS AFFECTING UNEMPLOYMENT RATES
Where You Live

Unemployment rates in the United States vary from state to state. In December 2007 the unemployment rate nationwide was 5%. (See Table 3.1.) Unemployment rates in some states, however, were at least one percentage point higher, including in Michigan (7.6%), Mississippi (6.8%), South Carolina (6.6%), Alaska (6.5%), California (6.1%), the District of Columbia (6.1%), and Ohio

(6.0%). Other states with higher unemployment rates than the nationwide average included Arkansas (5.8%) and Nevada (5.8%).

On the other hand, some states had unemployment rates as much as two percentage points below the national average. Both Idaho and South Dakota had unemployment rates of only 3%. (See Table 3.1.) Wyoming (3.1%), Hawaii (3.2%), Nebraska (3.2%), Utah (3.2%), North Dakota (3.3%), and Virginia (3.5%) had unemployment rates one and a half percentage points or more below the national average. Other states with lower than average unemployment rates included Delaware (3.8%), Iowa (4%), Kansas (4.4%), Maryland (3.8%), Montana (3.6%), New Hampshire (3.6%), New Mexico (3.7%), Texas (4.5%), and Vermont (4%).

Metropolitan areas tend to have lower unemployment rates than states as a whole, indicating that unemployment is a bigger problem in rural areas. For example, notes the BLS in *Metropolitan Area Employment and Unemployment: December 2007* (January 29, 2008, http://www.bls.gov/news.release/archives/metro_01292008.pdf), in December 2007 Mississippi had a high unemployment rate, at 6.8%; in the Mississippi city of Jackson, however, the unemployment rate was close to the national average, at 5.1%. South Carolina also had a high unemployment rate, at 6.6%, but the unemployment rate in the cities of Charleston (5%) and Greenville (5.5%) were much lower. The same held true in Alaska, where overall the unemployment rate was 6.5%. In Alaska's cities of Anchorage and Fairbanks, however, the unemployment rate was 5.7%, significantly lower than statewide. The exception to this rule is in Michigan. The unemployment rate in that state was 7.6%, but the unemployment rate in its two principal cities, Detroit (8%) and Flint (8.3%), was much higher. This is mainly due to the loss of industrial jobs in these once dominantly industrial cities.

The same pattern of lower unemployment rates in cities holds true for states with low unemployment rates

FIGURE 3.1

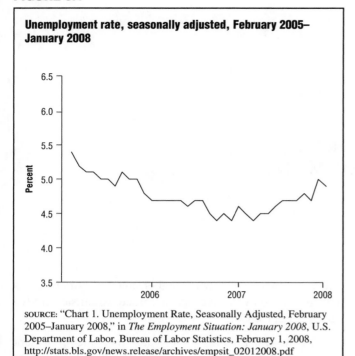

Unemployment rate, seasonally adjusted, February 2005– January 2008

SOURCE: "Chart 1. Unemployment Rate, Seasonally Adjusted, February 2005–January 2008," in *The Employment Situation: January 2008*, U.S. Department of Labor, Bureau of Labor Statistics, February 1, 2008, http://stats.bls.gov/news.release/archives/empsit_02012008.pdf (accessed March 8, 2008)

TABLE 3.1

States with unemployment rates significantly different from that of the United States as a whole, December 2007, seasonally adjusted

State	Rate
United States	5.0
Alaska	6.5
Arkansas	5.9
California	6.1
Delaware	3.8
District of Columbia	6.1
Hawaii	3.2
Idaho	3.0
Iowa	4.0
Kansas	4.4
Maryland	3.8
Michigan	7.6
Mississippi	6.8
Montana	3.6
Nebraska	3.2
Nevada	5.8
New Hampshire	3.6
New Mexico	3.7
North Dakota	3.3
Ohio	6.0
South Carolina	6.6
South Dakota	3.0
Texas	4.5
Utah	3.2
Vermont	4.0
Virginia	3.5
Wyoming	3.1

SOURCE: "Table A. States with Unemployment Rates Significantly Different from That of the U.S., December 2007, Seasonally Adjusted," in *Regional and State Employment and Unemployment: December 2007*, U.S. Department of Labor, Bureau of Labor Statistics, January 18, 2008, http://www.bls.gov/news.release/archives/laus_01182008.pdf (accessed February 8, 2008)

as well. The BLS notes that the unemployment rate in Idaho in December 2007 was a low 3%; the unemployment rates of Boise (2.9%) and Idaho Falls (2.2%) were even lower. In South Dakota the unemployment rate of Rapid City matched that of the state as a whole (3%), but the unemployment rate of Sioux Falls was half a percentage point lower (2.5%). In Wyoming, where the unemployment rate of the state was 3.1%, the unemployment rate in Casper was 2.9%.

Age

Unemployment does not occur evenly in all occupations or sectors of society. Workers under twenty-five years of age are far more likely than older workers to be unemployed. The jobs held by younger workers are often more marginal, younger workers tend to have less education than older workers, and they leave their jobs more often than older workers. In addition, workers under age twenty-five also have less seniority to protect them against layoffs. These workers have less work experience than older workers as well, which can work against them when looking for a new job.

During 2007, for example, as noted by the BLS in *Employment and Earnings*, the unemployment rate among those sixteen years of age and older was greatest among sixteen- to nineteen-year-olds (15.7% of those in the labor force). It was higher for men in that age group (17.6%) than it was for women (13.8%). In contrast, the unemployment rate for men ages twenty to twenty-four years old was

8.9%, and for men ages twenty-five to fifty-four years it was only 3.7%. The unemployment rate for women ages twenty to twenty-four years was 7.3%, and for those ages twenty-five to fifty-four years it was only 3.8%.

Race, Gender, and Marital Status

Unemployment does not affect all demographic groups equally. Many African-Americans, for instance, work in occupations that have suffered as the American economy has changed from an industrial to a service economy, and, as in the overall unemployment picture, the youngest workers are particularly affected. In addition, African-Americans sometimes face discrimination in employment that can keep them from finding employment as quickly as members of other groups. According to the BLS in *Employment and Earnings*, African-American teenagers aged sixteen to nineteen experienced an unemployment rate of 29.4% in 2007, compared with an unemployment rate of 13.9% for white teenagers and 12.7% for Asian teens. African-American male teenagers (33.8%) were more likely to be unemployed in 2007 than were African-American female teenagers (25.3%), although the rates for both were very high.

TABLE 3.2

Unemployed persons by marital status, race, Hispanic ethnicity, age, and sex, 2006–07

Marital status, race, Hispanic or Latino ethnicity, and age	Men				Women			
	Thousands of persons		Unemployment rates		Thousands of persons		Unemployment rates	
	2006	2007	2006	2007	2006	2007	2006	2007
Total, 16 years and over	**3,753**	**3,882**	**4.6**	**4.7**	**3,247**	**3,196**	**4.6**	**4.5**
Married, spouse present	1,142	1,206	2.4	2.5	1,042	1,049	2.9	2.8
Widowed, divorced, or separated	545	544	5.2	5.3	709	724	4.9	5.0
Single (never married)	2,067	2,132	8.6	8.8	1,496	1,422	7.7	7.2
White, 16 years and over	**2,730**	**2,869**	**4.0**	**4.2**	**2,271**	**2,274**	**4.0**	**4.0**
Married, spouse present	896	965	2.2	2.4	839	830	2.7	2.6
Widowed, divorced, or separated	407	421	4.7	4.9	523	547	4.7	4.9
Single (never married)	1,428	1,483	7.5	7.8	909	897	6.4	6.3
Black or African American, 16 years and over	**774**	**752**	**9.5**	**9.1**	**775**	**693**	**8.4**	**7.5**
Married, spouse present	166	156	4.7	4.3	121	123	4.4	4.3
Widowed, divorced, or separated	105	92	8.3	7.5	155	135	6.4	5.7
Single (never married)	502	504	15.2	15.0	499	435	12.5	10.8
Asian, 16 years and over	**110**	**119**	**3.0**	**3.1**	**95**	**110**	**3.1**	**3.4**
Married, spouse present	49	54	2.2	2.2	55	61	2.9	3.1
Widowed, divorced, or separated	11	9	3.5	3.0	12	12	2.7	2.7
Single (never married)	49	56	4.9	5.2	29	37	3.8	4.4
Hispanic or Latino ethnicity, 16 years and over	**601**	**695**	**4.8**	**5.3**	**480**	**525**	**5.9**	**6.1**
Married, spouse present	201	247	3.0	3.5	177	191	4.5	4.7
Widowed, divorced, or separated	73	85	4.2	5.1	97	110	5.5	6.0
Single (never married)	327	363	7.8	8.3	206	224	8.2	8.3
Total, 25 years and over	**2,426**	**2,538**	**3.5**	**3.6**	**2,221**	**2,198**	**3.7**	**3.6**
Married, spouse present	1,088	1,152	2.4	2.5	955	959	2.7	2.7
Widowed, divorced, or separated	520	515	5.1	5.1	667	683	4.8	4.9
Single (never married)	819	871	6.1	6.3	599	556	5.7	5.2
White, 25 years and over	**1,798**	**1,907**	**3.1**	**3.3**	**1,578**	**1,579**	**3.3**	**3.3**
Married, spouse present	854	919	2.2	2.3	765	756	2.6	2.5
Widowed, divorced, or separated	389	401	4.6	4.8	494	516	4.5	4.7
Single (never married)	555	587	5.3	5.5	320	307	4.5	4.3
Black or African American, 25 years and over	**473**	**457**	**7.0**	**6.6**	**505**	**453**	**6.5**	**5.8**
Married, spouse present	156	149	4.5	4.1	113	113	4.2	4.1
Widowed, divorced, or separated	102	85	8.2	7.3	145	129	6.1	5.5
Single (never married)	214	222	10.6	10.5	247	211	9.2	7.7
Asian, 25 years and over	**80**	**92**	**2.4**	**2.7**	**75**	**87**	**2.7**	**3.0**
Married, spouse present	48	53	2.1	2.2	53	59	2.8	3.0
Widowed, divorced, or separated	11	9	3.4	2.8	10	12	2.3	2.7
Single (never married)	21	30	3.1	4.0	13	17	2.7	3.1
Hispanic or Latino ethnicity, 16 years and over	**387**	**455**	**3.8**	**4.2**	**330**	**355**	**4.9**	**5.1**
Married, spouse present	189	234	3.0	3.5	154	166	4.2	4.3
Widowed, divorced, or separated	67	77	4.1	4.9	91	100	5.3	5.7
Single (never married)	131	144	5.7	5.8	85	89	6.4	6.1

Note: Estimates for the above race groups (white, black or African American, and Asian) do not sum to totals because data are not presented for all races. Persons whose ethnicity is identified as Hispanic or Latino may be of any race. Updated population controls are introduced annually with the release of January data.

SOURCE: "24. Unemployed Persons by Marital Status, Race, Hispanic or Latino Ethnicity, Age, and Sex," in *Employment and Earnings*, U.S. Department of Labor, Bureau of Labor Statistics, January 2008, http://www.bls.gov/cps/cpsaat24.pdf (accessed February 2, 2008)

Table 3.2 shows unemployment rates for men and women of different races and ethnicities. Among all ages, African-Americans and Hispanics were more likely than non-Hispanic whites or Asians to be unemployed. In 2007 African-American men age sixteen and older had an unemployment rate of 9.1%, while African-American women had an unemployment rate of 7.5%. Among Hispanics age sixteen and older, 5.3% of males and 5.9% of females were unemployed. In contrast, among non-Hispanic whites age sixteen and older, 4.2% of males and 4% of females were unemployed in 2007. Among Asians age sixteen and over, only 3.1% of males and 3.4% of females were unemployed. Among all men and women age sixteen and over, unemployment rates were similar in all ethnic groups except among African-Americans, where women were much less likely to be unemployed than were men in 2007.

Among men and women age twenty-five and over, unemployment rates for non-Hispanic whites were the same for men and women (3.3%). (See Table 3.2.) Among African-Americans, the unemployment rate for women was again lower than for men (5.8% and 6.6%, respectively). Among Asians and Hispanics, however, women age twenty-five and over were more likely to be unemployed than were men of the same age. Asian men had an unemployment rate of 2.7% in 2007, while Asian women had an unemployment rate of 3%. Hispanic men had an unemployment rate of 4.2%, while Hispanic women had an unemployment rate of 5.1%.

Marital status is also correlated with unemployment. A married person was much less likely to be unemployed than a single, widowed, or divorced individual in 2007. This observation held true across all races and ethnic groups. In 2007 single, never-married males aged sixteen and over had more than three times the unemployment rate of married males of the same age (8.8% and 2.5%, respectively). (See Table 3.2.) Widowed, divorced, or separated males (5.3%) had more than twice the unemployment rate of married men. Although only 2.4% of white, married men were unemployed in 2007, 7.8% of never-married white men and 4.9% of widowed, divorced, or separated white males were out of work. Among African-Americans, 4.3% of married men aged sixteen years and older were unemployed in 2007, compared with 7.5% of widowed, divorced, or separated men and 15% of never-married men.

The same correlation between marital status and employment was true for women. Although only 2.8% of married women age sixteen and over were unemployed in 2007, the unemployment rate of widowed, divorced, or separated women was 5%. Among never-married females, 7.2% were unemployed in 2007. (See Table 3.2.) This pattern held true across all races and ethnic groups. For example, never-married white women over the age of sixteen were markedly more likely to be out of work than married white women (6.3% and 2.6%, respectively), and never-married African-American women were significantly more likely to be unemployed than married African-American women (10.8% and 4.3%, respectively).

Education and Unemployment

The more education an individual possesses, the less likely it is that he or she will be unemployed. In the *Occupational Outlook Quarterly* ("More Education: Lower Unemployment, Higher Pay," Fall 2004, http://www.bls.gov/opub/ooq/2004/fall/oochart.pdf), the BLS theorizes that potential employers are more likely to hire more educated applicants because they see the ability to earn an academic degree as "an indicator of assets—such as organizational skills and aptitude—that a potential worker will bring to the job."

According to the BLS in *Employment and Earnings*, the unemployment rate of the population dropped with educational attainment. In 2007 high school dropouts with no diploma had an unemployment rate of 7.1%, while people with a bachelor's, master's, professional, and doctoral degrees had an unemployment rate of only 2%. High school graduates with no college had an unemployment rate of 4.4%, while those with some college, but no degree, had an unemployment rate of 3.8%.

People who achieve graduate degrees have even lower unemployment rates than people who have completed bachelor's degrees. The BLS notes in its Current Population Survey ("Education Pays," April 15, 2008, http://www.bls.gov/emp/emptab7.htm) that in 2007 the unemployment rate for those with bachelor's degrees was 2.2%. People with master's degrees had an unemployment rate of 1.8%, people with doctoral degrees had an unemployment rate of 1.4%, and people with a professional degree had an unemployment rate of 1.3%.

Occupations and Industries

Workers in some occupations are more susceptible to unemployment than workers in others. In general, occupations that require more education have lower unemployment rates than occupations that have only basic educational requirements. For example, in 2007 the unemployment rate for people employed in managerial and professional specialties (2.1%) was much lower than the rate for people employed in production, transportation, and material moving occupations (5.8%). (See Table 3.3.)

Within each occupational grouping, significant differences can exist. In natural resources, construction, and maintenance occupations, 6.3% of workers were unemployed overall. (See Table 3.3.) The unemployment rate was highest in the farming, fishing, and forestry occupations (8.5%), while the rate was quite low in the installation, maintenance, and repair occupations (3.4%). Even within the professional ranks, unemployment was comparatively high for those in arts, design, entertainment, sports, and media occupations (4.4%), while it was comparatively low among health care techs and practitioners (1.3%).

Gender also plays a role in variations of unemployment rates in different occupations. In 2007 women in sales occupations had an unemployment rate of 5.7%, compared with a rate of only 3.8% for men. (See Table 3.3.) Although women and men had similar unemployment rates in managerial and professional specialty fields, more female workers in production, transportation, and material moving occupations were out of work (7.3%) than their male counterparts (5.4%). Similarly, 10.4% of women workers in natural resources, construction, and maintenance occupations were unemployed in 2007, compared with only 6.1% of men in that category. It may be that because women traditionally did not work in these fields, at times of high

TABLE 3.3

Unemployed persons by occupation and sex, 2006–07

| Occupation | Thousands of persons Total | | Unemployment rates | | | | | |
| | | | Total | | Men | | Women | |
	2006	2007	2006	2007	2006	2007	2006	2007
Total, 16 years and over*	7,001	7,078	4.6	4.6	4.6	4.7	4.6	4.5
Management, professional, and related occupations	1,065	1,090	2.1	2.1	1.9	2.0	2.2	2.2
Management, business, and financial operations occupations	427	429	2.0	1.9	1.8	1.7	2.2	2.2
Management occupations	279	278	1.8	1.8	1.7	1.7	2.0	1.9
Business and financial operations occupations	148	151	2.4	2.4	2.3	2.1	2.5	2.7
Professional and related occupations	638	662	2.1	2.1	2.1	2.1	2.2	2.1
Computer and mathematical occupations	80	76	2.4	2.1	2.5	2.1	2.3	2.3
Architecture and engineering occupations	49	47	1.7	1.6	1.6	1.5	2.6	1.9
Life, physical, and social science occupations	27	28	1.8	2.0	1.7	1.7	2.0	2.4
Community and social services occupations	50	53	2.3	2.3	2.4	1.9	2.2	2.6
Legal occupations	22	40	1.3	2.3	.9	1.4	1.8	3.2
Education, training, and library occupations	196	198	2.4	2.3	2.4	2.3	2.4	2.3
Arts, design, entertainment, sports, and media occupations	115	127	4.0	4.4	4.3	5.0	3.8	3.7
Healthcare practitioner and technical occupations	98	93	1.4	1.3	.7	1.3	1.6	1.3
Service occupations	1,485	1,521	5.9	5.9	6.0	6.0	5.8	5.9
Healthcare support occupations	152	147	4.6	4.5	5.8	4.1	4.5	4.5
Protective service occupations	105	118	3.4	3.7	2.9	3.0	5.3	6.0
Food preparation and serving related occupations	590	626	7.2	7.5	7.5	7.9	6.9	7.2
Building and grounds cleaning and maintenance occupations	402	392	7.0	6.7	6.9	6.6	7.0	6.8
Personal care and service occupations	235	238	4.7	4.8	4.9	4.9	4.7	4.7
Sales and office occupations	1,667	1,638	4.4	4.3	3.9	4.2	4.7	4.4
Sales and related occupations	812	835	4.7	4.8	3.4	3.8	5.9	5.7
Office and administrative support occupations	856	804	4.2	4.0	4.9	4.9	4.0	3.7
Natural resources, construction, and maintenance occupations	1,007	1,052	6.0	6.3	5.8	6.1	9.1	10.4
Farming, fishing, and forestry occupations	101	89	9.5	8.5	8.4	7.0	13.2	13.8
Construction and extraction occupations	699	781	6.8	7.6	6.7	7.5	9.9	11.2
Installation, maintenance, and repair occupations	207	182	3.7	3.4	3.7	3.3	4.3	5.6
Production, transportation, and material moving occupations	1,127	1,128	5.8	5.8	5.3	5.4	7.5	7.3
Production occupations	544	564	5.5	5.7	4.7	5.0	7.2	7.2
Transportation and material moving occupations	583	564	6.2	6.0	5.9	5.7	8.0	7.7
No previous work experience	616	627	—	—	—	—	—	—
16 to 19 years	435	419	—	—	—	—	—	—
20 to 24 years	90	115	—	—	—	—	—	—
25 years and over	91	93	—	—	—	—	—	—

*Includes a small number of persons whose last job was in the Armed Forces.
Note: Updated population controls are introduced annually with the release of January data. Dash indicates no data or data that do not meet publication criteria.

SOURCE: "25. Unemployed Persons by Occupation and Sex," in *Employment and Earnings*, U.S. Department of Labor, Bureau of Labor Statistics, January 2008, http://www.bls.gov/cps/cpsaat25.pdf (accessed February 2, 2008)

unemployment, women are more likely to lose their jobs and be unable to find another.

Unemployment also varies by industry. The BLS breaks down nonagricultural private wage workers into eleven industry categories: mining, construction, manufacturing (durable and nondurable goods), wholesale and retail trade, transportation and utilities, information services, financial activities, professional and business services, education and health services, leisure and hospitality, and other services. According to the BLS in *Employment and Earnings*, workers in leisure and hospitality suffered from the highest unemployment rate in 2007 (7.4%), while people in the finance industry (3%) and education and health services (3%) faced the lowest unemployment rates.

In the industries with low unemployment rates, women and men faced similar unemployment rates. On the other hand, in industries suffering from high unemployment rates, women usually had higher than average unemployment rates. For example, the BLS reports in *Employment and Earnings* that in manufacturing, the unemployment rate among women was 5.4% in 2007, while the unemployment rate for men was 3.8%. In the wholesale and retail trade, the unemployment rate for women was 5.4%, while the unemployment rate for men was only 4.2%. In transportation and utilities, the unemployment rate for women was 4.5%, while

TABLE 3.4

Unemployed persons by age, sex, race, Hispanic ethnicity, marital status, and duration of unemployment, 2007

	2007							
	Thousands of persons						Weeks	
				15 weeks and over				
Characteristic	Total	Less than 5 weeks	5 to 14 weeks	Total	15 to 26 weeks	27 weeks and over	Average (mean) duration	Median duration
Age and sex								
Total, 16 years and over	7,078	2,542	2,232	2,303	1,061	1,243	16.8	8.5
16 to 19 years	1,101	509	355	237	131	106	11.2	5.5
20 to 24 years	1,241	492	402	347	174	174	14.4	7.6
25 to 34 years	1,544	550	501	493	229	265	16.4	8.5
35 to 44 years	1,225	403	386	436	194	242	17.9	9.4
45 to 54 years	1,135	331	340	464	196	268	21.2	11.0
55 to 64 years	642	186	192	264	110	154	21.9	11.0
65 years and over	190	73	55	62	28	34	18.5	7.8
Men, 16 years and over	3,882	1,370	1,228	1,284	578	706	17.3	8.7
16 to 19 years	623	288	198	137	70	67	11.6	5.5
20 to 24 years	721	270	238	212	101	112	15.6	8.0
25 to 34 years	856	297	278	281	137	144	16.4	8.7
35 to 44 years	634	216	198	220	98	122	17.7	9.2
45 to 54 years	591	169	180	241	98	144	22.0	11.1
55 to 64 years	349	92	106	150	58	92	23.4	11.9
65 years and over	108	37	29	42	17	25	22.1	9.2
Women, 16 years and over	3,196	1,172	1,004	1,020	483	537	16.2	8.4
16 to 19 years	478	221	157	100	61	39	10.6	5.5
20 to 24 years	520	221	164	135	73	62	12.8	6.9
25 to 34 years	688	252	223	213	92	121	16.3	8.3
35 to 44 years	591	187	188	216	96	121	18.2	9.7
45 to 54 years	544	161	160	222	98	124	20.4	10.9
55 to 64 years	293	94	86	114	52	62	20.0	9.9
65 years and over	81	35	26	20	11	9	13.6	6.2
Race and Hispanic or Latino ethnicity								
White, 16 years and over	5,143	1,947	1,634	1,562	747	814	15.7	7.9
Men	2,869	1,070	913	886	413	474	16.3	8.0
Women	2,274	877	721	675	335	341	15.1	7.8
Black or African American, 16 years and over	1,445	413	442	590	253	337	20.7	11.1
Men	752	205	228	318	133	185	21.6	11.7
Women	693	208	214	272	120	152	19.8	10.4
Asian, 16 years and over	229	81	72	76	29	48	17.5	8.7
Men	119	40	39	40	15	25	17.8	8.9
Women	110	40	33	37	14	23	17.2	8.5
Hispanic or Latino ethnicity, 16 years and over	1,220	495	381	344	169	175	14.9	7.3
Men	695	285	222	187	93	94	14.6	7.2
Women	525	210	158	157	76	80	15.5	7.5
Marital status								
Men, 16 years and over								
Married, spouse present	1,206	414	379	413	188	225	17.6	9.0
Widowed, divorced, or separated	544	177	168	199	87	112	19.3	9.8
Single (never married)	2,132	780	681	671	303	368	16.7	8.2
Women, 16 years and over								
Married, spouse present	1,049	385	332	332	147	185	16.6	8.2
Widowed, divorced, or separated	724	231	227	266	130	137	18.2	9.8
Single (never married)	1,422	557	445	421	206	215	14.9	7.8

Note: Estimates for the above race groups (white, black or African American, and Asian) do not sum to totals because data are not presented for all races. Persons whose ethnicity is identified as Hispanic or Latino may be of any race. Updated population controls are introduced annually with the release of January data.

SOURCE: "31. Unemployed Persons by Age, Sex, Race, Hispanic or Latino Ethnicity, Marital Status, and Duration of Unemployment," in *Employment and Earnings*, U.S. Department of Labor, Bureau of Labor Statistics, January 2008, http://www.bls.gov/cps/cpsaat31.pdf (accessed February 2, 2008)

the unemployment rate for men was 3.8%. The exception to this rule was in construction, where women suffered a high unemployment rate of 6.6% in 2007, but men faced an even higher unemployment rate of 7.5%.

HOW LONG DOES UNEMPLOYMENT LAST?

According to historical data compiled by the BLS from the Current Population Survey (http://www.bls.gov/webapps/legacy/cpsatab9.htm), the average length of unemployment in 2007 was 16.8 weeks, down from 19.6 weeks in 2004, but up from 12.6 weeks in 2000. The median duration of unemployment in 2007 was 8.5 weeks. (See Table 3.4.) In 2007 about 2.5 million of the nation's 7.1 million unemployed workers (35.9%) had been unemployed for less than five weeks, and 2.2 million (31.5%) had been out of work for five to fourteen weeks. About 2.3 million unemployed workers (32.5%) had been out of work for fifteen weeks or more. Over one million of these workers had been out of work for twenty-seven weeks or more. However, these statistics varied by gender, age, race and ethnicity, marital status, occupation, and industry.

Gender and Age

Both gender and age have some effect on the length of unemployment. Women typically spent less time unemployed than did men. In 2007 men were unemployed for an average of 17.3 weeks, while women were unemployed for an average of 16.2 weeks. (See Table 3.4.) In addition, generally the older the job seeker, the longer it took to find work. Because better-paying jobs usually take longer to find, men forty-five years and older, who are most likely to be seeking higher-paying employment than either women or younger people, remained unemployed longer. Young men and women aged sixteen to nineteen years old were unemployed an average of 11.6 weeks and 10.6 weeks, respectively, compared with 23.4 weeks for men and 20 weeks for women who were aged fifty-five to sixty-four.

Race and Ethnicity

Race and ethnicity also affects the duration of unemployment. Hispanic workers were unemployed, on average, for the least amount of time in 2007 (14.9 weeks), possibly because Hispanic workers tend to be concentrated in low-paid service occupations, a growing industry. Unlike in other race and ethnic groups, Hispanic women spent a longer average time unemployed than did Hispanic men—15.5 and 14.6, respectively. (See Table 3.4.)

Whites spent the next shortest average time unemployed in 2007 (15.7 weeks). (See Table 3.4.) White women spent an average of 15.1 weeks unemployed, while white men spent an average of 16.3 weeks unemployed. Asians spent an average of 17.5 weeks unemployed; Asian men spent on average a slightly longer time than Asian women looking for work (17.8 weeks and 17.2 weeks, respectively). African-Americans spent the longest time looking for work; their average length of unemployment, 20.7 weeks, was nearly six weeks longer than the average length of unemployment for Hispanics. African-American men spent, on average, 21.6 weeks unemployed, while African-American women averaged 19.8 weeks unemployed.

Marital Status

Although never-married persons have a higher unemployment rate than married persons, married persons spend, on average, a longer time unemployed than do never-married persons. Widowed, divorced, or separated persons spend the longest average time unemployed of all. Among never-married men, the average length of a stint of unemployment was 16.7 weeks in 2007. (See Table 3.4.) Married men, on the other hand, spent an average of 17.6 weeks unemployed, while widowed, divorced, or separated men spent, on average, 19.3 weeks unemployed.

A similar pattern was true among women. Never-married women spent an average of 14.9 weeks unemployed in 2007. (See Table 3.4.) Married women spent, on average, a week and a half longer unemployed (16.6 weeks). Widowed, divorced, or separated women were unemployed longest of all; they spent, on average, 18.2 weeks unemployed, more than three weeks longer than never-married women did.

Occupation and Industry

People working in management, professional, and related occupations and production, transportation, and material moving occupations had a longer average duration of unemployment than did people in other occupations in 2007. Professionals averaged 18.1 weeks out of work, while managers averaged 17.6 weeks out of work. (See Table 3.5.) Those in production occupations averaged 18.1 weeks out of work, while those in transportation and material moving occupations averaged 17.7 weeks out of work. Natural resources, construction, and maintenance occupations had a relatively low average duration of unemployment (15.1 weeks). People working in sales averaged unemployment durations of 16.9 weeks, while those in service occupations averaged 16.3 weeks out of work. People with no previous work experience averaged a duration of 17.3 weeks looking for work.

The length of unemployment also varied by industry. The construction industry averaged the shortest duration of unemployment in 2007, at 14.1 weeks. The leisure and hospitality industry and "other services" industry also averaged fairly short durations of unemployment in that year (15.2 weeks and 15.9 weeks, respectively). The information industry averaged the longest duration of unemployment, at 22.1 weeks, followed by the public administration industry (20.3 weeks) and manufacturing (19.5 weeks). (See Table 3.5.)

REASONS FOR UNEMPLOYMENT

In 2007 nearly 7.1 million workers experienced unemployment in the United States, according to the Bureau of Labor Statistics in *Employment and Earnings.* Nearly half of those had lost their jobs or had completed temporary jobs (3.5 million, or 49.7%), including 976,000 who were on temporary layoff. (See Table 3.6.) Another 2.1 million people (30.3%) had left the labor force at one time and were now returning and searching for work; the BLS calls these people "reentrants." Another 793,000 people (11.2%) were unemployed because they had voluntarily left their jobs. Only 627,000 (8.9%) were new entrants to the labor force.

Reasons for unemployment varied greatly by gender. A larger proportion of men who were unemployed had lost their jobs permanently; 31.1% of unemployed men over the

TABLE 3.5

Unemployed persons by occupation, industry, and duration of unemployment, 2007

	2007							
	Thousands of persons						Weeks	
				15 weeks and over				
Occupation and industry	Total	Less than 5 weeks	5 to 14 weeks	Total	15 to 26 weeks	27 weeks and over	Average (mean) duration	Median duration
Occupation								
Management, professional, and related occupations	1,090	379	344	368	161	207	17.9	8.8
Management, business, and financial operations occupations	429	138	141	150	68	82	17.6	9.4
Professional and related occupations	662	240	203	218	93	126	18.1	8.4
Service occupations	1,521	560	478	482	232	251	16.3	8.3
Sales and office occupations	1,638	570	508	560	276	285	16.9	8.9
Sales and related occupations	835	302	255	277	136	142	16.2	8.7
Office and administrative support occupations	804	268	253	283	140	143	17.5	9.2
Natural resources, construction, and maintenance occupations	1,052	408	345	299	142	157	15.1	7.6
Farming, fishing, and forestry occupations	89	30	32	27	13	13	16.5	8.6
Construction and extraction occupations	781	316	253	212	100	112	14.4	7.1
Installation, maintenance, and repair occupations	182	62	60	60	28	32	17.2	9.1
Production, transportation, and material moving occupations	1,128	383	361	384	164	219	17.9	9.0
Production occupations	564	187	183	193	83	110	18.1	9.2
Transportation and material moving occupations	564	196	177	191	81	109	17.7	8.8
Industry[a]								
Agriculture and related industries	82	28	29	25	12	14	17.6	8.7
Mining	25	9	10	6	3	3	[b]	[b]
Construction	769	299	255	215	109	107	14.1	7.5
Manufacturing	710	229	222	259	108	152	19.5	9.7
Durable goods	439	139	139	162	69	93	19.1	9.8
Nondurable goods	271	90	83	97	39	58	20.2	9.4
Wholesale and retail trade	987	341	311	334	163	171	16.8	9.0
Transportation and utilities	262	83	84	95	37	58	18.8	9.5
Information	124	40	36	49	19	29	22.1	10.1
Financial activities	295	101	94	100	50	50	17.2	8.9
Professional and business services	752	262	242	247	117	130	16.9	8.8
Education and health services	807	300	255	253	121	132	16.2	8.1
Leisure and hospitality	929	361	294	274	132	142	15.2	7.6
Other services	245	95	71	80	37	43	15.9	8.1
Public administration	133	40	42	51	22	29	20.3	10.0
No previous work experience	627	237	190	201	83	118	17.3	8.1

[a]Includes wage and salary workers only.
[b]Data not shown where base is less than 35,000.
Note: Updated population controls are introduced annually with the release of January data.

SOURCE: "32. Unemployed Persons by Occupation, Industry, and Duration of Unemployment," in *Employment and Earnings*, U.S. Department of Labor, Bureau of Labor Statistics, January 2008, http://www.bls.gov/cps/cpsaat32.pdf (accessed February 2, 2008)

age of twenty compared with 25.6% of unemployed women over the age of twenty were in this position, as indicated by Table 3.6. Women, on the other hand, were more likely to have voluntarily left their positions (12.9% of women who were unemployed and 11.4% of men who were unemployed). In addition, women were much more likely than men to be reentering the job market after some time away; 36.2% of unemployed women were reentrants, compared with only 22.2% of men. This reflects the reality that women workers often leave their jobs for a period of time to care for young children or elderly parents.

Duration by Reason of Unemployment

According to the BLS in *Employment and Earnings*, in 2007 people on temporary layoff were most likely to be out of work for less than five weeks, while people who had permanently lost their jobs were most likely to be out of work for fifteen weeks or more. In that year, slightly over one-third (37%) of workers aged sixteen and over who had lost their jobs or who had completed temporary jobs were unemployed less than five weeks, while 30.7% were unemployed fifteen weeks or more. More than one-half (55.8%) of those who were on temporary layoff were out of work for five weeks or less. Of those who had permanently lost their jobs in 2005, more than two out of five (41.3%) remained unemployed fifteen weeks or more.

A worker's age also had an impact on the amount of time spent unemployed. About two-thirds (62.9%) of all new entrants into the job market found work within fourteen weeks, 32.8% of them finding employment within five

TABLE 3.6

Unemployed persons by reason for unemployment, sex, and age, 2006–07

[Numbers in thousands]

Reason	Total, 16 years and over		Men, 20 years and over		Women, 20 years and over		Both sexes, 16 to 19 years	
	2006	2007	2006	2007	2006	2007	2006	2007
Number of unemployed								
Total unemployed	7,001	7,078	3,131	3,259	2,751	2,718	1,119	1,101
Job losers and persons who completed temporary jobs	3,321	3,515	1,927	2,064	1,249	1,276	145	176
On temporary layoff	921	976	540	580	324	333	57	63
Not on temporary layoff	2,400	2,539	1,387	1,483	925	943	88	113
Permanent job losers	1,686	1,781	948	1,013	685	696	53	72
Persons who completed temporary jobs	714	758	439	470	240	247	35	42
Job leavers	827	793	368	371	380	351	78	71
Reentrants	2,237	2,142	757	723	1,019	984	461	435
New entrants	616	627	78	101	103	107	435	419
Percent distribution								
Total unemployed	100.0	100.0	100.0	100.0	100.0	100.0	100.0	100.0
Job losers and persons who completed temporary jobs	47.4	49.7	61.6	63.3	45.4	46.9	13.0	16.0
On temporary layoff	13.2	13.8	17.3	17.8	11.8	12.2	5.1	5.7
Not on temporary layoff	34.3	35.9	44.3	45.5	33.6	34.7	7.9	10.3
Job leavers	11.8	11.2	11.7	11.4	13.8	12.9	7.0	6.5
Reentrants	32.0	30.3	24.2	22.2	37.0	36.2	41.2	39.5
New entrants	8.8	8.9	2.5	3.1	3.7	3.9	38.9	38.0
Unemployed as a percent of the civilian labor force								
Job losers and persons who completed temporary jobs	2.2	2.3	2.5	2.6	1.9	1.9	2.0	2.5
Job leavers	.5	.5	.5	.5	.6	.5	1.1	1.0
Reentrants	1.5	1.4	1.0	.9	1.5	1.5	6.3	6.2
New entrants	.4	.4	.1	.1	.2	.2	6.0	6.0

Note: Updated population controls are introduced annually with the release of January data.

SOURCE: "27. Unemployed Persons by Reason for Unemployment, Sex, and Age," in *Employment and Earnings*, U.S. Department of Labor, Bureau of Labor Statistics, January 2008, http://www.bls.gov/cps/cpsaat27.pdf (accessed February 2, 2008)

weeks, according to the BLS. Younger unemployed people and temporary workers tended to find jobs more quickly than older workers. Among sixteen- to nineteen-year-olds, nearly two-thirds (61.9%) of those who had lost their jobs or who had completed temporary jobs had found work within five weeks or less. Men age twenty and over were more likely than women of the same age to spend fifteen weeks or more unemployed (35.2% and 33.8%, respectively), while women were more likely than men to find work within five weeks (35% and 33.2%, respectively).

WITHDRAWN FROM THE LABOR FORCE

In addition to people who are working, the labor force includes all of the unemployed people who are looking for work. People who stop looking for work are considered to have left the labor force, regardless of their age or reason for not looking for work. They are not counted among the unemployed by the Department of Labor. In 2007 more than half of the 78.7 million people who were not in the labor force were aged fifty-five or older (42.2 million, or 53.6%). (See Table 3.7.) Approximately 21.3 million (27.1%) were between the ages of

twenty-five and fifty-four and another 15.2 million (19.3%) were aged sixteen to twenty-four. More than six of every ten people not in the labor force (61.9%) were women, reflecting the fact that many women take care of their families rather than work.

Most of the people not in the labor force (74 million, or 94%) did not want a job at the time they were surveyed by the U.S. Department of Labor. (See Table 3.7.) Of the approximately 4.7 million people who were out of the labor force but did still want a job, nearly two million (41.6%) had looked for work during the previous year. Men who were not in the labor force were more likely to want a job (2.1 million of 30 million, or 7.1%) than were women who were not in the labor force (2.6 million of 48.7 million, or 5.3%).

Reasons for Not Working

The reasons people were not looking for work included school or family responsibilities, ill health or disability, and discouragement over job prospects. Women's reasons for being out of the labor force differed markedly from those reported by men. Of the 669,000 women who were avail-

TABLE 3.7

Persons not in the labor force, by desire and availability for work, age, and sex, 2007

[In thousands]

Category	Total	Age			Sex	
		16 to 24 years	25 to 54 years	55 years and over	Men	Women
	2007	2007	2007	2007	2007	2007
Total not in the labor force	**78,743**	**15,192**	**21,343**	**42,207**	**30,036**	**48,707**
Do not want a job now[a]	74,040	13,510	19,256	41,275	27,914	46,126
Want a job[a]	4,703	1,683	2,088	933	2,122	2,581
Did not search for work in previous year	2,748	931	1,148	668	1,173	1,575
Searched for work in previous year[b]	1,955	751	939	264	950	1,005
Not available to work now	560	272	234	53	223	336
Available to work now	1,395	479	705	211	726	669
Reason not currently looking						
Discouragement over job prospects[c]	369	110	199	61	226	143
Reasons other than discouragement	1,026	370	506	150	500	526
Family responsibilities	160	31	109	21	37	123
In school or training	180	149	27	3	102	78
Ill health or disability	114	11	66	37	57	58
Other[d]	572	178	304	90	305	267

[a]Includes some persons who are not asked if they want a job.
[b]Persons who had a job in the prior 12 months must have searched since the end of that job.
[c]Includes believes no work available, could not find work, lacks necessary schooling or training, employer thinks too young or old, and other types of discrimination.
[d]Includes those who did not actively look for work in the prior 4 weeks for such reasons as child care and transportation problems, as well as a small number for which reason for nonparticipation was not ascertained.
Note: Updated population controls are introduced annually with the release of January data.

SOURCE: Adapted from "35. Persons Not in the Labor Force by Desire and Availability for Work, Age, and Sex," in *Employment and Earnings*, U.S. Department of Labor, Bureau of Labor Statistics, January 2008, http://www.bls.gov/cps/cpsaat35.pdf (accessed February 2, 2008)

able to work but not currently looking for a job in 2007, 123,000 (18.4%) cited taking care of their home or family as their reason for not working; 78,000 (11.7%) were in school; and 58,000 (8.7%) were either ill or disabled. (See Table 3.7.) In contrast, among the 726,000 men who were available to work but out of the labor force in 2007, only 37,000 (5.1%) were taking care of their family or home; 102,000 (14%) were in school or training; and 57,000 (7.9%) were ill or disabled. Nearly a third (226,000 of 726,000, or 31.1%) of the men available to work but not currently looking for work reported discouragement over job prospects as the reason. Discouragement over job prospects was reported by only 143,000 of 669,000 women (21.4%) not currently looking for work.

CHAPTER 4
THE EDUCATION OF AMERICAN WORKERS

Education is an investment in skills, and like all investments, it involves both costs and returns. The cost to the student of finishing high school is quite low. However, the cost to the student of attending college is higher because it includes tuition, books, fees, and the earnings a student potentially gives up either by not working at all during college or by working only part-time. However, according to a report by Kathleen Porter of the ERIC Clearinghouse on Higher Education ("The Value of a College Degree," *ERIC Digest*, 2002, http://www.ericdigests.org/2003-3/value.htm), over an adult's working life, those with a high school degree will earn on average $1.2 million, those with an associate's degree will earn an average of $1.6 million, and those with a bachelor's degree will earn about $2.1 million. These figures put the costs of higher education in perspective. In addition, it is important to remember that while the returns from a high school or college education can be measured economically, there are invaluable social, emotional, and intellectual returns as well.

Although some returns from education accrue for the individual, others benefit society and the nation in general. Returns related to the economy—specifically the labor market—include better job opportunities and jobs that are less sensitive to general economic conditions. Other societal returns often attributed to higher education include a greater interest and participation in civil affairs among well-educated individuals. Porter also noted that individuals with higher educational attainment contribute more to general tax revenues, are more productive, and are less likely to rely on governmental financial support, all important benefits for society as a whole.

A BETTER-EDUCATED NATION

American workers are better educated than ever before. Before the end of World War II (1939–1945), with the exception of doctors, lawyers, engineers, teachers, and a few other professionals, only a small number of people earned higher degrees for the purpose of preparing for a career or vocation. Most colleges were private, four-year schools with limited enrollments. Therefore, a person who wanted training for a job or an occupation usually went to a vocational high school or became an apprentice, learning a trade from a highly skilled mentor.

The G.I. Bill of Rights, introduced after World War II, changed the way Americans viewed higher education. The soldiers, sailors, and pilots returning to civilian life wanted to make better lives for themselves, and the U.S. government was willing to pay to give them the chance. Federal money paid to America's returning veterans opened up and enlarged trade and vocational schools and filled college classrooms across the nation.

Approximately 2.2 million veterans, or about one-third of all American veterans returning from World War II, enrolled in colleges and universities under the G.I. Bill between 1944 and 1960, according to Jennifer Ann Adams of Pennsylvania State University in "The G.I. Bill and the Changing Place of U.S. Higher Education after World War II" (November 18, 2000, http://www.personal.psu.edu/jaa144/ashe2000.PDF). This influx of students represented a massive democratization of education. Existing colleges and universities expanded, and nearly 1,700 new institutions were founded across the nation during the fifty years following the passage of the G.I. Bill. Most of these schools were two-year colleges, providing a new option in higher education for many people. In the postwar period, American colleges, universities, and junior colleges graduated increasing numbers of engineers, accountants, scientists, business people, technicians, nurses, and others with similar professional and technical careers.

How Well Educated Are Americans?

According to the National Center for Education Statistics (NCES) in *Digest of Education Statistics, 2007*

(September 2007), significant increases were registered during the twentieth century in the number of years of school completed by students. The median number of school years completed (half of the students completed more, and half completed less) by American students increased from 8.4 years in 1930 to 13 years by 1993. (The NCES no longer publishes data on median number of years completed.) In 1930 fewer than one in five Americans aged twenty-five and over (19.1%) were high school graduates, and only 3.9% held a bachelor's degree or higher. (See Table 4.1.) Since that time these proportions have steadily increased. By March 1970 over half (55.2%) of adults aged twenty-five and over had completed high school, and 11% had a bachelor's degree. By 1990 more than three-quarters (77.6%) of adults had a high school diploma, and over one in five (21.3%) had a bachelor's degree. By March 2007, 85.7% of all adults aged twenty-five and over had completed high school, and over a quarter (28.7%) had a bachelor's degree or higher. These percentages were the highest recorded since statistics began to be compiled in 1910.

Who Is in College?

In 1970, 8.6 million high school graduates were enrolled in degree-granting institutions including colleges and universities. By 2006, 17.7 million people were enrolled in degree-granting institutions. Projections by the NCES in *Digest of Education Statistics, 2007* estimate that in 2011, enrollment will surpass 19.1 million, and by 2016, 20.4 million students will be enrolled in college, graduate, or professional school. (See Table 4.2.)

GENDER. Not only have enrollment numbers burgeoned, but the demographic characteristics of students—including gender, age, and minority status—have shifted. Since the 1970s a dramatic change has been seen in the gender makeup of fall enrollees at degree-granting institutions. In 1970 male students predominated on college campuses; 5 million of the 8.6 million (58.8%) fall enrollees that year were males. A decade later females outnumbered males on college campuses; 6.2 million of the 12.1 million enrollees (51.4%) were females that year. This trend of increasing proportions of female enrollment continued through subsequent years. By 2000, 8.6 million of 15.3 million (56.1%) college or graduate students were female. In 2006, 10.2 million college or graduate students were female, compared with 7.5 million males; females made up 57.7% of enrollment. This trend is expected to continue. The NCES projects that in 2016, 12.2 million of 20.4 million enrolled students, or 59.8%, will be females. (See Table 4.2.)

Increased female enrollment has contributed to overall growth in college enrollment. From 1990 through 2006 male enrollment increased from 6.3 million to 7.5 million, an 18.9% increase, while the number of females rose from 7.5 million to 10.2 million, a 35.4% increase. Between 2006 and 2016 female enrollment is projected to rise from 10.2 million to 12.2 million, an increase of 19.8%, while male enrollment is expected to rise from 7.5 million to 8.2 million, an increase of only 10.1%. (See Table 4.2.)

OLDER STUDENTS. Since 1970 there has been a significant increase in the percentage of older students enrolled in college. In 1970, 1.1 million students were between the ages of twenty-five and twenty-nine, 487,000 were between the ages of thirty and thirty-four, and 823,000 were aged thirty-five or older. (See Table 4.2.) These nontraditional students made up 27.8% of the 8.6 million students enrolled in degree-granting institutions that year. By 2006, 2.5 million students were between the ages of twenty-five and twenty-nine, 1.3 million were between thirty and thirty-four years old, and nearly 3.1 million were aged thirty-five and older. By that year, these older students made up 38.9% of the student bodies.

The increased enrollment of older students may reflect the higher education levels required by many occupations and the return to school of those who had previously left school to work. Historically, older students generally begin or return to degree programs in order to handle involuntary career transitions or to upgrade their skills in order to advance at their current jobs or prepare to seek new employment.

MINORITY ENROLLMENT. The enrollment of minority students (African-Americans, Hispanics, Asians, Pacific Islanders, Native Americans, and Alaskan Natives) in higher education has been rising steadily. In 1970, of the 1.4 million students who had recently completed high school and then enrolled in degree-granting institutions, 1.3 million (89.7%) were non-Hispanic whites. By 2006 nearly 1.8 million recent high school completers had enrolled in college, and only 1.2 million of them (69.7%) were non-Hispanic whites. In that year, there were 177,000 African-American recent high school completers who were enrolled in college (10%) and 222,000 Hispanic recent high school completers who were enrolled in college (12.5%). Probably most of the remaining 7.8% of the recent high school completers enrolled in college were Asians. (See Table 4.3.)

Although non-Hispanic white students still comprise a large majority of college students (11.5 million of 17.5 million students in 2005), the trend is toward more racial and ethnic diversity on campuses. The NCES reported in *Digest of Education Statistics, 2007* (http://nces.ed.gov/ programs/digest/d07/tables/dt07_216.asp) that in 1976 white students made up 82.6% of higher education enrollment. In 2005, of the 17.5 million people attending college, 65.7% were non-Hispanic whites, 12.7% were African-Americans, 10.8% were Hispanics, 6.5% were Asians/Pacific Islanders, and 1% were Native Americans.

TABLE 4.1

Percentage of persons aged 25 years and over by race/ethnicity, years of school completed, and sex, selected years, 1910–2007

Sex, age, and year	Total			White[a]			Black[a]			Hispanic		
	Less than 5 years of elementary school	High school completion or higher[b]	Bachelor's or higher degree[c]	Less than 5 years of elementary school	High school completion or higher[b]	Bachelor's or higher degree[c]	Less than 5 years of elementary school	High school completion or higher[b]	Bachelor's or higher degree[c]	Less than 5 years of elementary school	High school completion or higher[b]	Bachelor's or higher degree[c]
1	2	3	4	5	6	7	8	9	10	11	12	13
Total, 25 and over												
1910[d]	23.8	13.5	2.7	—	—	—	—	—	—	—	—	—
1920[d]	22.0	16.4	3.3	—	—	—	—	—	—	—	—	—
1930[d]	17.5	19.1	3.9	—	—	—	—	—	—	—	—	—
April 1940	13.7	24.5	4.6	10.9	26.1	4.9	41.8	7.7	—	—	—	—
April 1950	11.1	34.3	6.2	8.9	36.4	6.6	32.6	13.7	1.3	—	—	—
April 1960	8.3	41.1	7.7	6.7	43.2	8.1	23.5	21.7	2.2	—	—	—
March 1970	5.3	55.2	11.0	4.2	57.4	11.6	14.7	36.1	3.5	—	—	—
March 1980	3.4	68.6	17.0	1.9	71.9	18.4	9.1	51.4	6.1	15.8	44.5	7.6
March 1990	2.4	77.6	21.3	1.1	81.4	23.1	5.1	66.2	7.9	12.3	50.8	9.2
March 2000	1.6	84.1	25.6	0.5	88.4	28.1	1.6	78.9	11.3	8.7	57.0	10.6
March 2005	1.6	85.2	27.6	0.5	90.1	30.5	1.5	81.5	16.6	7.9	58.5	12.0
March 2006	1.5	85.5	28.0	0.4	90.5	31.0	1.5	81.2	17.7	7.6	59.3	12.4
March 2007	1.5	85.7	28.7	0.4	90.6	31.8	1.2	82.8	18.6	6.9	60.3	12.7
Males, 25 and over												
April 1940	15.1	22.7	5.5	12.0	24.2	5.9	46.2	6.9	1.4	—	—	—
April 1950	12.2	32.6	7.3	9.8	34.6	7.9	36.9	12.6	2.1	—	—	—
April 1960	9.4	39.5	9.7	7.4	41.6	10.3	27.7	20.0	3.5	—	—	—
March 1970	5.9	55.0	14.1	4.5	57.2	15.0	17.9	35.4	6.8	—	—	—
March 1980	3.6	69.2	20.9	2.0	72.4	22.8	11.3	51.2	7.7	16.5	44.9	9.2
March 1990	2.7	77.7	24.4	1.3	81.6	26.7	6.4	65.8	11.9	12.9	50.3	9.8
March 2000	1.6	84.2	27.8	0.6	88.5	30.8	2.1	79.1	16.4	8.2	56.6	10.7
March 2005	1.7	84.9	28.9	0.5	89.9	32.3	1.7	81.4	16.1	8.0	58.0	11.8
March 2006	1.6	85.0	29.2	0.4	90.2	32.8	1.7	80.7	17.5	7.8	58.5	11.9
March 2007	1.6	85.0	29.5	0.4	90.2	33.2	1.3	82.5	18.1	7.3	58.2	11.8
Females, 25 and over												
April 1940	12.4	26.3	3.8	9.8	28.1	4.0	37.5	8.4	1.2	—	—	—
April 1950	10.0	36.0	5.2	8.1	38.2	5.4	28.6	14.7	2.4	—	—	—
April 1960	7.4	42.5	5.8	6.0	44.7	6.0	19.7	23.1	3.6	—	—	—
March 1970	4.7	55.4	8.2	3.9	57.7	8.6	11.9	36.6	5.6	—	—	—
March 1980	3.2	68.1	13.6	1.8	71.5	14.4	7.4	51.5	8.1	15.3	44.2	6.2
March 1990	2.2	77.5	18.4	1.0	81.3	19.8	4.0	66.5	10.8	11.7	51.3	8.7
March 2000	1.5	84.0	23.6	0.4	88.4	25.5	1.1	78.7	16.8	9.3	57.5	10.6
March 2005	1.5	85.4	26.5	0.4	90.3	28.9	1.3	81.5	18.9	7.8	58.9	12.1
March 2006	1.5	85.9	26.9	0.4	90.8	29.3	1.3	81.5	19.5	7.4	60.1	12.9
March 2007	1.4	86.4	28.0	0.4	91.0	30.6	1.1	83.0	19.2	6.6	62.5	13.7

TABLE 4.1

Percentage of persons aged 25 years and over by race/ethnicity, years of school completed, and sex, selected years, 1910–2007 [CONTINUED]

—Not available.

[F]Rounds to zero.

[a]Includes persons of Hispanic ethnicity for years prior to 1980.

[b]Data for years prior to 1993 are for persons with 4 or more years of high school. Data for later years are for high school completers—i.e., those persons who graduated from high school with a diploma, as well as those who completed high school through equivalency programs.

[c]Data for years prior to 1993 are for persons with 4 or more years of college.

[d]Estimates based on Census Bureau retrojection of 1940 census data on education by age.

SOURCE: Adapted from "Table 8. Percentage of Persons Age 25 and Over and 25 to 29, by Race/Ethnicity, Years of School Completed, and Sex: Selected Years, 1910 through 2007," in *Digest of Education Statistics, 2007,* U.S. Department of Education, National Center for Education Statistics, September 2007, http://nces.ed.gov/programs/digest/d07/tables/dt07_008.asp (accessed February 11, 2008)

TABLE 4.2

Total fall enrollment in degree-granting institutions by sex, age, and attendance status, selected years, 1970–2016

[In thousands]

Sex, age, and attendance status	1970	1980	1990	1995	2000	2001	2002	2003*	2004	2005*	2006*	Projected 2011	Projected 2016
	2	3	4	5	6	7	8	9	10	11	12	13	14
Males and females	**8,581**	**12,097**	**13,819**	**14,262**	**15,312**	**15,928**	**16,612**	**16,911**	**17,272**	**17,487**	**17,672**	**19,105**	**20,442**
14 to 17 years old	259	247	177	148	145	133	202	151	200	199	172	176	190
18 and 19 years old	2,600	2,901	2,950	2,894	3,531	3,595	3,571	3,479	3,578	3,610	3,710	3,996	4,010
20 and 21 years old	1,880	2,424	2,761	2,705	3,045	3,408	3,366	3,473	3,651	3,778	3,855	4,294	4,299
22 to 24 years old	1,457	1,989	2,144	2,411	2,617	2,760	2,932	3,482	3,036	3,072	3,060	3,364	3,715
25 to 29 years old	1,074	1,871	1,982	2,120	1,960	2,014	2,102	2,106	2,386	2,384	2,452	2,729	3,168
30 to 34 years old	487	1,243	1,322	1,236	1,265	1,290	1,300	1,368	1,329	1,354	1,331	1,501	1,741
35 years old and over	823	1,421	2,484	2,747	2,749	2,727	3,139	2,852	3,092	3,090	3,092	3,046	3,319
Males	5,044	5,874	6,284	6,343	6,722	6,961	7,202	7,260	7,387	7,456	7,470	7,967	8,222
14 to 17 years old	130	99	87	61	63	54	82	60	78	78	80	80	82
18 and 19 years old	1,349	1,375	1,421	1,338	1,583	1,629	1,616	1,558	1,551	1,592	1,626	1,727	1,687
20 and 21 years old	1,095	1,259	1,368	1,282	1,382	1,591	1,562	1,492	1,743	1,778	1,792	1,966	1,919
22 to 24 years old	964	1,064	1,107	1,153	1,293	1,312	1,342	1,605	1,380	1,355	1,330	1,428	1,516
25 to 29 years old	783	993	940	962	862	905	890	930	1,045	978	989	1,082	1,198
30 to 34 years old	308	576	537	561	527	510	547	592	518	545	530	589	660
35 years old and over	415	507	824	986	1,012	961	1,164	1,025	1,073	1,130	1,122	1,095	1,161
Females	3,537	6,223	7,535	7,919	8,591	8,967	9,410	9,651	9,885	10,032	10,202	11,139	12,220
14 to 17 years old	129	148	90	87	82	79	121	91	122	121	91	96	108
18 and 19 years old	1,250	1,526	1,529	1,557	1,948	1,966	1,955	1,922	2,027	2,018	2,084	2,269	2,323
20 and 21 years old	786	1,165	1,392	1,424	1,663	1,817	1,804	1,981	1,908	2,000	2,064	2,328	2,380
22 to 24 years old	493	925	1,037	1,258	1,324	1,448	1,590	1,877	1,657	1,717	1,730	1,936	2,199
25 to 29 years old	291	878	1,043	1,159	1,099	1,110	1,212	1,177	1,341	1,406	1,463	1,646	1,970
30 to 34 years old	179	667	784	675	738	780	753	776	812	809	801	912	1,081
35 years old and over	409	914	1,659	1,760	1,736	1,767	1,976	1,827	2,018	1,960	1,970	1,951	2,159
Full-time	**5,816**	**7,098**	**7,821**	**8,129**	**9,010**	**9,448**	**9,946**	**10,326**	**10,610**	**10,797**	**10,982**	**12,222**	**13,325**
14 to 17 years old	242	223	144	123	125	122	161	121	165	131	107	112	125
18 and 19 years old	2,406	2,669	2,548	2,387	2,932	2,929	2,942	2,953	3,028	3,037	3,126	3,401	3,469
20 and 21 years old	1,647	2,075	2,151	2,109	2,401	2,662	2,759	2,767	2,911	3,030	3,099	3,495	3,567
22 to 24 years old	881	1,121	1,350	1,517	1,653	1,757	1,922	2,144	2,074	2,097	2,098	2,357	2,679
25 to 29 years old	407	577	770	908	878	883	1,013	1,072	1,131	1,136	1,179	1,360	1,676
30 to 34 years old	100	251	387	430	422	494	465	512	490	549	545	639	790
35 years old and over	134	182	471	653	599	602	684	758	812	818	828	858	1,019
Males	3,505	3,689	3,808	3,807	4,111	4,300	4,501	4,638	4,739	4,803	4,836	5,231	5,377
14 to 17 years old	124	87	71	54	51	43	65	50	63	36	43	43	44
18 and 19 years old	1,265	1,270	1,230	1,091	1,250	1,329	1,327	1,307	1,313	1,357	1,387	1,478	1,452
20 and 21 years old	990	1,109	1,055	999	1,106	1,249	1,275	1,218	1,385	1,460	1,473	1,624	1,595
22 to 24 years old	650	665	742	789	839	854	936	1,041	960	951	935	1,012	1,083
25 to 29 years old	327	360	401	454	415	397	467	503	509	439	445	494	558
30 to 34 years old	72	124	156	183	195	216	183	242	201	238	233	262	300
35 years old and over	75	74	152	238	256	212	247	277	310	321	320	318	346

TABLE 4.2

TABLE 4.2

Total fall enrollment in degree-granting institutions by sex, age, and attendance status, selected years, 1970–2016 [CONTINUED]

[In thousands]

Sex, age, and attendance status	1970	1980	1990	1995	2000	2001	2002	2003*	2004	2005*	2006*	Projected 2011	Projected 2016
	2	3	4	5	6	7	8	9	10	11	12	13	14
Females	2,311	3,409	4,013	4,321	4,899	5,148	5,445	5,688	5,871	5,994	6,146	6,991	7,948
14 to 17 years old	117	136	73	69	74	78	96	71	103	94	64	69	80
18 and 19 years old	1,140	1,399	1,318	1,296	1,682	1,600	1,615	1,646	1,716	1,680	1,739	1,923	2,017
20 and 21 years old	657	966	1,096	1,111	1,296	1,413	1,484	1,549	1,526	1,569	1,626	1,871	1,973
22 to 24 years old	231	456	608	729	814	903	985	1,103	1,113	1,146	1,164	1,345	1,596
25 to 29 years old	80	217	369	455	463	486	546	569	622	697	733	866	1,118
30 to 34 years old	28	127	231	247	227	277	282	270	289	311	312	377	491
35 years old and over	59	108	319	415	343	390	437	481	502	497	508	540	673
Part-time	**2,765**	**4,999**	**5,998**	**6,133**	**6,303**	**6,480**	**6,665**	**6,585**	**6,662**	**6,690**	**6,689**	**6,883**	**7,117**
14 to 17 years old	17	38	32	25	20	11	41	30	35	68	65	64	65
18 and 19 years old	194	418	402	507	599	666	628	526	549	573	584	595	542
20 and 21 years old	233	441	610	596	644	746	607	706	741	748	756	799	732
22 to 24 years old	576	844	794	894	964	1,003	1,010	1,338	963	976	962	1,008	1,036
25 to 29 years old	668	1,209	1,213	1,212	1,083	1,132	1,088	1,034	1,255	1,248	1,273	1,369	1,493
30 to 34 years old	388	905	935	805	843	796	835	856	839	805	787	862	950
35 years old and over	689	1,145	2,012	2,093	2,150	2,126	2,456	2,094	2,280	2,272	2,264	2,187	2,301
Males	1,540	2,185	2,476	2,535	2,611	2,661	2,701	2,622	2,648	2,653	2,634	2,736	2,845
14 to 17 years old	5	17	16	7	11	11	17	10	15	41	38	37	37
18 and 19 years old	84	202	191	246	333	300	288	250	239	235	239	249	235
20 and 21 years old	105	201	313	283	276	342	287	274	358	318	319	342	324
22 to 24 years old	314	392	365	365	454	458	405	564	419	405	396	416	433
25 to 29 years old	456	594	539	508	447	508	423	427	536	539	544	588	640
30 to 34 years old	236	397	381	378	332	294	364	350	317	306	298	327	360
35 years old and over	340	382	672	748	757	749	917	748	764	809	802	777	815
Females	1,225	2,814	3,521	3,598	3,692	3,820	3,964	3,963	4,014	4,038	4,056	4,148	4,272
14 to 17 years old	12	20	17	18	9	1	24	20	19	27	27	27	27
18 and 19 years old	110	215	211	261	266	366	340	276	311	338	344	346	306
20 and 21 years old	128	240	297	313	368	404	320	433	382	430	437	457	407
22 to 24 years old	262	452	429	529	510	545	605	774	543	571	566	592	603
25 to 29 years old	212	616	674	704	636	624	666	608	720	709	729	781	852
30 to 34 years old	151	507	554	427	511	502	471	507	523	499	489	535	590
35 years old and over	349	762	1,340	1,345	1,393	1,377	1,539	1,346	1,516	1,464	1,462	1,411	1,486

*Some data have been revised from previously published figures.

Note: Distributions by age are estimates based on samples of the civilian noninstitutional population from the U.S. Census Bureau's Current Population Survey. Data through 1995 are for institutions of higher education, while later data are for degree-granting institutions. Degree-granting institutions grant associate's or higher degrees and participate in Title IV federal financial aid programs. The degree-granting classification is very similar to the earlier higher education classification, but it includes more 2-year colleges and excludes a few higher education institutions that did not grant degrees. Detail may not sum to totals because of rounding.

SOURCE: "Table 181. Total Fall Enrollment in Degree-Granting Institutions, by Sex, Age, and Attendance Status: Selected Years, 1970 through 2016," in *Digest of Education Statistics, 2007*, U.S. Department of Education, National Center for Education Statistics, August 2007, http://nces.ed.gov/programs/digest/d07/tables/dt07_181.asp (accessed February 11, 2008)

TABLE 4.3

College enrollment and enrollment rates of recent high school completers, by race/ethnicity, selected years, 1960–2006

[Numbers in thousands]

											Enrolled in college[b]			
													Hispanic[c]	
														Percent
	Number of high school completers[a]				Total		White		Black[c]					
Year	Total	White	Black[c]	Hispanic[c]	Number	Percent	Number	Percent	Number	Percent	Number	Annual	3-year moving average
1	2	3	4	5	6	7	8	9	10	11	12	13	14
1960	1,679	1,565	—	—	758	45.1	717	45.8	—	—	—	—	—
1970	2,758	2,461	—	—	1,427	51.7	1,280	52.0	—	—	—	—	—
1980	3,088	2,554	350	130	1,523	49.3	1,273	49.8	149	42.7	68	52.3	49.8
1990	2,362	1,819	331	121	1,420	60.1	1,147	63.0	155	46.8	52	42.7	51.7
2000	2,756	1,938	393	300	1,745	63.3	1,272	65.7	216	54.9	159	52.9	49.0
2005[d]	2,675	1,799	345	390	1,834	68.6	1,317	73.2	192	55.7	211	54.0	57.9
2006[d]	2,692	1,805	318	382	1,776	66.0	1,237	68.5	177	55.5	222	57.9	—

—Not available.

[a]Individuals ages 16 to 24 who graduated from high school or completed a GED during the preceding 12 months.

[b]Enrollment in college as of October of each year for individuals ages 16 to 24 who completed high school during the preceding 12 months.

[c]Due to the small sample size, data are subject to relatively large sampling errors.

[d]White and black data exclude persons identifying themselves as multiracial.

Note: High school completion data in this table differ from figures appearing in other tables because of varying survey procedures and coverage. High school completers include GED recipients. Moving averages are used to produce more stable estimates. Race categories exclude persons of Hispanic ethnicity.

SOURCE: Adapted from "Table 192. College Enrollment and Enrollment Rates of Recent High School Completers, by Race/Ethnicity: 1960 through 2006," in *Digest of Education Statistics, 2007,* U.S. Department of Education, National Center for Education Statistics, September 2007, http://nces.ed.gov/programs/digest/d07/tables/dt07_192.asp (accessed February 11, 2008)

NCES statistics further reveal that enrollment of minority students increased at a faster pace than the enrollment of non-Hispanic white students between 1976 and 2005. The number of non-Hispanic white students rose from 9.1 million in 1976 to 11.5 million in 2005, an increase of 26.7%. The number of African-American students rose from 1 million in 1976 to 2.2 million in 2005, an increase of an astounding 114.3%. Other minority groups increased their enrollment by even higher proportions. In 1976, 76,000 Native Americans were enrolled in college; by 2005 that number had risen to 176,000, an increase of 131.6%. In 1976, 383,000 Hispanics were enrolled in college; by 2005 that number had risen to 1.9 million, an increase of 391.4%. The number of Asian/Pacific Islander students increased from 197,000 in 1976 to 1.1 million in 2005, an increase of 475.6%.

Types of Degrees

Students can earn a variety of vocational certifications and college degrees in institutions for higher education. Associate degrees are usually awarded by junior colleges or community colleges after about two years of course work. Private institutions, as well as government-funded community and junior colleges, award vocational degrees. These degrees prepare people for specific jobs, such as court reporter, legal assistant, or computer programmer. Bachelor's degrees usually take a minimum of four years to complete, and typically include a broader liberal arts education in addition to training for a particular career. Private and public universities also award advanced master's, doctoral, or professional (doctor or lawyer) degrees. These advanced degrees prepare students to enter a specific profession.

HOW MANY? At the end of the 2005–06 school year, according to the NCES in *Digest of Education Statistics, 2007* (http://nces.ed.gov/programs/digest/d07/tables/dt07_266.asp), a total of 713,066 associate degrees (557,134 from public institutions and 155,932 from private institutions) and nearly 1.5 million bachelor's degrees (955,369 from public institutions and 529,873 from private institutions) were awarded. In addition, 594,065 master's degrees, 87,655 first professional degrees, and 56,067 doctoral degrees were awarded.

Just as women have increased their enrollment in college, they have also increased as a proportion of those receiving degrees. In 1976–77, 494,424 of 917,900 bachelor's degrees conferred (53.9%) were awarded to males. By 2005–06 only 630,600 of nearly 1.5 million degrees conferred (42.5%) were awarded to males. (See Table 4.4.) In *Digest of Education Statistics, 2007*, the NCES further reported that while six out of ten master's degrees awarded in 2005–06 were awarded to women (356,169 of 594,065 master's degrees awarded), slightly more men than women received first professional degrees (44,038 males and 43,617 females) and doctoral degrees (28,634 males and 27,433 females), although women were closing the gap.

Despite their increasing enrollment in higher education, African-American and Hispanic students were underrepresented in attaining four-year college degrees. According to NCES data released in *Digest of Education Statistics,*

TABLE 4.4

Bachelor's degrees conferred by race/ethnicity and sex of student, selected years, 1976–77 through 2005–06

Year and sex	Number of degrees conferred								Percentage distribution of degrees conferred						
	Total	White	Black	Hispanic	Asian/ Pacific Islander	American Indian/ Alaska Native	Non- resident alien	Total	White	Black	Hispanic	Asian/ Pacific Islander	American Indian/ Alaska Native	Non- resident alien
1	2	3	4	5	6	7	8	9	10	11	12	13	14	15
Total														
1976–77 [a]	917,900	807,688	58,636	18,743	13,793	3,326	15,714	100.0	88.0	6.4	2.0	1.5	0.4	1.7
1980–81 [b]	934,800	807,319	60,673	21,832	18,794	3,593	22,589	100.0	86.4	6.5	2.3	2.0	0.4	2.4
1990–91	1,094,538	914,093	66,375	37,342	42,529	4,583	29,616	100.0	83.5	6.1	3.4	3.9	0.4	2.7
1995–96	1,164,792	905,846	91,496	58,351	64,433	6,976	37,690	100.0	77.8	7.9	5.0	5.5	0.6	3.2
2000–01	1,244,171	927,357	111,307	77,745	78,902	9,049	39,811	100.0	74.5	8.9	6.2	6.3	0.7	3.2
2005–06	1,485,242	1,075,561	142,420	107,588	102,376	10,940	46,357	100.0	72.4	9.6	7.2	6.9	0.7	3.1
Males														
1976–77 [a]	494,424	438,161	25,147	10,318	7,638	1,804	11,356	100.0	88.6	5.1	2.1	1.5	0.4	2.3
1980–81 [b]	469,625	406,173	24,511	10,810	10,107	1,700	16,324	100.0	86.5	5.2	2.3	2.2	0.4	3.5
1990–91	504,045	421,290	24,800	16,598	21,203	1,938	18,216	100.0	83.6	4.9	3.3	4.2	0.4	3.6
1995–96	522,454	409,565	32,974	25,029	30,669	2,885	21,332	100.0	78.4	6.3	4.8	5.9	0.6	4.1
2000–01	531,840	401,780	38,103	31,368	35,865	3,700	21,024	100.0	75.5	7.2	5.9	6.7	0.7	4.0
2005–06	630,600	467,467	48,079	41,814	45,809	4,203	23,228	100.0	74.1	7.6	6.6	7.3	0.7	3.7
Females														
1976–77 [a]	423,476	369,527	33,489	8,425	6,155	1,522	4,358	100.0	87.3	7.9	2.0	1.5	0.4	1.0
1980–81 [b]	465,175	401,146	36,162	11,022	8,687	1,893	6,265	100.0	86.2	7.8	2.4	1.9	0.4	1.3
1990–91	590,493	492,803	41,575	20,744	21,326	2,645	11,400	100.0	83.5	7.0	3.5	3.6	0.4	1.9
1995–96	642,338	496,281	58,522	33,322	33,764	4,091	16,358	100.0	77.3	9.1	5.2	5.3	0.6	2.5
2000–01	712,331	525,577	73,204	46,377	43,037	5,349	18,787	100.0	73.8	10.3	6.5	6.0	0.8	2.6
2005–06	854,642	608,094	94,341	65,774	56,567	6,737	23,129	100.0	71.2	11.0	7.7	6.6	0.8	2.7

[a]Excludes 1,121 males and 528 females whose racial/ethnic group was not available.
[b]Excludes 258 males and 82 females whose racial/ethnic group was not available.
[c]Data have been revised from previously published figures.
Note: Race categories exclude persons of Hispanic ethnicity. For 1989–90 and later years, reported racial/ethnic distributions of students by level of degree, field of degree, and sex were used to estimate race/ethnicity for students whose race/ethnicity was not reported. Detail may not sum to totals because of rounding.

SOURCE: Adapted from "Table 274. Bachelor's Degrees Conferred by Degree-Granting Institutions, by Race/Ethnicity and Sex of Student: Selected Years, 1976–77 through 2005–06," in *Digest of Education Statistics, 2007,* U.S. Department of Education, National Center for Education Statistics, June 2007, http://nces.ed.gov/programs/digest/d07/tables/dt07_274.asp (accessed February 11, 2008)

2007, in the 2005–06 school year only 9.6% of all bachelor's degrees were awarded to African-Americans and only 7.2% were awarded to Hispanics. These proportions were lower than the proportions of minority students among those who had recently completed high school and enrolled in college, indicating that African-American and Hispanic students were more likely to drop out of college than their non-Hispanic white counterparts. (See Table 4.4.) Similarly, minorities were underrepresented at the master's, doctoral, and first-professional degree levels.

According to the NCES, of the nearly 1.5 million bachelor's degrees conferred during the 2005–06 school year, by far the largest number, 318,042 (21.4%), were awarded for business; in addition, 161,485 (10.9%) were awarded for social sciences and history, and 107,238 (7.2%) were for education. Computer and information sciences accounted for 47,480 bachelor's degrees (3.2%), down from a high of 59,488 awarded in 2003–04. More than 55,000 bachelor's degrees (3.7%) were awarded for English language and literature, 88,134 (5.9%) were awarded in psychology, and 91,973 (6.2%) were awarded in the health professions and related clinical sciences. (See http://nces.ed.gov/programs/digest/d07/tables/dt07_261.asp for historical data on numbers of degrees conferred by discipline.)

LABOR FORCE PARTICIPATION

Data gathered by the NCES show that adults with higher levels of education are more likely to participate in the labor force than those with less education. As reported in *Digest of Education Statistics, 2007*, about 85.9% of adults with a bachelor's degree between the ages of twenty-five and sixty-four participated in the labor force in 2006, compared with 76.5% of high school graduates who had not gone on to college and just 63.8% of those who had not completed high school. (See Table 4.5.)

The labor force participation rate varied by gender and race/ethnicity. Nine out of ten (91.8%) males ages twenty-five to sixty-four who had earned a bachelor's degree or higher participated in the labor force, compared with only about eight out of every ten (80.2%) females. Only half (49.1%) of females who had not completed high school worked, compared with 76.9% of males. Two-thirds (68.3%) of females who had completed high school worked, compared with 84.5% of males. These figures represent the greater likelihood that women will stay home to care for children or elderly relatives, regardless of educational attainment, although women with lower levels of education are more likely to remain out of the labor force than are women with more education. (See Table 4.5.)

African-Americans with a college degree were more likely to participate in the labor force (87.9%) than non-Hispanic whites (86.2%), Hispanics (85.6%), or Asians (81.8%) with college degrees in 2006. However, among high school graduates, African-Americans were least likely to be participating in the labor force (73.8%), compared with Asians (74%), non-Hispanic whites (76.8%), and Hispanics (78.9%). (See Table 4.5.)

As might be expected, NCES data also reveal that people with lower levels of education are more likely to be unemployed than those with higher levels of education. *Digest of Education Statistics, 2007* reveals that the unemployment rate for adults aged twenty-five and older who had not completed high school was 6.8% in 2006. In comparison, only 4.3% of those who had completed high school were unemployed, as were 2% of those who had attained a bachelor's degree or higher. (See Table 4.6.) Unemployment was a bigger problem among less-educated African-Americans twenty-five years of age or older than it was for those in other racial or ethnic groups. As Table 4.6 also shows, African-American adults aged twenty-five and older in 2006 who had not completed high school had the highest percentage of unemployment (13%), compared with non-Hispanic whites (6.5%), Hispanics (5.5%), and Asians (3.8%).

HIGH SCHOOL DROPOUTS

High school dropouts have significant difficulties successfully entering the job market. Without prior job experience or specialized training, dropouts often have difficulty finding jobs. According to the Bureau of Labor Statistics (BLS) in *College Enrollment and Work Activity of 2006 High School Graduates* (April 26, 2007, http://www.bls.gov/news.release/pdf/hsgec.pdf), between October 2005 and October 2006 about 444,000 high school students dropped out of school. Only slightly more than half (51.4%) of these youth were in the labor force, meaning they were either employed or they were looking for work, compared with three-quarters (76.4%) of high school graduates who were not enrolled in college. These recent dropouts had an unemployment rate of 23.1%.

Labor force participation rates among high school dropouts varies by gender and race/ethnicity. In 2006 male high school dropouts were more likely than female dropouts to be in the labor force (57.5% and 46.5%, respectively). One reason why the labor force participation rate might be so much lower among female dropouts is that often girls leave high school because they are pregnant; these girls may remain out of the labor force to take care of their infants. In addition, the unemployment rate among male dropouts (19.4%) was lower than among female dropouts (30.6%). (See Table 4.7.)

In 2005, the latest year for which complete data on race and ethnicity were available from the BLS, Hispanic students who had dropped out of high school were most likely to be participating in the labor force (64.3%), followed by non-Hispanic whites (60.3%), and African-Americans (42.5%). (See Table 4.7.)

TABLE 4.5

Labor force participation rates and employment to population ratios of persons 16 to 64 years old, by highest level of education, age, sex, and race/ethnicity, 2006

Age, sex, and race/ethnicity	Labor force participation rate[a]				College		Employment to population ratio[b]				College	
	Total	Less than high school completion[c]	High school completion	Some college, no degree	Associate's degree	Bachelor's or higher degree	Total	Less than high school completion[c]	High school completion	Some college, no degree	Associate's degree	Bachelor's or higher degree
1	2	3	4	5	6	7	8	9	10	11	12	13
16 to 19 years old[d]	**43.7**	**35.6**	**62.8**	**58.2**	**‡**	**‡**	**36.9**	**29.4**	**53.0**	**53.5**	**‡**	**‡**
Male	43.7	35.8	65.9	55.9	‡	‡	36.3	29.1	54.7	50.6	‡	‡
Female	43.7	35.4	59.6	59.9	‡	‡	37.6	29.7	51.2	55.6	‡	‡
White	48.9	41.0	67.2	61.5	‡	‡	42.6	35.0	58.5	57.2	‡	‡
Black	33.6	25.9	54.3	47.9	‡	‡	23.5	17.2	37.2	41.1	‡	‡
Hispanic	38.3	29.9	61.8	57.8	‡	‡	32.2	24.4	53.2	51.8	‡	‡
Asian	24.6	17.6	32.5	38.9	‡	‡	21.3	15.1	26.4	35.7	‡	‡
20 to 24 years old[d]	**74.6**	**66.2**	**78.5**	**70.1**	**83.7**	**83.0**	**68.5**	**56.7**	**70.2**	**65.9**	**79.4**	**78.8**
Male	79.6	79.7	86.0	71.4	86.2	84.5	72.7	69.9	76.9	66.9	80.6	79.7
Female	69.5	48.8	69.1	68.9	81.6	81.9	64.2	39.7	62.0	65.1	78.4	78.2
White	77.0	66.6	81.0	71.6	87.2	84.5	71.8	56.3	73.6	68.0	83.8	80.5
Black	68.7	54.2	71.9	67.8	74.0	84.6	57.4	38.2	58.2	60.2	63.5	77.4
Hispanic	74.4	71.0	78.3	71.6	79.1	81.1	69.0	64.4	72.3	67.8	75.6	77.8
Asian	58.7	47.8	66.0	51.1	64.0	68.5	55.3	42.7	62.4	48.3	59.6	65.0
25 to 64 years old	**79.1**	**63.8**	**76.5**	**79.8**	**83.5**	**85.9**	**76.2**	**59.4**	**73.1**	**76.7**	**81.0**	**84.1**
Male	86.5	76.9	84.5	86.5	89.1	91.8	83.4	72.1	80.8	83.5	86.5	90.0
Female	71.9	49.1	68.3	73.8	79.2	80.2	69.2	45.0	65.3	70.6	76.7	78.5
White	80.1	59.5	76.8	79.8	83.7	86.2	77.7	55.3	73.9	77.2	81.4	84.5
Black	75.8	54.2	73.8	78.8	82.9	87.9	70.6	46.9	67.8	73.5	78.5	85.5
Hispanic	77.6	71.2	78.9	82.4	83.5	85.6	74.3	67.3	75.7	79.2	81.1	83.6
Asian	78.0	63.2	74.0	75.9	81.4	81.8	76.0	60.8	71.6	73.0	79.5	80.0

‡Reporting standards not met.
[a]Percentage of the civilian population who are employed or seeking employment.
[b]Number of persons employed as a percentage of the civilian population.
[c]Includes persons reporting no school years completed.
[d]Excludes persons enrolled in school.
Note: Race categories exclude persons of Hispanic ethnicity.

SOURCE: "Table 368. Labor Force Participation Rates and Employment to Population Ratios of Persons 16 to 64 Years Old, by Highest Level of Education, Age, Sex, and Race/Ethnicity: 2006," in *Digest of Education Statistics, 2007*, U.S. Department of Education, National Center for Education Statistics, August 2007, http://nces.ed.gov/programs/digest/d07/tables/dt07_368.asp (accessed February 11, 2008)

TABLE 4.6

Unemployment rate of persons 16 years old and over, by age, sex, race/ethnicity, and educational attainment, 2006

Sex, race/ethnicity, and educational attainment	Unemployment rate, 2006			
	16- to 24-year-olds*			
	Total	16 to 19 years	20 to 24 years	25 years old and over
All persons, all education levels	**10.5**	**15.4**	**8.2**	**3.6**
Less than high school completion	16.6	17.5	14.3	6.8
High school completion, no college	12.0	15.7	10.5	4.3
Some college, no degree	6.3	8.1	5.9	3.9
Associate's degree	5.2	‡	5.1	3.0
Bachelor's or higher degree	5.1	‡	5.1	2.0
Male, all education levels	**11.2**	**16.9**	**8.7**	**3.5**
Less than high school completion	16.4	18.7	12.3	6.1
High school completion, no college	12.3	17.0	10.6	4.3
Some college, no degree	6.8	9.5	6.3	3.5
Associate's degree	6.4	‡	6.5	3.0
Bachelor's or higher degree	5.7	‡	5.7	1.9
Female, all education levels	**9.7**	**13.8**	**7.6**	**3.7**
Less than high school completion	16.8	16.3	18.7	7.9
High school completion, no college	11.5	14.2	10.3	4.3
Some college, no degree	5.9	7.1	5.5	4.3
Associate's degree	4.1	‡	3.9	3.1
Bachelor's or higher degree	4.7	‡	4.6	2.1
White, all education levels	**8.9**	**12.8**	**6.8**	**3.0**
Less than high school completion	14.9	14.7	15.5	6.5
High school completion, no college	10.3	12.9	9.2	3.7
Some college, no degree	5.4	6.9	5.0	3.3
Associate's degree	4.0	‡	3.9	2.7
Bachelor's or higher degree	4.9	‡	4.8	1.9
Black, all education levels	**20.5**	**29.9**	**16.4**	**6.8**
Less than high school completion	32.2	33.6	29.5	13.0
High school completion, no college	22.2	31.5	19.1	8.0
Some college, no degree	11.7	14.1	11.2	6.7
Associate's degree	15.3	‡	14.2	5.3
Bachelor's or higher degree	8.7	‡	8.4	2.8
Hispanic, all education levels	**9.7**	**15.9**	**7.2**	**4.2**
Less than high school completion	13.1	18.4	9.3	5.5
High school completion, no college	9.2	13.9	7.7	4.1
Some college, no degree	6.2	10.3	5.2	3.9
Associate's degree	4.5	‡	4.5	2.9
Bachelor's or higher degree	3.7	‡	4.1	2.2
Asian, all education levels	**7.4**	**13.7**	**5.6**	**2.6**
Less than high school completion	13.5	‡	‡	3.8
High school completion, no college	8.8	‡	5.4	3.1
Some college, no degree	5.9	‡	5.4	3.8
Associate's degree	‡	‡	6.7	2.3
Bachelor's or higher degree	‡	‡	5.1	2.1

‡Reporting standards not met.
*Excludes persons enrolled in school.
Note: The unemployment rate is the percentage of individuals in the labor force who are not working and who made specific efforts to find employment sometime during the prior 4 weeks. The labor force includes both employed and unemployed persons. Race categories exclude persons of Hispanic ethnicity. Some data have been revised from previously published figures.

SOURCE: Adapted from "Table 369. Unemployment Rate of Persons 16 Years Old and over, by Age, Sex, Race/Ethnicity, and Educational Attainment: 2004, 2005, and 2006," in *Digest of Education Statistics, 2007*, U.S. Department of Education, National Center for Education Statistics, September 2007, http://nces.ed.gov/programs/digest/d07/tables/dt07_369.asp (accessed February 11, 2008)

EDUCATION AND EARNINGS

Many people decide to attend college because they understand that a college degree will help them get a better job and increase their earnings potential. In fact, individuals with a higher level of education are generally more likely to be working, and they are likely to be earning more than those with lower levels of education. As reported by the National Center for Education Statistics in the *Digest of Educational Statistics, 2007* (http://nces.ed.gov/programs/digest/d07/tables/dt07_372.asp), in 2006 the median earnings of male college graduates aged twenty-five and over was $55,430, compared with male high school graduates, who earned a median of $33,070, and male high school dropouts, who earned a median of $24,090. (See Chapter 6 for complete discussion of earnings and benefits.)

Although better educated females also make more than their less-educated counterparts, there is a big difference between the earnings of males and females with the same educational background. Males generally earn more than females across all levels of education. The differential is most pronounced at the professional degree level (for example, medical doctor or law school graduate). In 2006 the median annual income of a male aged twenty-five or older with a master's degree was $67,990, whereas the median income for females with the same level of education was $47,590, or 70% of what men earned. Men with doctoral degrees earned a median of $91,050, compared with $60,450 (66.4% of what men earned) for equally educated women. Men aged twenty-five and older with a professional degree secured a median income of $100,000 in 2006; women with the same level of education earned a median income of only $65,110, or 65.1% of what their male counterparts earned.

However, the disparity in pay extends across all education levels. In 2006 female high school dropouts earned a median of $15,160, about 62.9% of what male dropouts earned, while female high school graduates earned a median of $21,610, about 65.3% of what males earned.

Researchers such as Linda Levine of the Congressional Research Service in "The Gender Wage Gap and Pay Equity: Is Comparable Worth the Next Step?" (June 5, 2001, http://digitalcommons.ilr.cornell.edu/cgi/viewcontent.cgi?article=1026&context=key_workplace) and Seth Kuhn of Furman University in "Examining a Changing Gender Wage Gap: The Role of Human Capital," (2006, http://economics.furman.edu/SethKuhnPaper.pdf) conclude that the wage gap cannot be explained by a single factor, but instead is attributable to the interrelated effects of many issues, including continuing discrimination against women that works against promotions and equal pay, the segregation of the female workforce into female-dominated jobs with lower wages, and the effects of females being less committed to staying in the workforce, as they are the family members who usually take time out of the labor force to care for small children.

TABLE 4.7

Labor force status of high school dropouts, by sex and race/ethnicity, selected years, 1980–2006

Year, sex, and race or ethnicity	Dropouts					Dropouts in civilian labor force[a]				Dropouts not in labor force (in thousands)
	Number (in thousands)	Percent of total	Percentage distribution of population			Number (in thousands)	Labor force participation rate	Unemployed		
			Employed	Unemployed	Not in labor force			Number (in thousands)	Unemployment rate	
1	2	3	4	5	6	7	8	9	10	11
All dropouts[b]										
1980	739	100.0	43.6	20.2	36.3	471	63.7	149	31.6	268
1985	612	100.0	43.5	24.0	32.5	413	67.5	147	35.6	199
1990	405	100.0	46.9	22.2	31.0	280	69.0	90	32.3	125
1995	604	100.0	47.7	20.0	32.3	409	67.7	121	29.6	195
2000	515	100.0	48.7	19.2	32.0	350	68.0	99	28.1	165
2002	401	100.0	47.4	20.2	32.3	271	67.7	81	29.8	129
2003	457	100.0	40.9	18.4	40.7	271	59.3	84	30.8	186
2004	496	100.0	32.5	21.4	46.3	267	53.7	106	39.9	229
2005	407	100.0	38.3	18.9	42.8	233	57.2	77	32.9	174
2006	445	100.0	40.3	12.5	47.2	235	52.8	55	23.6	210
Male										
1980	422	57.1	50.2	22.0	27.7	305	72.3	93	30.5	117
1985	321	52.5	50.8	30.5	18.7	261	81.3	98	37.5	60
1990	215	53.1	51.2	29.3	19.8	173	80.2	63	36.2	42
1995	339	56.1	52.8	21.2	26.0	251	74.0	72	28.7	88
2000	295	57.3	56.3	18.3	25.6	220	74.4	54	24.5	76
2002	214	53.4	53.3	16.4	30.5	149	69.5	35	23.4	65
2003	242	53.0	43.8	21.9	34.4	159	65.6	53	33.2	83
2004	278	56.0	35.6	24.1	40.1	166	59.9	67	40.4	112
2005	227	55.8	38.3	21.6	40.3	136	59.7	49	35.9	91
2006	256	57.6	46.3	11.2	42.5	147	57.5	29	19.4	109
Female										
1980	317	42.9	34.7	17.7	47.6	166	52.4	56	33.7	151
1985	291	47.5	35.4	16.8	47.8	152	52.2	49	32.2	139
1990	190	46.9	41.6	14.7	43.7	107	56.3	28	26.1	83
1995	265	43.9	40.8	18.5	40.5	157	59.5	49	30.9	107
2000	220	42.7	39.1	20.5	40.6	131	59.4	45	34.2	90
2002	187	46.6	40.6	24.6	34.4	122	65.6	46	37.6	64
2003	215	47.0	37.7	14.4	47.9	112	52.1	31	27.6	103
2004	218	44.0	28.0	17.9	54.1	100	45.9	39	38.9	118
2005	180	44.2	38.3	15.6	46.0	97	54.0	28	28.8	83
2006	189	42.4	32.3	14.2	53.5	88	46.5	27	30.6	101
White										
1980[c]	580	78.5	49.3	18.3	32.4	392	67.6	106	27.0	188
1985[c]	458	74.8	46.7	25.3	27.9	330	72.1	116	35.2	128
1990[c]	303	74.8	51.2	18.5	30.2	211	69.8	56	26.3	92
1995	316	52.3	51.6	18.3	30.1	221	69.9	58	26.2	95
2000	288	55.9	60.2	16.5	23.4	221	76.6	47	21.5	67
2002	190	47.4	54.3	13.4	32.3	129	67.7	25	19.8	61
2003	226	49.4	48.0	18.2	33.8	149	66.2	41	27.4	76
2004	239	48.2	36.1	14.9	49.0	122	51.0	36	29.2	117
2005	194	47.6	40.3	20.0	39.7	117	60.3	39	33.2	77
2006	214	48.0	48.9	8.2	42.8	122	57.2	18	14.4	92

TABLE 4.7

Labor force status of high school dropouts, by sex and race/ethnicity, selected years, 1980–2006 [CONTINUED]

Year, sex, and race or ethnicity	Dropouts		Percentage distribution of population			Dropouts in civilian labor force[a]				
	Number (in thousands)	Percent of total	Employed	Unemployed	Not in labor force	Number (in thousands)	Labor force participation rate	Unemployed Number (in thousands)	Unemployed Unemployment rate	Dropouts not in labor force (in thousands)
1	2	3	4	5	6	7	8	9	10	11
Black										
1980[c]	146	19.8	22.6	27.4	50.0	73	50.0	40	‡	73
1985[c]	132	21.6	29.5	22.7	47.7	69	52.3	30	‡	63
1990[c]	86	21.2	30.2	34.9	34.7	56	65.3	30	‡	30
1995	104	17.2	33.5	25.8	40.8	62	59.2	27	‡	42
2000	106	20.6	26.7	25.5	47.8	55	52.2	27	‡	51
2002	77	19.1	33.2	35.4	31.3	53	68.7	27	‡	24
2003	81	17.8	29.1	22.9	48.0	42	52.0	19	‡	39
2004	86	17.3	9.9	44.9	45.2	47	54.8	39	‡	39
2005	108	26.5	26.5	16.0	57.5	46	42.5	17	‡	62
2006	69	‡	‡	‡	‡	36	‡	17	‡	33
Hispanic										
1980	91	12.3	47.3	18.7	34.1	60	65.9	17	‡	31
1985	106	17.3	37.7	31.1	31.1	73	68.9	33	‡	33
1990	67	16.5	‡	‡	‡	32	‡	10	‡	35
1995	174	28.8	48.5	20.1	31.4	119	68.6	35	29.3	55
2000	101	19.6	39.0	22.2	38.9	62	61.1	22	‡	39
2002	94	23.4	42.2	24.3	33.5	62	66.5	23	‡	31
2003	124	27.1	40.7	13.8	45.5	68	54.5	17	‡	57
2004	154	31.0	39.3	17.4	43.2	87	56.8	27	30.7	67
2005	86	21.1	45.1	19.2	35.7	55	64.3	17	‡	31
2006	136	30.5	35.3	12.6	52.2	65	47.8	17	‡	71

‡Reporting standards not met.

[a]The labor force includes all employed persons plus those seeking employment. The labor force participation rate is the percentage of persons either employed or seeking employment. The unemployment rate is the percentage of persons in the labor force who are seeking employment.

[b]Persons 16 to 24 years old who dropped out of school in the 12-month period ending in October of years shown.

[c]Includes persons of Hispanic ethnicity.

Note: Data are based on sample surveys of the civilian noninstitutional population. Includes dropouts from any grade, including a small number from elementary and middle schools. Race categories exclude persons of Hispanic ethnicity unless otherwise noted. Totals include race categories not separately shown. Some data have been revised from previously published figures. Detail may not sum to totals because of rounding.

SOURCE: "Table 376. Labor Force Status of High School Dropouts, by Sex and Race/Ethnicity: Selected Years, 1980 through 2006," in *Digest of Education Statistics, 2007*, U.S. Department of Education, National Center for Education Statistics, August 2007, http://nces.ed.gov/programs/digest/d07/tables/dt07_376.asp (accessed February 11, 2008)

Beyond the Bachelor's Degree

Having a bachelor's degree opens the door to many occupational options, but a degree itself does not guarantee that a graduate will enter a high-paying career. In general, graduates who major in business, computer sciences, and engineering will find that occupations in their subject areas pay higher salaries than do occupations in education, the humanities, and social and behavioral sciences. For example, the median weekly earnings of network systems and data communication analysts ($1,039) and network and computer systems administrators ($1,180) were considerably higher than those for elementary and middle school teachers ($863), librarians ($861), salaried writers ($999), or social workers ($757) in 2007. (See Table 6.2 in Chapter 6.)

In fact, the National Association of Colleges and Employers reported in "Year-End Report Shows Salary Gains for Class of 2007" (September 12, 2007, http://www.naceweb .org/press/display.asp?year=2007&prid=264) that the starting salaries for engineers and computer scientists graduating with a bachelor's degree in May 2007 surpassed the median annual earnings of many other professions. Class of 2007 graduates with a chemical engineering degree could expect a starting salary of $59,218 and those with a mechanical engineering degree could expect a starting salary of $54,057. Grads with computer science degrees could expect a salary offer of $53,051. In contrast, history majors could expect only $35,092 and English majors could expect only $31,924 to start.

The lifelong earnings potential of a college degree makes a four-year bachelor's degree attractive to both recent high school graduates and adults returning to formal education to advance their careers. In some fast-growing occupational fields, including health care and education, the highest-paying jobs now require formal education beyond the bachelor's degree for entry or advancement. Figure 4.1 presents a list of twenty large-growth occupations that require a master's, doctoral, or first-professional degree for employment, their median annual wages, and the projected change in employment in these occupations from 2006 through 2016. Although the huge growth in available positions for postsecondary teachers reflects expanding college enrollments, most of the other high growth occupations are in the health-care field.

EDUCATION AND POVERTY

In general, as individuals attain higher educational levels, the risk of living in poverty falls markedly. Of all those sixteen years of age and older in the labor force during 2005, those with less than a high school diploma had a much higher poverty rate (14.1%) than did high school graduates (6.6%), according to the BLS in *A Profile of the Working Poor, 2005*. The lowest poverty rates were reported by workers with an associate degree (3.4%) or bachelor's degree or higher (1.7%). (See Table 4.8.)

Historically, poverty rates are higher for African-American and Hispanic workers than for non-Hispanic white workers at all educational levels. This trend held true in 2005. The poverty rates of African-American and Hispanic high school dropouts were 22.2% and 16.5%, respectively, while the poverty rates of non-Hispanic whites and Asians with comparable education were 13% and 10%, respectively. (See Table 4.8.) Even among those with a bachelor's degree, poverty rates were higher for Hispanics and African-Americans. The poverty rate for African-Americans with a bachelor's degree or higher was 2.7% in 2005; for Hispanics it was 2.6%. On the other hand, the poverty rate for non-Hispanic whites with a bachelor's degree or higher was only 1.5%.

FIGURE 4.1

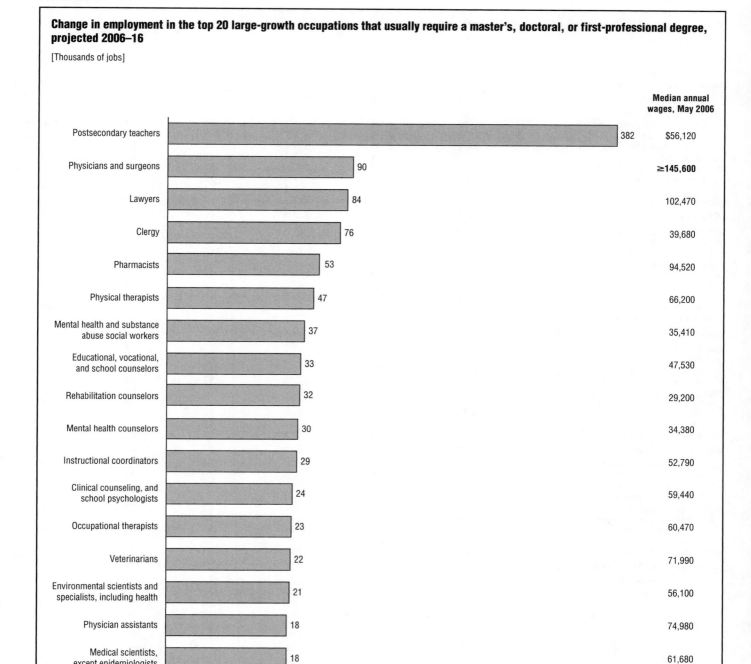

Change in employment in the top 20 large-growth occupations that usually require a master's, doctoral, or first-professional degree, projected 2006–16

[Thousands of jobs]

		Median annual wages, May 2006
Postsecondary teachers	382	$56,120
Physicians and surgeons	90	≥145,600
Lawyers	84	102,470
Clergy	76	39,680
Pharmacists	53	94,520
Physical therapists	47	66,200
Mental health and substance abuse social workers	37	35,410
Educational, vocational, and school counselors	33	47,530
Rehabilitation counselors	32	29,200
Mental health counselors	30	34,380
Instructional coordinators	29	52,790
Clinical counseling, and school psychologists	24	59,440
Occupational therapists	23	60,470
Veterinarians	22	71,990
Environmental scientists and specialists, including health	21	56,100
Physician assistants	18	74,980
Medical scientists, except epidemiologists	18	61,680
Dentists, general	13	132,140
Speech-language pathologists	12	57,710
Chiropractors	8	65,220

SOURCE: "Occupations That Have the Most Growth and That Usually Require a Master's, Doctoral, or First-Professional Degree, Projected 2006–16," in "Occupational Employment," *Occupational Outlook Quarterly*, vol. 51, no. 3, Fall 2007, http://www.bls.gov/opub/ooq/2007/fall/art02.pdf (accessed February 11, 2008)

TABLE 4.8

Poverty status of workers by educational attainment, race/ethnicity, and sex, 2005

[Numbers in thousands]

Educational attainment, race, and Hispanic or Latino ethnicity	Total	Men	Women	Rate[a] Total	Rate[a] Men	Rate[a] Women
Total, 16 years and older	142,824	77,329	65,495	5.4	4.8	6.1
Less than a high school diploma	15,961	10,136	5,825	14.1	12.6	16.8
Less than 1 year of high school	5,020	3,494	1,526	16.0	15.4	17.3
1–3 years of high school	8,918	5,401	3,517	14.2	11.9	17.8
4 years of high school, no diploma	2,022	1,241	782	9.1	7.8	11.3
High school graduates, no college[b]	42,947	24,154	18,793	6.6	5.6	8.0
Some college or associate degree	41,514	20,570	20,944	4.7	3.7	5.6
Some college, no degree	27,930	14,212	13,718	5.3	4.2	6.4
Associate degree	13,583	6,358	7,226	3.4	2.7	4.0
Bachelor's degree and higher[c]	42,402	22,469	19,933	1.7	1.6	1.7
White, 16 years and older	117,078	64,603	52,475	4.7	4.4	5.0
Less than a high school diploma	12,939	8,495	4,444	13.0	12.0	14.8
Less than 1 year of high school	4,309	3,073	1,236	15.7	15.1	17.2
1–3 years of high school	7,083	4,433	2,651	12.5	11.1	14.9
4 years of high school, no diploma	1,547	990	557	7.8	6.8	9.6
High school graduates, no college[b]	34,885	19,938	14,947	5.5	4.9	6.3
Some college or associate degree	34,111	17,221	16,890	4.0	3.3	4.6
Some college, no degree	22,643	11,754	10,889	4.5	3.8	5.3
Associate degree	11,468	5,467	6,001	2.8	2.4	3.2
Bachelor's degree and higher[c]	35,143	18,949	16,194	1.5	1.4	1.6
Black or African American, 16 years and older	16,122	7,482	8,640	10.5	7.7	13.0
Less than a high school diploma	1,956	1,035	922	22.2	15.8	29.4
Less than 1 year of high school	307	194	112	18.7	16.2	22.9
1–3 years of high school	1,323	674	649	24.5	16.3	33.0
4 years of high school, no diploma	327	166	161	16.1	13.0	19.3
High school graduates, no college[b]	5,778	2,898	2,881	12.7	8.5	17.0
Some college or associate degree	5,050	2,151	2,899	8.6	5.7	10.8
Some college, no degree	3,698	1,606	2,091	9.3	6.0	11.8
Associate degree	1,352	545	808	6.7	4.9	7.9
Bachelor's degree and higher[c]	3,337	1,398	1,938	2.7	3.0	2.4
Asian, 16 years and older	6,290	3,396	2,894	4.7	5.0	4.4
Less than a high school diploma	568	303	265	10.0	11.9	7.8
Less than 1 year of high school	255	126	129	12.2	10.8	13.5
1–3 years of high school	217	126	91	9.7	15.2	2.1
4 years of high school, no diploma	97	51	46	[d]	[d]	[d]
High school graduates, no college[b]	1,243	690	552	7.3	8.6	5.6
Some college or associate degree	1,208	618	590	6.1	5.4	6.7
Some college, no degree	755	409	346	5.9	5.7	6.0
Associate degree	453	209	244	6.4	4.8	7.7
Bachelor's degree and higher[c]	3,271	1,785	1,487	2.4	2.3	2.5
Hispanic or Latino ethnicity, 16 years and older	18,905	11,557	7,348	10.5	10.4	10.6
Less than a high school diploma	6,651	4,604	2,047	16.5	15.6	18.5
Less than 1 year of high school	3,527	2,526	1,001	17.4	16.9	18.7
1–3 years of high school	2,534	1,672	861	16.4	14.8	19.6
4 years of high school, no diploma	591	406	185	11.4	11.1	12.0
High school graduates, no college[b]	5,747	3,524	2,223	9.4	9.1	10.0
Some college or associate degree	4,141	2,207	1,935	6.8	5.9	7.8
Some college, no degree	2,930	1,607	1,322	7.4	6.7	8.4
Associate degree	1,212	599	612	5.2	3.7	6.6
Bachelor's degree and higher[c]	2,365	1,222	1,143	2.6	2.9	2.4

[a]Number below the poverty level as a percent of the total in the labor force for 27 weeks or more.
[b]Includes people with a high school diploma or equivalent.
[c]Includes people with bachelor's, master's, professional, and doctoral degrees.
[d]Data not shown where base is less than 80,000.
Note: Estimates for the above race groups (white, black or African American, and Asian) do not sum to totals because data are not presented for all races. In addition, people whose ethnicity is identified as Hispanic or Latino may be of any race and, therefore, are classified by ethnicity as well as by race.

SOURCE: Adapted from "Table 3. People in the Labor Force for 27 Weeks or More: Poverty Status by Educational Attainment, Race, Hispanic or Latino Ethnicity, and Sex, 2005," in *A Profile of the Working Poor, 2005*, U.S. Department of Labor, Bureau of Labor Statistics, September 2007, http://www.bls.gov/cps/cpswp2005.pdf (accessed February 8, 2008)

CHAPTER 5
THE WORKFORCE OF TOMORROW

Making informed career decisions requires reliable information about what employment opportunities will be available in the future. Job opportunities result from the relationships between the population, the labor force, and the demand for goods and services. Population ultimately limits the size of the labor force, which, in turn, drives how much can be produced. Demand for various goods and services determines employment in the industries providing them. Occupational employment opportunities then result from skills needed within specific industries. Opportunities for registered nurses and other health-related specialists, for example, have surged in response to the rapid growth in demand for health services as the American population has aged. Likewise, the growth in the demand for college teachers has been exponential as college enrollment has soared.

Based on population and economic growth, the U.S. Department of Labor's Bureau of Labor Statistics (BLS) predicts where future job growth is expected, by industry and occupation, and what the demographic makeup of the workforce is likely to be. The latest predictions released are for the decade 2006 to 2016. These ten-year projections are widely used for studying long-range economic and employment trends, planning education and training programs, and developing career information.

LABOR FORCE

The civilian labor force is made up of individuals aged sixteen and older who are either working or looking for work. These are the workers available to fill any new or vacated jobs. According to the BLS, both the population of the country and labor force will continue to grow over the 2006 to 2016 period at a slightly slower rate than they grew over the previous ten-year period. Figure 5.1 compares growth in the labor force with growth in the population of working-age individuals in the United States during the period 1996 through 2016. The labor

force is projected to increase by 12.8 million (8.5%) between 2006 and 2016, reaching 164.2 million workers in 2016. (See Table 5.1.) The population is expected to grow at a slightly higher rate (9.6%) than the labor force, reflecting the aging of the U.S. population—a higher proportion of the population will be retired.

Older Workers

The demographic makeup of the labor force is changing. Workers over age fifty-five make up an increasing number of people in the labor force. In 2006, 22.4 million of 151.4 million workers (14.8%) were ages sixteen to twenty-four. (See Table 5.1.) Another 103.6 million workers (68.4%) were between ages twenty-five and fifty-four. A large proportion of workers (25,468, or 16.8%) were age fifty-five or older. These figures indicated the aging of American workers as the baby-boom generation (those born between 1946 and 1964) nears retirement age.

By 2016 most of the workers counted in the fifty-five and older group in 2006 will have retired from the labor force. However, an even larger number of workers (37,354, or 22.7% of all workers) than in 2006 are projected to be age fifty-five and older by that year. (See Table 5.1.) Although the number of workers age twenty-four and younger is projected to decrease by 6.9% between 2006 and 2016, and the number of workers age twenty-five to fifty-four is expected to increase by only 2.4%, the number of workers age fifty-five and older is projected to rise by an astounding 46.7% over the course of the decade.

Gender

Historically, married women have typically stayed home to care for children and the home; therefore, there have always been fewer females than males in the civilian labor force. When married women began working outside of the home in large numbers in the 1960s and

FIGURE 5.1

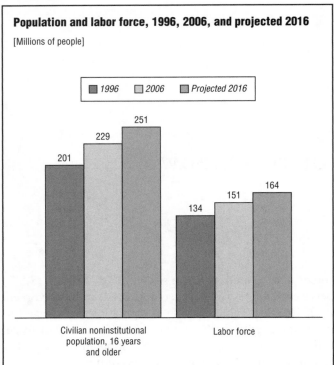

Population and labor force, 1996, 2006, and projected 2016

[Millions of people]

■ 1996　□ 2006　▨ Projected 2016

SOURCE: "Population and Labor Force, 1996, 2006, and Projected 2016," in "Labor Force," *Occupational Outlook Quarterly*, vol. 51, no. 3, Fall 2007, http://www.bls.gov/opub/ooq/2007/fall/art04.pdf (accessed February 14, 2008)

1970s, they often did so in order to supplement their husbands' incomes. By 2000, however, married women were much less likely than they had been in 1980 to leave the labor force if their husbands received pay wages or to increase their labor force participation if their husbands' wages were cut. According to Francine D. Blau and Lawrence M. Kahn for the National Bureau of Economic Research (NBER), in "Changes in the Labor Supply Behavior of Married Women: 1980–2000" (February 2005, http://papers.nber.org/papers/w11230), women's work decisions became much less sensitive to their husbands' incomes than they had been in the past. In "Changing Work Behavior of Married Women" (2005, http://www.nber.org/digest/nov05/w11230.html), David R. Francis for the NBER speculates on the reasons for this shift: "Married women apparently are becoming accustomed to working outside the home. Maybe they like having their own careers. Or maybe they worry that, with a high divorce rate, they might split from their husband and need a separate income and career." For whatever reason, married women now often work outside the home, helping to narrow the gaps in the labor force participation rates between men and women.

In 2006 women made up 46.3% of the labor force. As shown in Table 5.1, while women will continue to compose less than one-half of the labor force in 2016 (46.6%),

TABLE 5.1

Civilian labor force by age, sex, race, and Hispanic origin, 1996, 2006, and projected 2016

[In thousands]

Age, sex, race, and ethnicity	Level			Change		Percent change		Percent distribution			Annual growth rate (percent)	
	1996	2006	2016	1996–2006	2006–2016	1996–2006	2006–2016	1996	2006	2016	1996–2006	2006–2016
Total, 16 years and older	133,943	151,428	164,232	17,485	12,804	13.1	8.5	100.0	100.0	100.0	1.2	0.8
Age, years												
16 to 24	21,183	22,394	20,852	1,211	−1,542	5.7	−6.9	15.8	14.8	12.7	.6	−.7
25 to 54	96,786	103,566	106,026	6,780	2,460	7.0	2.4	72.3	68.4	64.6	.7	.2
55 and older	15,974	25,468	37,354	9,494	11,886	59.4	46.7	11.9	16.8	22.7	4.8	3.9
Sex												
Men	72,087	81,255	87,781	9,168	6,526	12.7	8.0	53.8	53.7	53.4	1.2	.8
Women	61,857	70,173	76,450	8,316	6,277	13.4	8.9	46.2	46.3	46.6	1.3	.9
Race												
White	113,108	123,834	130,665	10,726	6,831	9.5	5.5	84.4	81.8	79.6	.9	.5
Black	15,134	17,314	20,121	2,180	2,807	14.4	16.2	11.3	11.4	12.3	1.4	1.5
Asian	5,701	6,727	8,741	1,026	2,014	18.0	29.9	4.3	4.4	5.3	1.7	2.7
All other groups*	—	3,553	4,705	—	1,152	—	32.4	—	2.3	2.9	—	2.8
Ethnicity												
Hispanic origin	12,774	20,694	26,889	7,920	6,195	62.0	29.9	9.5	13.7	16.4	4.9	2.7
Other than Hispanic origin	121,169	130,734	137,343	9,565	6,609	7.9	5.1	90.5	86.3	83.6	.8	.5
White non-Hispanic	100,915	104,629	106,133	3,714	1,504	3.7	1.4	75.3	69.1	64.6	.4	.1

*The "all other groups" category includes (1) those classified as being of multiple racial origin and (2) the race categories of (2a) American Indian and Alaska Native and (2b) Native Hawaiian and other Pacific Islanders.
Note: Dash indicates no data collected for category.

SOURCE: "Table 10. Civilian Labor Force by Age, Sex, Race, and Hispanic Origin, 1996, 2006, and Projected 2016," in *Employment Projections: 2006–16*, U.S. Department of Labor, Bureau of Labor Statistics, December 4, 2007, http://www.bls.gov/news.release/pdf/ecopro.pdf (accessed February 14, 2008)

FIGURE 5.2

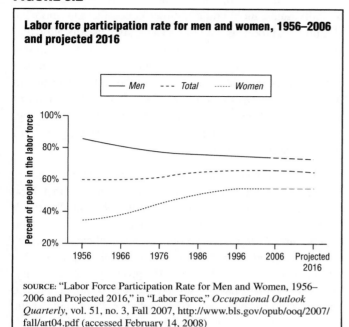

Labor force participation rate for men and women, 1956–2006 and projected 2016

SOURCE: "Labor Force Participation Rate for Men and Women, 1956–2006 and Projected 2016," in "Labor Force," *Occupational Outlook Quarterly*, vol. 51, no. 3, Fall 2007, http://www.bls.gov/opub/ooq/2007/fall/art04.pdf (accessed February 14, 2008)

FIGURE 5.3

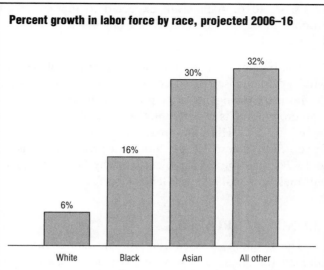

Percent growth in labor force by race, projected 2006–16

SOURCE: "Percent Growth in Labor Force by Race, Projected 2006–16," in "Labor Force," *Occupational Outlook Quarterly*, vol. 51, no. 3, Fall 2007, http://www.bls.gov/opub/ooq/2007/fall/art04.pdf (accessed February 14, 2008)

their representation in the labor force will continue to grow at a faster rate than men's between 2006 and 2016 (8.9% and 8%, respectively). Figure 5.2 shows the historic shifts in participation rates by gender in the American labor force since the 1950s, when only about one-third of women worked outside the home. By 2016 about six out of every ten women are expected to be in the labor force, compared with about 72% of men.

Race and Ethnicity

The demographic makeup of the United States has changed in recent decades due largely to the effects of immigration. These demographic changes are reflected in the growing participation of minorities in the labor force. According to the BLS, participation in the labor force by Hispanics and Asians will increase much faster than that of non-Hispanic whites and African-Americans between 2006 and 2016. Workers of Hispanic and Asian ethnicity are projected to be the fastest-growing group in the labor force this period, both with a projected 30% growth, followed by African-Americans, whose labor force participation is expected to grow by 16%. (See Figure 5.3 and Figure 5.4.) The group "All Others," whose labor participation rate is projected to increase by 32%, includes people who do not identify themselves as white, Hispanic, African-American, or Asian, including Native Americans, Alaska Natives, Native Hawaiians, Pacific Islanders, and multiracial individuals. Non-Hispanic whites' labor force participation is projected to grow by only 6% during this period.

As a result of the high rate of growth among minority groups, the composition of the labor force will change by

FIGURE 5.4

Percent growth in labor force by Hispanic ethnicity, projected 2006–16

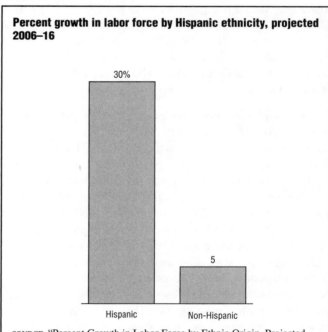

SOURCE: "Percent Growth in Labor Force by Ethnic Origin, Projected 2006–16," in "Labor Force," *Occupational Outlook Quarterly*, vol. 51, no. 3, Fall 2007, http://www.bls.gov/opub/ooq/2007/fall/art04.pdf (accessed February 14, 2008)

2016. Whites will continue to make up the majority of the labor force, although that proportion is dropping. In 1996 whites made up 84.4% of the labor force. (See Table 5.1.) By 2006 that proportion had dropped to 81.8%, and it was projected to drop still further to 79.6% in 2016. African-Americans are projected to increase their proportion of the labor force from 11.4% in 2006 to 12.3% in 2016. Asians are expected to increase their proportion of the labor market from 4.4% in 2006 to 5.3% in 2016.

The biggest change in the makeup of the labor force will be the increased presence of Hispanics. Hispanics are the fastest-growing minority group in the country. This high growth rate is reflected in their presence in the labor force. In 1996 Hispanics made up 9.5% of the labor force. (See Table 5.1.) By 2006 that proportion was up to 13.7%, and the BLS projects that by 2016 Hispanics will make up 16.4% of the labor force.

ECONOMIC GROWTH

The economy's need for workers stems from the demand for goods and services, which is measured by the national gross domestic product (GDP; the total value of goods and services produced during the year). According to BLS projections in the Fall 2007 *Occupational Outlook Quarterly* ("Overall Economy," http://www.bls.gov/opub/ooq/2007/fall/art05.pdf), the GDP is projected to reach approximately $14.9 trillion (in 2000 dollars) by 2016, growing at a rate of 2.8% annually, which is slightly lower than the annual growth rate of the 1996–2006 period (3.1%) and the 1986–96 period (2.9%). The growth in exports is expected to be particularly high, at a rate of 5.5% annual growth, and the growth in the values of governmental services is expected to be particularly low, with a projected annual growth of 1.4%.

Although the labor force is expected to grow by 8.5% over the 2006–16 period, the BLS reports in the *Occupational Outlook Quarterly* that most of the growth in GDP is expected to be achieved through higher productivity (more output per worker) rather than through a growing labor force. Compared with an output valued at about $30 per hour per worker in 1986, productivity in 2016 will approach $60 per hour per worker. Advanced technology and new equipment will enable workers to produce goods and services more efficiently, increasing output at a faster rate than a company's workforce. In the competitive global economy, high-productivity companies are more likely to prosper and thereby increase their output even further by being able to hire additional workers or invest in technologies that will allow them to achieve more production from existing workers.

Domestic and foreign consumers, including individuals, businesses, and governments, purchase millions of American products each year. Shifts in consumer tastes and government priorities can affect the growth of and demand for different kinds of goods and services. Technical changes in products also affect demand. For example, the use of more plastics instead of steel in automobiles increases demand for plastics and decreases demand for steel. Such changes can have a significant effect on industry employment.

Personal consumption expenditures are purchases made by individuals, including consumer goods like automobiles, clothing, and food, as well as services, such as education and health care. Although personal consumption expenditures are projected to increase only about 2.9% per year in the 2006–16 period, they make up 70% of the GDP, according to the BLS in the *Occupational Outlook Quarterly*. Traditionally, households have spent most of their income on housing, transportation, and medical care; this spending pattern should continue through 2016.

The largest growth in personal expenditures on goods will be on computers and software; the BLS reports that these purchases are expected to increase by 16.8%, annually, much faster than the 2.9% growth rate in personal consumption expenditures in general. Spending on medical care and insurance is expected to increase by 3.6% annually, while expenditures on recreation are expected to grow by 4.5% annually, the largest growth rates of all the services components. The large growth in these sectors is fueled in large part by the aging of the American population; older Americans both need more medical care and have more time for recreation.

EMPLOYMENT BY INDUSTRY

The BLS develops projections of employment for the industries and industry groups that make up the economy as a whole. Because of expected shifts in consumer and business spending, employment growth rates vary significantly among industries. As a consequence, the structure of industry employment will change over the period 2006 through 2016.

Changes in demand for an industry's products constitute the most important cause of differences in employment growth rates among industries. Technological change is another factor affecting industry employment. For example, automated equipment in manufacturing plants enables fewer workers to produce more goods, and its use is a major reason for declining employment in manufacturing. This decline in generally better-paying blue-collar jobs in manufacturing is a major reason that the earnings of less-educated Americans have been falling since the 1980s. According to the BLS in *Highlights of Women's Earnings in 2006* (September 2007, http://www.bls.gov/cps/cpswom2006.pdf), between 1979 and 2006 average weekly earnings for men employed full-time with less than a high school education declined by nearly 30%, from $648 to $469, and weekly earnings for men with a high school diploma and no college declined by about 15%, from $793 to $678, in constant 2006 dollars.

Changes in business practices also have an impact on employment. When businesses use contractors or temporary help services, they reduce their total employment. At the same time, employment rises for contractors and the temporary help services industry. This often means a loss of better-paying jobs and a gain in lower-paying jobs.

One way the government measures employment projections is by looking at industries. For analytical purposes, industries fall into the goods-producing sector and the services-producing sector. The divisions within the goods-producing sector are construction, manufacturing, and natural resources and mining, which includes agriculture. In the services-producing sector, the divisions are educational services, financial activities, health care and social assistance, information, leisure and hospitality, professional and business services, public administration, and trade, transportation, and utilities. Workers are grouped into these industries according to the goods or services their employers provide, rather than according to what jobs they do. For example, teachers, computer specialists, and janitors who all work in a school are all part of the educational services industry, while maids, front-desk clerks, and accountants who work in a hotel are all part of the leisure and hospitality industry.

The BLS projects in the Fall 2007 *Occupational Outlook Quarterly* ("Industry Employment," http://www.bls.gov/opub/ooq/2007/fall/art03.pdf) that services-producing industries will account for all of the growth of wage and salary employment over the 2006 to 2016 period, with goods-producing employment actually declining from twenty-four million in 2006 to twenty-three million in 2016. Wage and salary employment in the services-producing sector (114 million jobs) accounted for 82.6% of the 138 million American jobs in 2006. Over the 2006 to 2016 period, services-sector jobs are projected to increase by about sixteen million, to about 85% of the job market. Goods-producing employment, meanwhile, is projected to decline over the same period, shrinking from about 17.8% to about 15% of the job market.

Figure 5.5 and Figure 5.6 show projected wage and salary employment growth and decline from 2006 to 2016 in the various industry sectors. Professional and business services and health care and social assistance are the industry groups expected to have the largest wage and salary employment growth by 2016, with the professional and business services sector projected to create nearly 4.1 million new jobs, an increase of 23%, and the health care and social assistance sector projected to create over 4 million new jobs, an increase of 25%. Employment in manufacturing is expected to decline by 1.5 million jobs, a decrease of 11%, and 113,000 job losses are expected in natural resources and mining, a decrease of 6%.

Figure 5.7 shows the specific industries in which the largest wage-and-salary worker declines are predicted. Gasoline stations, which are becoming increasingly automated, are expected to lose 146,000 jobs between 2006 and 2016, the largest number of any detailed industry. Printing and related support activities are becoming obsolete with the enhanced ability of home computer users to print their own materials; this sector is expected to lose 139,000 jobs in the coming decade. Motor vehicle parts manufacturing

FIGURE 5.5

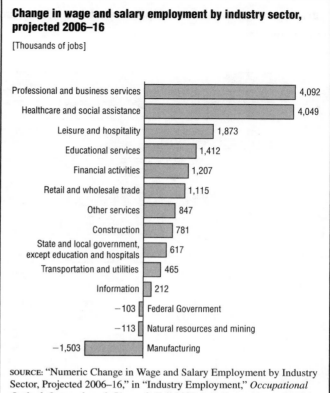

Change in wage and salary employment by industry sector, projected 2006–16

[Thousands of jobs]

SOURCE: "Numeric Change in Wage and Salary Employment by Industry Sector, Projected 2006–16," in "Industry Employment," *Occupational Outlook Quarterly*, vol. 51, no. 3, Fall 2007, http://www.bls.gov/opub/ooq/2007/fall/art03.pdf (accessed February 14, 2008)

FIGURE 5.6

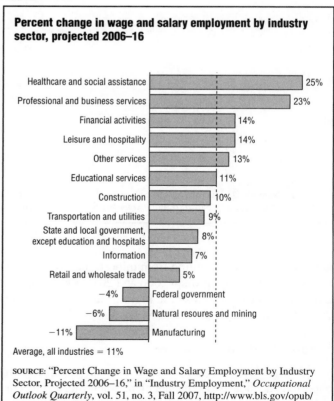

Percent change in wage and salary employment by industry sector, projected 2006–16

Average, all industries = 11%

SOURCE: "Percent Change in Wage and Salary Employment by Industry Sector, Projected 2006–16," in "Industry Employment," *Occupational Outlook Quarterly*, vol. 51, no. 3, Fall 2007, http://www.bls.gov/opub/ooq/2007/fall/art03.pdf (accessed February 14, 2008)

FIGURE 5.7

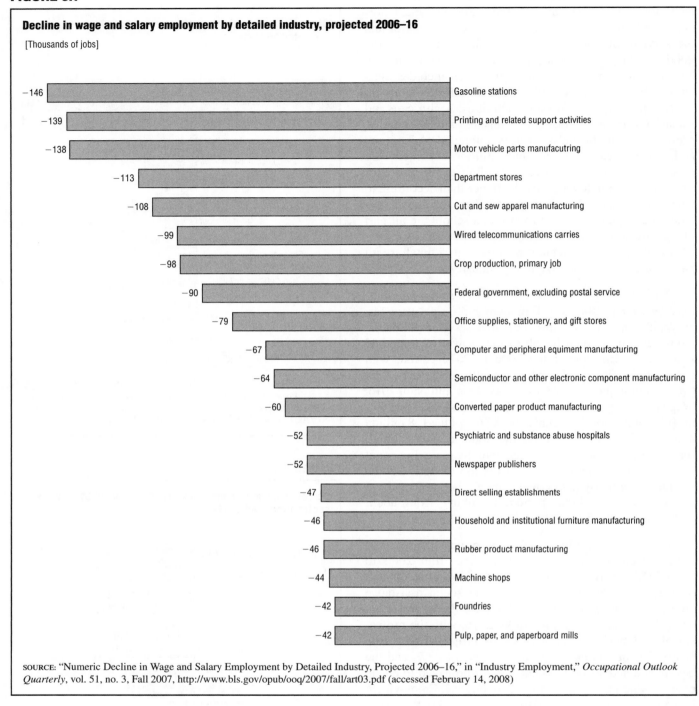

Decline in wage and salary employment by detailed industry, projected 2006–16

[Thousands of jobs]

−146	Gasoline stations
−139	Printing and related support activities
−138	Motor vehicle parts manufacutring
−113	Department stores
−108	Cut and sew apparel manufacturing
−99	Wired telecommunications carries
−98	Crop production, primary job
−90	Federal government, excluding postal service
−79	Office supplies, stationery, and gift stores
−67	Computer and peripheral equiment manufacturing
−64	Semiconductor and other electronic component manufacturing
−60	Converted paper product manufacturing
−52	Psychiatric and substance abuse hospitals
−52	Newspaper publishers
−47	Direct selling establishments
−46	Household and institutional furniture manufacturing
−46	Rubber product manufacturing
−44	Machine shops
−42	Foundries
−42	Pulp, paper, and paperboard mills

SOURCE: "Numeric Decline in Wage and Salary Employment by Detailed Industry, Projected 2006–16," in "Industry Employment," *Occupational Outlook Quarterly*, vol. 51, no. 3, Fall 2007, http://www.bls.gov/opub/ooq/2007/fall/art03.pdf (accessed February 14, 2008)

has been hurt by competition from imports, and is expected to lose 138,000 jobs between 2006 and 2016. Of the twenty industries projected to lose the highest number of jobs by 2016, ten are in the manufacturing sector.

Services-Producing Industries

With a 78% increase in wage-and-salary employment expected, the industry of management, scientific, and technical consulting services is predicted to be the fastest-growing industry sector between 2006 and 2016. (See Figure 5.8.)

Services for the elderly and persons with disabilities are also projected to increase quickly, with a projected job growth of 74% over the decade. This growth is fueled by the aging of the American population. Other industries expecting to add to employment by 50% or more include gambling industries (66%), home health care services (55%), educational support services (53%), and community care for the elderly (50%).

Figure 5.9 shows the twenty industries projected to have the greatest numerical growth (increase in the total

FIGURE 5.8

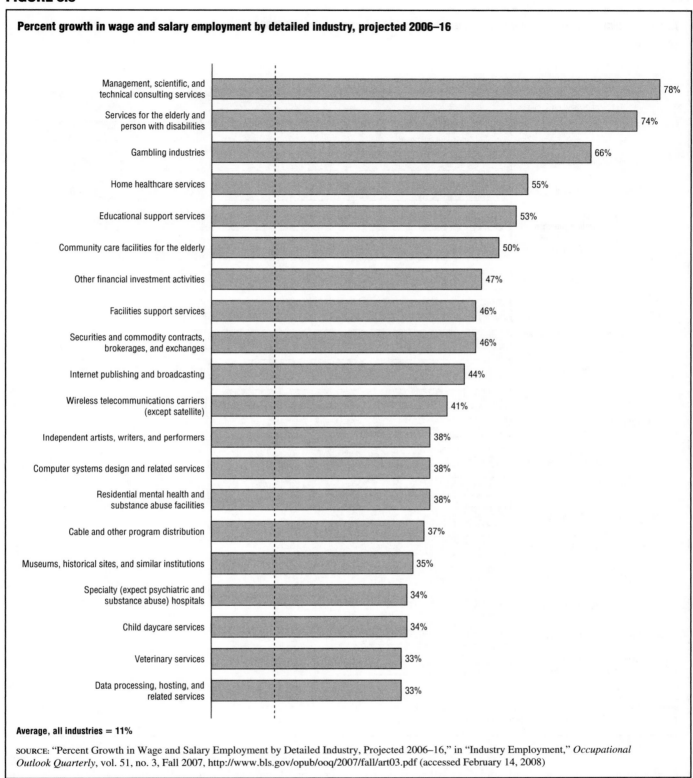

Percent growth in wage and salary employment by detailed industry, projected 2006–16

Industry	Percent
Management, scientific, and technical consulting services	78%
Services for the elderly and person with disabilities	74%
Gambling industries	66%
Home healthcare services	55%
Educational support services	53%
Community care facilities for the elderly	50%
Other financial investment activities	47%
Facilities support services	46%
Securities and commodity contracts, brokerages, and exchanges	46%
Internet publishing and broadcasting	44%
Wireless telecommunications carriers (except satellite)	41%
Independent artists, writers, and performers	38%
Computer systems design and related services	38%
Residential mental health and substance abuse facilities	38%
Cable and other program distribution	37%
Museums, historical sites, and similar institutions	35%
Specialty (expect psychiatric and substance abuse) hospitals	34%
Child daycare services	34%
Veterinary services	33%
Data processing, hosting, and related services	33%

Average, all industries = 11%

SOURCE: "Percent Growth in Wage and Salary Employment by Detailed Industry, Projected 2006–16," in "Industry Employment," *Occupational Outlook Quarterly*, vol. 51, no. 3, Fall 2007, http://www.bls.gov/opub/ooq/2007/fall/art03.pdf (accessed February 14, 2008)

number of jobs) between 2006 and 2016. Management, scientific, and technical consulting services, which help businesses respond to and cope with globalization and technological changes, will add a projected 718,000 new jobs between 2006 and 2016. Employment services will add 692,000 jobs, general medical and surgical hospitals will add 691,000 new jobs, elementary and secondary schools will add 638,000 new jobs, and local government will add 612,000 new jobs. Eight of the top twenty industries with the largest numeric growth in employment are in

FIGURE 5.9

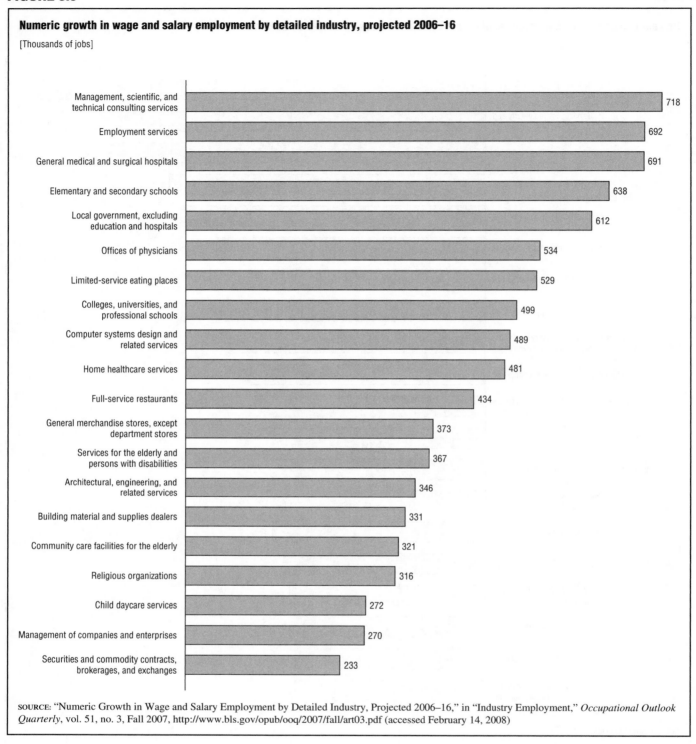

Numeric growth in wage and salary employment by detailed industry, projected 2006–16

[Thousands of jobs]

Industry	Jobs
Management, scientific, and technical consulting services	718
Employment services	692
General medical and surgical hospitals	691
Elementary and secondary schools	638
Local government, excluding education and hospitals	612
Offices of physicians	534
Limited-service eating places	529
Colleges, universities, and professional schools	499
Computer systems design and related services	489
Home healthcare services	481
Full-service restaurants	434
General merchandise stores, except department stores	373
Services for the elderly and persons with disabilities	367
Architectural, engineering, and related services	346
Building material and supplies dealers	331
Community care facilities for the elderly	321
Religious organizations	316
Child daycare services	272
Management of companies and enterprises	270
Securities and commodity contracts, brokerages, and exchanges	233

SOURCE: "Numeric Growth in Wage and Salary Employment by Detailed Industry, Projected 2006–16," in "Industry Employment," *Occupational Outlook Quarterly*, vol. 51, no. 3, Fall 2007, http://www.bls.gov/opub/ooq/2007/fall/art03.pdf (accessed February 14, 2008)

the education, health care, and social assistance sectors, reflecting a demand for services for an aging population as well as the rising enrollment in schools.

Goods-Producing Industries

The United States is increasingly a service-based economy. Employment in the goods-producing sector is projected to vary over the 2006 to 2016 period, with a general downward trend reflecting the shift away from manufacturing and toward the service industries. The construction industry is expected to add about 781,000 new jobs between 2006 and 2016, reflecting the continued demand for new homes and buildings. (See Figure 5.5.) However, natural resources and mining will lose approximately 113,000 jobs, while manufacturing will lose more than 1.5 million jobs.

EMPLOYMENT BY OCCUPATION

The economy's occupational and industrial structures form a close relationship. Workers in various occupations provide the skills needed in different industries. Nurses, physicians, orderlies, and medical-records technicians are needed in hospitals; cooks, waiters and waitresses, and food preparation workers are needed in restaurants. Consequently, the demand for the occupations concentrated in an industry often rises or falls with the fortunes of that industry. At the same time, it is important to remember that members of the same industry may not share the same concerns. For example, in the health industry, the objectives of the hospital administrator, the doctor, and the licensed practical nurse may differ dramatically.

Changes in technology usually affect how industries use workers. For example, technological advances will continue to reduce the need for typists, directory assistance telephone operators, and bookkeeping, accounting, and auditing clerks. Changes in business practices and operations also can affect occupational staffing and job skills required in the workforce. For example, many companies are eliminating middle managers, thereby tending to put more authority in the hands of nonmanagerial frontline workers.

The BLS analyzes these factors to project employment for more than five hundred detailed occupations. These occupations can be grouped in different ways to provide a better understanding of broad occupational employment trends. Two of the grouping methods used are by type of work performed and by education and training usually required.

Types of Work

The professional and related occupational group is expected to add nearly five million jobs between 2006 and 2016, about a 17% increase over its 2006 employment. (See Figure 5.10 and Figure 5.11.) This increase means that more than one of every five workers (20.9%) will be employed in a professional or related occupation by 2016. (See Table 5.2.) These occupations include broad categories, such as computer and mathematical occupations (for example, database administrators and mathematicians); architecture and engineering occupations (for example, surveyors, architects, and engineers); life, physical, and social science occupations (for example, economists, urban planners, and psychologists); community and social service occupations (for example, counselors and clergy); legal occupations (for example, lawyers, judges, and paralegals); education, training, and library occupations (for example teachers and their assistants and librarians); arts, design, entertainment, sports, and media occupations (for example, actors, editors, writers, and directors); and health care practitioner and technical occupations (for example, physicians, dentists, veterinarians, and nurses).

FIGURE 5.10

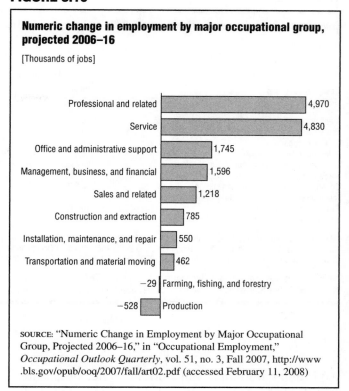

Numeric change in employment by major occupational group, projected 2006–16

[Thousands of jobs]

SOURCE: "Numeric Change in Employment by Major Occupational Group, Projected 2006–16," in "Occupational Employment," *Occupational Outlook Quarterly*, vol. 51, no. 3, Fall 2007, http://www.bls.gov/opub/ooq/2007/fall/art02.pdf (accessed February 11, 2008)

FIGURE 5.11

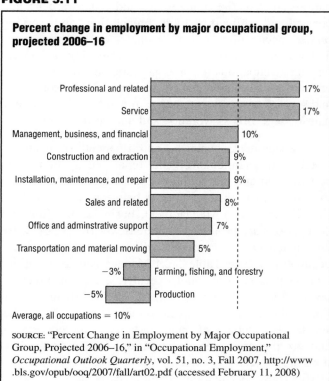

Percent change in employment by major occupational group, projected 2006–16

Average, all occupations = 10%

SOURCE: "Percent Change in Employment by Major Occupational Group, Projected 2006–16," in "Occupational Employment," *Occupational Outlook Quarterly*, vol. 51, no. 3, Fall 2007, http://www.bls.gov/opub/ooq/2007/fall/art02.pdf (accessed February 11, 2008)

Service occupations were also projected to grow by nearly 17% between 2006 and 2016. (See Figure 5.11.) Over 4.8 million service jobs are expected to be created

TABLE 5.2

Employment by major occupational group, 2006 and projected 2016

[In thousands]

Occupational group	Employment		Percent distribution		Change	
	2006	2016	2006	2016	Percent	Number
Total, all occupations	150,620	166,220	100.0	100.0	10.4	15,600
Management, business, and financial occupations[a]	15,397	16,993	10.2	10.2	10.4	1,596
Professional and related occupations[b]	29,819	34,790	19.8	20.9	16.7	4,970
Service occupations[c]	28,950	33,780	19.2	20.3	16.7	4,830
Sales and related occupations	15,985	17,203	10.6	10.3	7.6	1,218
Office and administrative support occupations	24,344	26,089	16.2	15.7	7.2	1,745
Farming, fishing, and forestry occupations	1,039	1,010	.7	.6	−2.8	−29
Construction and extraction occupations	8,295	9,079	5.5	5.5	9.5	785
Installation, maintenance, and repair occupations	5,883	6,433	3.9	3.9	9.3	550
Production occupations	10,675	10,147	7.1	6.1	−4.9	−528
Transportation and material moving occupations	10,233	10,695	6.8	6.4	4.5	462

[a]Major occupational groups 11–0000 through 13–0000 in the 2000 Standard Occupational Classification (SOC).
[b]Major occupational groups 15–0000 through 29–0000 in the 2000 Standard Occupational Classification (SOC).
[c]Major occupational groups 31–0000 through 39–0000 in the 2000 Standard Occupational Classification (SOC).

SOURCE: "Table 4. Employment by Major Occupational Group, 2006 and Projected 2016," in *Employment Projections: 2006–16*, U.S. Department of Labor, Bureau of Labor Statistics, December 4, 2007, http://www.bls.gov/news.release/pdf/ecopro.pdf (accessed February 14, 2008)

by 2016. (See Figure 5.10.) By that year, 20.3% of the nation's workforce will work in service occupations. (See Table 5.2.) Occupations in this group include health care support occupations (such as nursing aides, massage therapists, and dental assistants); protective service occupations (such as fire fighters, fish and game wardens, and correctional officers); food preparation and serving related occupations (such as chefs, cooks, bartenders, and waiters); building and grounds cleaning and maintenance occupations (such as janitors, pest control workers, and ground maintenance workers); and personal care and service occupations (such as funeral service workers, hairdressers, fitness workers, and animal trainers).

Management, business, and financial occupations, installation, maintenance, and repair occupations, and construction and extraction occupations are all expected to grow at about the average rate between 2006 and 2016. (See Figure 5.11.) Management, business, and financial occupations are projected to increase by 10.4%; by 2016, one in ten (10.2%) workers will work in one of these occupations. (See Table 5.2.) Management occupations include jobs such as chief executives, funeral directors, postmasters, and managers in all fields. Business and financial operations occupations include human resources specialists, accountants and auditors, loan counselors, and tax preparers. Construction and extraction occupations are projected to increase by 9.5% between 2006 and 2016. These occupations include carpenters, brickmasons, plasterers, roofers, mining machine operators, and building inspectors. Installation, maintenance, and repair occupations are projected to increase by 9.3%. These occupations include automotive mechanics, maintenance and repair workers, computer repairers, and locksmiths.

Table 5.3 presents what are projected to be the thirty fastest-growing occupations during the period of 2006 to 2016. Most of them are in the professional and related occupations or service occupations groups, reflecting the high rate of growth in these groups as a whole. Half of the thirty fastest-growing occupations require a bachelor's degree or higher, including network systems and data communications analysts, computer software engineers, physical therapists, mental health counselors, and physician assistants. Three of the occupations require only short-term on-the-job training (and all three are in the service occupations), including personal and home care aides and home health aides.

Demand for Information Technology Workers

One of the fastest-growing segments of the economy is the information technology (IT) industry. During the 1990s, when personal computers became ubiquitous in the home and the workplace and the Internet became an important part of many people's lives, there was explosive growth in computer-related jobs. Although this growth had slowed considerably by 2000, the IT industry has remained one of the most rapidly expanding parts of the job market and is expected to continue to grow, on the whole, faster than the average for all industries.

Triggering this growth are significant advances in networking and data communications technology and the increasing need for sophisticated security systems to protect networks and databases from viruses, hackers, and so-called cyber-terrorists. As technology advances, so does the need to apply it in business, to provide computer education and support to workers and clients, to develop and improve software, and to oversee the

TABLE 5.3

The thirty fastest-growing occupations, 2006–16

[In thousands]

Occupation	Occupational group	Employment 2006	Employment 2016	Change Percent	Change Number	Most significant source of postsecondary education or training[a]
Network systems and data communications analysts	Professional and related occupations[b]	262	402	53.4	140	Bachelor's degree
Personal and home care aides	Service occupations[c]	767	1,156	50.6	389	Short-term on-the-job training
Home health aides	Service occupations[c]	787	1,171	48.7	384	Short-term on-the-job training
Computer software engineers, applications	Professional and related occupations[b]	507	733	44.6	226	Bachelor's degree
Veterinary technologists and technicians	Professional and related occupations[b]	71	100	41.0	29	Associate degree
Personal financial advisors	Management, business, and financial occupations[d]	176	248	41.0	72	Bachelor's degree
Makeup artists, theatrical and performance	Service occupations[c]	2	3	39.8	1	Postsecondary vocational award
Medical assistants	Service occupations[c]	417	565	35.4	148	Moderate-term on-the-job training
Veterinarians	Professional and related occupations[b]	62	84	35.0	22	First professional degree
Substance abuse and behavioral disorder counselors	Professional and related occupations[b]	83	112	34.3	29	Bachelor's degree
Skin care specialists	Service occupations[c]	38	51	34.3	13	Postsecondary vocational award
Financial analysts	Management, business, and financial occupations[d]	221	295	33.8	75	Bachelor's degree
Social and human service assistants	Professional and related occupations[b]	339	453	33.6	114	Moderate-term on-the-job training
Gaming surveillance officers and gaming investigators	Service occupations[c]	9	12	33.6	3	Moderate-term on-the-job training
Physical therapist assistants	Service occupations[c]	60	80	32.4	20	Associate degree
Pharmacy technicians	Professional and related occupations[b]	285	376	32.0	91	Moderate-term on-the-job training
Forensic science technicians	Professional and related occupations[b]	13	17	30.7	4	Bachelor's degree
Dental hygienists	Professional and related occupations[b]	167	217	30.1	50	Associate degree
Mental health counselors	Professional and related occupations[b]	100	130	30.0	30	Master's degree
Mental health and substance abuse social workers	Professional and related occupations[b]	122	159	29.9	37	Master's degree
Marriage and family therapists	Professional and related occupations[b]	25	32	29.8	7	Master's degree
Dental assistants	Service occupations[c]	280	362	29.2	82	Moderate-term on-the-job training
Computer systems analysts	Professional and related occupations[b]	504	650	29.0	146	Bachelor's degree
Database administrators	Professional and related occupations[b]	119	154	28.6	34	Bachelor's degree
Computer software engineers, systems software	Professional and related occupations[b]	350	449	28.2	99	Bachelor's degree
Gaming and sports book writers and runners	Service occupations[c]	18	24	28.0	5	Short-term on-the-job training
Environmental science and protection technicians, including health	Professional and related occupations[b]	36	47	28.0	10	Associate degree
Manicurists and pedicurists	Service occupations[c]	78	100	27.6	22	Postsecondary vocational award
Physical therapists	Professional and related occupations[b]	173	220	27.1	47	Master's degree
Physician assistants	Professional and related occupations[b]	66	83	27.0	18	Master's degree

[a]An occupation is placed into 1 of 11 categories that best describes the postsecondary education or training needed by most workers to become fully qualified in that occupation.
[b]Major occupational groups 15-0000 through 29-0000 in the 2000 Standard Occupational Classification (SOC).
[c]Major occupational groups 31-0000 through 39-0000 in the 2000 Standard Occupational Classification (SOC).
[d]Major occupational groups 11-0000 through 13-0000 in the 2000 Standard Occupational Classification (SOC).

SOURCE: "Table 6. The 30 Fastest-Growing Occupations, 2006–16," in *Employment Projections: 2006–16*, U.S. Department of Labor, Bureau of Labor Statistics, December 4, 2007, http://www.bls.gov/news.release/pdf/ecopro.pdf (accessed February 14, 2008)

operations of large networks and databases. The BLS's *Occupational Outlook Handbook, 2007–2008* projects that employment in computer systems design and related services will grow 38% between 2006 and 2016, adding 489,000 jobs by 2016. Some occupations within this group will experience even stronger growth, such as network systems and data communications analysts, expected to grow by 82.3%; computer software engineers working in applications, expected to grow by 62%; and computer software engineers working in systems software, expected to grow by 48.5%. These jobs require at least bachelor's degrees and can pay approaching $50 per hour.

Factors that contribute to the slower growth in the twenty-first-century IT industry, as compared with the boom of the 1990s, include the increasing sophistication of software, widespread use of personal computers, and the outsourcing of many computing tasks overseas to low-paid workers. Newer software packages are able to do many jobs that were once only possible for human beings to do. In particular, such routine jobs as writing simple computer codes or entering data into a database system have been automated using bar-code scanners, voice recognition software, and character recognition readers (machines that are capable of reading printed text or handwriting). Typing jobs that were once given to typists are now being performed on desktop computers by the document authors themselves. In order to cut costs, many companies are sending routine data entry and information processing tasks, and even such highly skilled jobs as technology support and routine software engineering and programming, to overseas contractors in countries where labor costs are lower than in the United States. Because of these factors, a decline of 7% in data entry, information processing, and word processing jobs is expected during the period from 2006 through 2016. Demand for programmers and computer support specialists is expected to slow, and even growth in the market for software engineers—one of the fastest-growing sectors of the IT industry—will be tempered by these trends.

EDUCATION AND PROJECTED JOB GROWTH

Although jobs are available at all levels of education and training, most jobs do not require postsecondary education or training. As shown in Table 5.2, the economy will produce about 15.6 million new jobs between 2006 and 2016, a 10.4% increase in employment. Many of the occupations with the largest number of job openings due to growth or net replacements will require less education than a bachelor's degree. Table 5.4 lists the thirty occupations with the largest number of job openings. Of the top ten, nine require less education than a four-year college degree; the tenth, postsecondary teachers, requires a doctoral degree. Only four of the top thirty jobs require a bachelor's degree or higher. The other twenty-six positions generally offer much lower pay and fewer benefits than do the jobs requiring a postsecondary degree. Jobs that require an associate's degree, such as registered nurses, offer higher pay and benefits than do those that require on-the-job training only.

Bachelor's Degree or Higher

On the other hand, a bachelor's degree or more will be required for most of the higher-paying jobs that will be added to the job market between 2006 and 2016. Nearly 100,000 new jobs are expected to be created in the highest-paid field requiring a bachelor's degree: computer software engineering for systems software, which pays a median annual wage of $85,370. (See Figure 5.12.) Almost a quarter of a million (226,000) new jobs for computer software engineers working in applications are expected to be created by 2016; these positions have a median annual salary of $79,780. Other high-paying occupations requiring a bachelor's degree include construction managers (77,000 new jobs expected, with an annual median wage of $73,700), computer systems analysts (146,000 new jobs expected, with an annual median wage of $69,760), and civil engineers (46,000 new jobs expected, with an annual median wage of $68,600). The lowest-paying jobs among these high-growth occupations that require college degrees are child, family, and school social workers, which only receive a median annual wage of $37,480.

Postsecondary Vocational Training

Several occupations that usually require postsecondary vocational training—education beyond high school, but less than a four-year bachelor's degree—will have significant employment growth between 2006 and 2016, according to the BLS. Postsecondary vocational training may include special vocational certification, or the achievement of an associate's degree, usually a two-year program at a public community college or a private business or technical school. The fastest-growing occupation in this group by far is registered nurses; over half a million new positions (587,000) will be created between 2006 and 2016. (See Figure 5.13.) In addition, the annual wages of registered nurses are among the highest in this educational group, at $57,280. Other occupations with the most growth in this educational group include health-care aides, orderlies, and attendants (264,000 new jobs expected, with an annual median wage of $22,180), preschool teachers (115,000 new jobs expected, with an annual median wage of $22,680), automotive service technicians (110,000 new jobs expect, with an annual median wage of $33,780), and licensed practical and vocational nurses (105,000 new jobs expected, with an annual median wage of $36,550).

Postsecondary vocational training may also include supervised work experience or extended on-the-job training. Figure 5.14 shows the occupations with the most growth expected over the 2006 to 2016 period that require only work experience or extended on-the-job training. During the period 2006 through 2016, 239,000 executive secretary/administrative assistant jobs are expected to open up. These positions have a median annual wage of $37,240. Carpenters are also expected to have high job growth, with 150,000 new jobs added during the decade. These positions pay a median annual wage of $36,550. The highest-paid jobs in this group are sales representatives of technical and scientific products. About 51,000 of these jobs will open up, paying a median annual wage of $64,440. Other jobs in this category that will experience large growth in the decade include other sales representatives working in wholesale and manufacturing (131,000 new jobs expected, with an annual median wage of $49,610), cooks (98,000 new jobs expected, with an annual median wage of $20,340), and supervisors of food preparation and serving workers (92,000 new jobs expected, with an annual median wage of $26,980). Occupations requiring work experience or long-term on-the-job training vary dramatically in potential for earnings.

Twenty selected occupations that usually require short- or moderate-term on-the-job training are projected to increase employment between 2006 and 2016. Of the twenty occupations, the fastest-growing ones are expected to be retail sales workers (557,000 jobs), customer service representatives (545,000 jobs), food preparation and serving workers (452,000 jobs), office clerks (404,000 jobs), and personal and home health aides (389,000 jobs). Most of

TABLE 5.4

The thirty occupations with the largest number of job openings, projected 2006–16

[In thousands]

Occupation	Occupational group	Employment 2006	Employment 2016	Change Number	Net replacement needs	Total job openings due to growth and net replacements[a]	Most significant source of postsecondary education or training[b]
Retail salespersons	Sales and related occupations	4,477	5,034	557	1,378	1,935	Short-term on-the-job training
Cashiers, except gaming	Sales and related occupations	3,500	3,382	−118	1,664	1,664	Short-term on-the-job training
Waiters and waitresses	Service occupations[c]	2,361	2,615	255	1,282	1,537	Short-term on-the-job training
Customer service representatives	Office and administrative support occupations	2,202	2,747	545	613	1,158	Moderate-term on-the-job training
Registered nurses	Professional and related occupations[d]	2,505	3,092	587	413	1,001	Associate degree
Office clerks, general	Office and administrative support occupations	3,200	3,604	404	587	991	Short-term on-the-job training
Combined food preparation and serving workers, including fast food	Service occupations[c]	2,503	2,955	452	475	927	Short-term on-the-job training
Laborers and freight, stock, and material movers, hand	Transportation and material moving occupations	2,416	2,466	50	773	823	Short-term on-the-job training
Janitors and cleaners, except maids and housekeeping cleaners	Service occupations[c]	2,387	2,732	345	457	802	Short-term on-the-job training
Postsecondary teachers	Professional and related occupations[d]	1,672	2,054	382	280	662	Doctoral degree
Child care workers	Service occupations[c]	1,388	1,636	248	399	646	Short-term on-the-job training
Bookkeeping, accounting, and auditing clerks	Office and administrative support occupations	2,114	2,377	264	331	594	Moderate-term on-the-job training
Elementary school teachers, except special education	Professional and related occupations[d]	1,540	1,749	209	336	545	Bachelor's degree
Truck drivers, heavy and tractor-trailer	Transportation and material moving occupations	1,860	2,053	193	330	523	Moderate-term on-the-job training
Personal and home care aides	Service occupations[c]	767	1,156	389	130	519	Short-term on-the-job training
Executive secretaries and administrative assistants	Office and administrative support occupations	1,618	1,857	239	258	497	Work experience in a related occupation
Receptionists and information clerks	Office and administrative support occupations	1,173	1,375	202	287	489	Short-term on-the-job training
Sales representatives, wholesale and manufacturing, except technical and scientific products	Sales and related occupations	1,562	1,693	131	345	476	Work experience in a related occupation
Maids and housekeeping cleaners	Service occupations[c]	1,470	1,656	186	277	463	Short-term on-the-job training
Home health aides	Service occupations[c]	787	1,171	384	70	454	Short-term on-the-job training
Food preparation workers	Service occupations[c]	902	1,040	138	313	451	Short-term on-the-job training
Accountants and auditors	Management, business, and financial occupations[e]	1,274	1,500	226	224	450	Bachelor's degree
General and operations managers	Management, business, and financial occupations[e]	1,720	1,746	26	415	441	Bachelor's or higher degree, plus work experience
Counter attendants, cafeteria, food concession, and coffee shop	Service occupations[c]	533	587	54	370	424	Short-term on-the-job training
First-line supervisors/managers of retail sales workers	Sales and related occupations	1,676	1,747	71	352	423	Work experience in a related occupation
Stock clerks and order fillers	Office and administrative support occupations	1,705	1,574	−131	405	405	Short-term on-the-job training
Nursing aides, orderlies, and attendants	Service occupations[c]	1,447	1,711	264	130	393	Postsecondary vocational award
Security guards	Service occupations[c]	1,040	1,216	175	211	387	Short-term on-the-job training
Landscaping and groundskeeping workers	Service occupations[c]	1,220	1,441	221	161	382	Short-term on-the-job training
First-line supervisors/managers of office and administrative support workers	Office and administrative support occupations	1,418	1,500	82	293	374	Work experience in a related occupation

[a]Total job openings represent the sum of employment increases and net replacements. If employment change is negative, job openings due to growth are zero and total job openings equal net replacements.
[b]An occupation is placed into 1 of 11 categories that best describes the postsecondary education or training needed by most workers to become fully qualified in that occupation.
[c]Major occupational groups 31–0000 through 39–0000 in the 2000 Standard Occupational Classification (SOC).
[d]Major occupational groups 15–0000 through 29–0000 in the 2000 Standard Occupational Classification (SOC).
[e]Major occupational groups 11–0000 through 13–0000 in the 2000 Standard Occupational Classification (SOC).

SOURCE: "Table 7. The 30 Occupations with the Largest Number of Total Job Openings Due to Growth and Net Replacements, 2006–16," in *Employment Projections: 2006–16*, U.S. Department of Labor, Bureau of Labor Statistics, December 4, 2007, http://www.bls.gov/news.release/pdf/ecopro.pdf (accessed February 14, 2008)

FIGURE 5.12

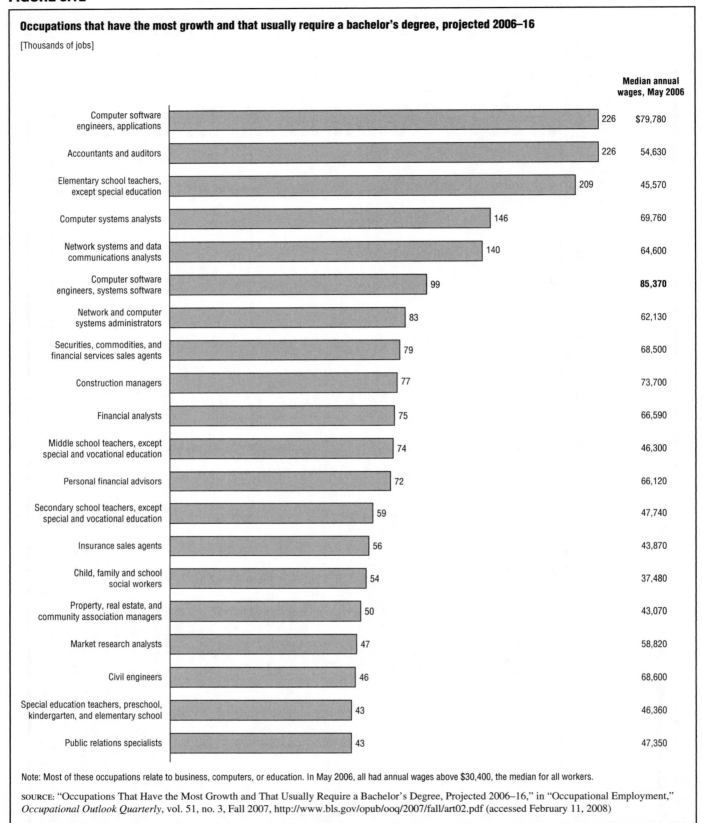

Occupations that have the most growth and that usually require a bachelor's degree, projected 2006–16

[Thousands of jobs]

Occupation	Jobs	Median annual wages, May 2006
Computer software engineers, applications	226	$79,780
Accountants and auditors	226	54,630
Elementary school teachers, except special education	209	45,570
Computer systems analysts	146	69,760
Network systems and data communications analysts	140	64,600
Computer software engineers, systems software	99	**85,370**
Network and computer systems administrators	83	62,130
Securities, commodities, and financial services sales agents	79	68,500
Construction managers	77	73,700
Financial analysts	75	66,590
Middle school teachers, except special and vocational education	74	46,300
Personal financial advisors	72	66,120
Secondary school teachers, except special and vocational education	59	47,740
Insurance sales agents	56	43,870
Child, family and school social workers	54	37,480
Property, real estate, and community association managers	50	43,070
Market research analysts	47	58,820
Civil engineers	46	68,600
Special education teachers, preschool, kindergarten, and elementary school	43	46,360
Public relations specialists	43	47,350

Note: Most of these occupations relate to business, computers, or education. In May 2006, all had annual wages above $30,400, the median for all workers.

SOURCE: "Occupations That Have the Most Growth and That Usually Require a Bachelor's Degree, Projected 2006–16," in "Occupational Employment," *Occupational Outlook Quarterly*, vol. 51, no. 3, Fall 2007, http://www.bls.gov/opub/ooq/2007/fall/art02.pdf (accessed February 11, 2008)

these jobs pay under $25,000 per year. The highest-paying position in this group are truck drivers, with a median annual wage of $35,040. Bookkeeping, accounting, and auditing clerks also make a fairly high median annual wage of $30,560. Waiters and waitresses only make about $14,850 annually. (See Figure 5.15.)

FIGURE 5.13

Occupations that have the most growth and that usually require an associate degree or postsecondary vocational award, projected 2006–16

[Thousands of jobs]

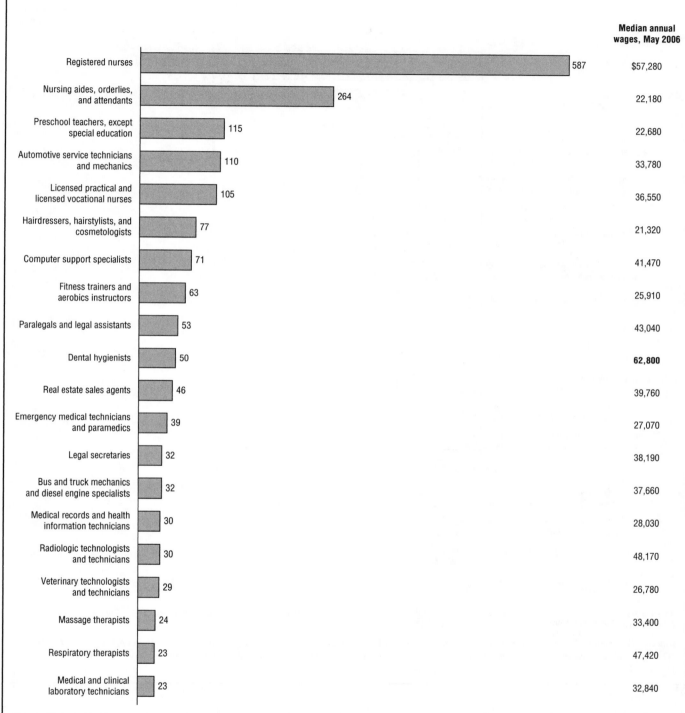

Occupation	Jobs	Median annual wages, May 2006
Registered nurses	587	$57,280
Nursing aides, orderlies, and attendants	264	22,180
Preschool teachers, except special education	115	22,680
Automotive service technicians and mechanics	110	33,780
Licensed practical and licensed vocational nurses	105	36,550
Hairdressers, hairstylists, and cosmetologists	77	21,320
Computer support specialists	71	41,470
Fitness trainers and aerobics instructors	63	25,910
Paralegals and legal assistants	53	43,040
Dental hygienists	50	**62,800**
Real estate sales agents	46	39,760
Emergency medical technicians and paramedics	39	27,070
Legal secretaries	32	38,190
Bus and truck mechanics and diesel engine specialists	32	37,660
Medical records and health information technicians	30	28,030
Radiologic technologists and technicians	30	48,170
Veterinary technologists and technicians	29	26,780
Massage therapists	24	33,400
Respiratory therapists	23	47,420
Medical and clinical laboratory technicians	23	32,840

Note: At this level of training, more than half of the occupations that are projected to gain the most jobs relate to healthcare, reflecting the growing medical needs of an aging population.

SOURCE: "Occupations That Have the Most Growth and That Usually Require an Associate Degree or Postsecondary Vocational Award, Projected 2006–16," in "Occupational Employment," *Occupational Outlook Quarterly*, vol. 51, no. 3, Fall 2007, http://www.bls.gov/opub/ooq/2007/fall/art02.pdf (accessed February 11, 2008)

FIGURE 5.14

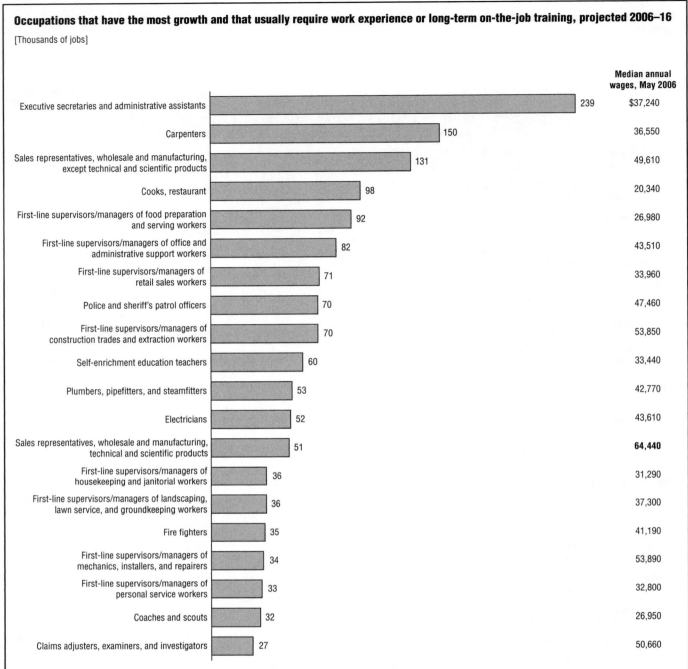

Occupations that have the most growth and that usually require work experience or long-term on-the-job training, projected 2006–16

[Thousands of jobs]

Occupation	Jobs	Median annual wages, May 2006
Executive secretaries and administrative assistants	239	$37,240
Carpenters	150	36,550
Sales representatives, wholesale and manufacturing, except technical and scientific products	131	49,610
Cooks, restaurant	98	20,340
First-line supervisors/managers of food preparation and serving workers	92	26,980
First-line supervisors/managers of office and administrative support workers	82	43,510
First-line supervisors/managers of retail sales workers	71	33,960
Police and sheriff's patrol officers	70	47,460
First-line supervisors/managers of construction trades and extraction workers	70	53,850
Self-enrichment education teachers	60	33,440
Plumbers, pipefitters, and steamfitters	53	42,770
Electricians	52	43,610
Sales representatives, wholesale and manufacturing, technical and scientific products	51	**64,440**
First-line supervisors/managers of housekeeping and janitorial workers	36	31,290
First-line supervisors/managers of landscaping, lawn service, and groundkeeping workers	36	37,300
Fire fighters	35	41,190
First-line supervisors/managers of mechanics, installers, and repairers	34	53,890
First-line supervisors/managers of personal service workers	33	32,800
Coaches and scouts	32	26,950
Claims adjusters, examiners, and investigators	27	50,660

Note: Increased activity in building and remodeling is expected to create growth in construction occupations. Supervisory occupations are also projected to gain many jobs over the 2006–16 decade.

SOURCE: "Occupations That Have the Most Growth and That Usually Require Work Experience or Long-Term On-the-Job Training, Projected 2006–16," in "Occupational Employment," *Occupational Outlook Quarterly*, vol. 51, no. 3, Fall 2007, http://www.bls.gov/opub/ooq/2007/fall/art02.pdf (accessed February 11, 2008)

WHICH WILL BE THE BEST JOBS?

Many criteria are used for determining job quality. Occupational characteristics generally accepted as a measure of future job quality include whether the number of jobs in that field will increase, how much the position pays, and whether a high percentage of those in that field are unemployed. In addition, individuals have personal desires and values that bring other factors into play in determining job quality, such as opportunities for self-employment for those who want to be their own boss, the availability of flexible work schedules for people who want to set their own hours, or the opportunity to travel for those who are adventurous.

FIGURE 5.15

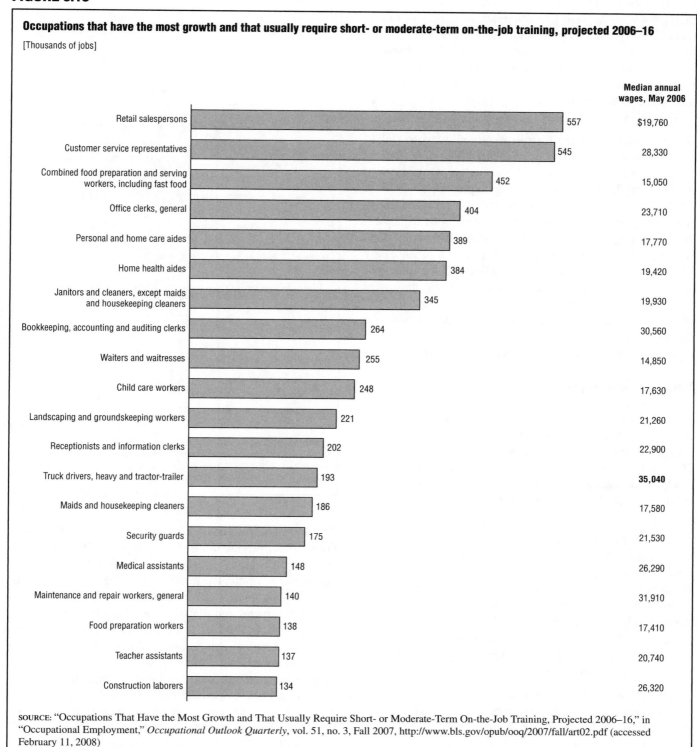

Occupations that have the most growth and that usually require short- or moderate-term on-the-job training, projected 2006–16

[Thousands of jobs]

Occupation	Jobs	Median annual wages, May 2006
Retail salespersons	557	$19,760
Customer service representatives	545	28,330
Combined food preparation and serving workers, including fast food	452	15,050
Office clerks, general	404	23,710
Personal and home care aides	389	17,770
Home health aides	384	19,420
Janitors and cleaners, except maids and housekeeping cleaners	345	19,930
Bookkeeping, accounting and auditing clerks	264	30,560
Waiters and waitresses	255	14,850
Child care workers	248	17,630
Landscaping and groundskeeping workers	221	21,260
Receptionists and information clerks	202	22,900
Truck drivers, heavy and tractor-trailer	193	**35,040**
Maids and housekeeping cleaners	186	17,580
Security guards	175	21,530
Medical assistants	148	26,290
Maintenance and repair workers, general	140	31,910
Food preparation workers	138	17,410
Teacher assistants	137	20,740
Construction laborers	134	26,320

SOURCE: "Occupations That Have the Most Growth and That Usually Require Short- or Moderate-Term On-the-Job Training, Projected 2006–16," in "Occupational Employment," *Occupational Outlook Quarterly*, vol. 51, no. 3, Fall 2007, http://www.bls.gov/opub/ooq/2007/fall/art02.pdf (accessed February 11, 2008)

Figure 5.12 shows twenty high-paying occupations generally requiring a bachelor's degree or higher that are predicted to have the most projected employment growth over the 2006 to 2016 period. Most of these high-growth occupations have high earnings and low unemployment rates, although employment opportunities, especially in fields like education, will vary from state to state depending on population trends.

Workers who responded to a 2006 Gallup survey by Jeffrey M. Jones (*Personal Fulfillment Frequently Cited as a Top Job 'Like'*, The Gallup Organization, August 7, 2006, http://www.gallup.com/poll/24010/Personal-Fulfillment-Frequently-Cited-Top-Job-Like.aspx) cited various reasons they liked or loved their jobs, giving insight into the attributes that can make a job satisfying. According to the poll, the most common reasons workers stated that they liked their jobs were that their jobs offered them a sense of fulfillment (18%), provided opportunities to help people (15%), or offered them freedom or flexibility (13%). College graduates were more likely than others to find their job fulfilling. On the other hand, 14% of American workers dislike their work schedules, 13% think they do not get paid well enough, and 11% say there are too many politics in the workplace.

According to Joseph Carroll, nearly all workers (94%) surveyed by Gallup in 2007 (*U.S. Workers Remain Largely Satisfied with Their Jobs*, The Gallup Organization, November 27, 2007, http://www.gallup.com/poll/102898/US-Workers-Remain-Largely-Satisfied-Their-Jobs.aspx) said they were at least somewhat satisfied with their jobs; 46% said they were completely satisfied. In recent years, workers' satisfaction in two areas has gone up. In 1992 only 17% of workers were completely satisfied with the amount of on-the-job stress; by 2007, 32% of workers said they were completely satisfied on this measure. Also in 1992, only 39% of workers said they were completely satisfied with the flexibility of their hours; by 2007, 68% said they were completely satisfied with this aspect of their work.

Employment Prospects

Employment prospects are influenced by more than the rate of growth within an industry. New workers are also needed to replace those who leave an occupation. In part because of the aging of the American workforce, between 2006 and 2016 it is expected that the need for replacement workers will create more jobs than will the addition of new positions to the labor market. (See Figure 5.16.)

The two occupational groups with the largest replacement needs are service occupations and professional and related occupations. The BLS projects that there will be more than 12.2 million job openings in service occupations between 2006 and 2016; more than half of them will be open because current workers have left permanently. (See Figure 5.16.) The BLS projects that there will be approximately 11.1 million job openings in professional and related occupations; over half of these will open when current workers leave.

Some occupational groups will have job openings even though there will be little, if any, job growth between 2006 and 2016. For example, although the BLS projects that there will be very few new production jobs created over the course of the decade, it also projects that more than two million workers will be needed to replace those who retire or leave the industry. (See Figure 5.16.)

EMPLOYMENT DECLINES. An occupation's employment total can decline because it is concentrated in a declining industry or because of changes to occupational staffing patterns. Office automation and other technological advances, declining industry employment, and changing legislation have adversely affected the occupations with

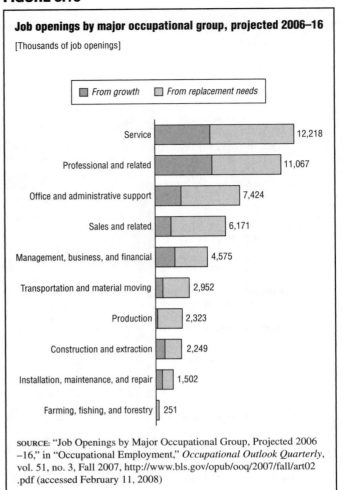

FIGURE 5.16

Job openings by major occupational group, projected 2006–16

[Thousands of job openings]

☐ From growth ☐ From replacement needs

Service	12,218
Professional and related	11,067
Office and administrative support	7,424
Sales and related	6,171
Management, business, and financial	4,575
Transportation and material moving	2,952
Production	2,323
Construction and extraction	2,249
Installation, maintenance, and repair	1,502
Farming, fishing, and forestry	251

SOURCE: "Job Openings by Major Occupational Group, Projected 2006–16," in "Occupational Employment," *Occupational Outlook Quarterly*, vol. 51, no. 3, Fall 2007, http://www.bls.gov/opub/ooq/2007/fall/art02.pdf (accessed February 11, 2008)

the largest projected employment declines. As shown in Figure 5.17, production and agriculture-related jobs, such as sewing-machine operators (−63,000 jobs), electrical and electronic equipment assemblers (−57,000 jobs), cutting, punching, and press machine setters, operators, and tenders working in metal and plastic (−40,000 jobs), and farmers and ranchers (−90,000), are examples of occupations that will lose employment between 2006 and 2016 due to declining needs in some goods-producing industries. Employment among such traditional administrative occupations as stock clerks and order fillers (−131,000 jobs), cashiers (−118,000 jobs), packers and packagers (−104,000 jobs), file clerks (−97,000 jobs), and order clerks (−66,000 jobs) will decline dramatically because of productivity improvements in office automation and the increased use of computer technology by professional and managerial employees. For this reason, these occupations would offer few opportunities for new workers.

BEST OPPORTUNITIES FOR SELF-EMPLOYMENT

Many types of jobs provide opportunities for self-employment, and the percentage of workers who are self-

FIGURE 5.17

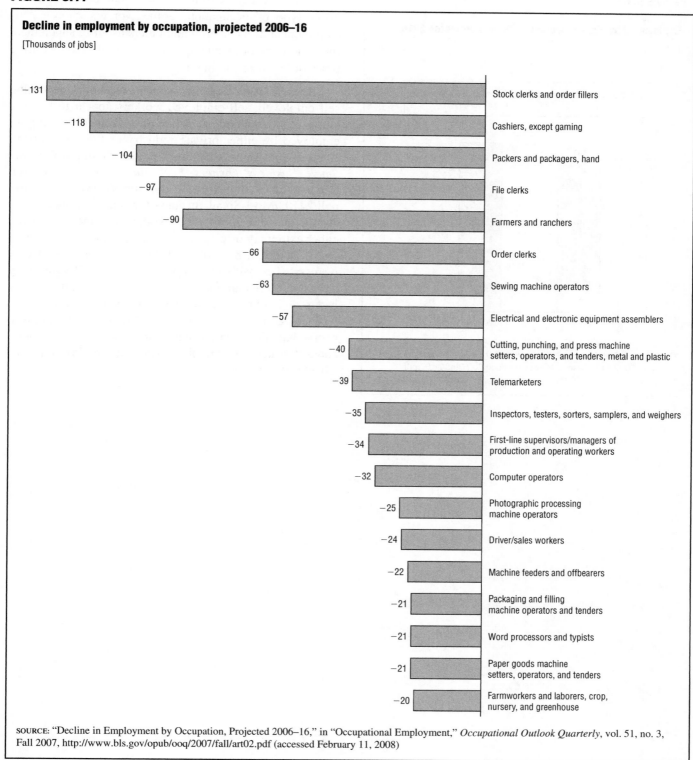

Decline in employment by occupation, projected 2006–16

[Thousands of jobs]

Occupation	Value
Stock clerks and order fillers	−131
Cashiers, except gaming	−118
Packers and packagers, hand	−104
File clerks	−97
Farmers and ranchers	−90
Order clerks	−66
Sewing machine operators	−63
Electrical and electronic equipment assemblers	−57
Cutting, punching, and press machine setters, operators, and tenders, metal and plastic	−40
Telemarketers	−39
Inspectors, testers, sorters, samplers, and weighers	−35
First-line supervisors/managers of production and operating workers	−34
Computer operators	−32
Photographic processing machine operators	−25
Driver/sales workers	−24
Machine feeders and offbearers	−22
Packaging and filling machine operators and tenders	−21
Word processors and typists	−21
Paper goods machine setters, operators, and tenders	−21
Farmworkers and laborers, crop, nursery, and greenhouse	−20

SOURCE: "Decline in Employment by Occupation, Projected 2006–16," in "Occupational Employment," *Occupational Outlook Quarterly*, vol. 51, no. 3, Fall 2007, http://www.bls.gov/opub/ooq/2007/fall/art02.pdf (accessed February 11, 2008)

employed is projected to rise slightly, from 12% in 2006 to 13% in 2016. (See Figure 5.18.) Farmers and ranchers, at 969,000 workers, make up the occupational group projected to have the most self-employed workers in 2016. (See Figure 5.19.) Managers of retail sales workers, including those who own retail establishments with employees, will make up the next largest group of self-

employed workers in 2016, at 589,000. Child care workers (506,000), carpenters (495,000), and hairdressers and cosmetologists (316,000) round out the top five categories of projected self-employed workers.

The twenty occupations listed in Figure 5.19 represent only the largest occupational categories of self-employed

FIGURE 5.18

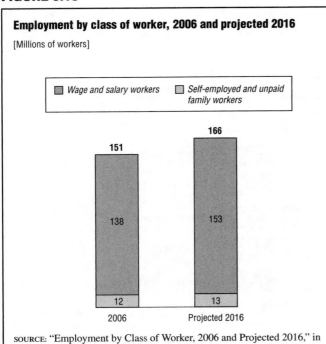

Employment by class of worker, 2006 and projected 2016

[Millions of workers]

Legend: ■ Wage and salary workers □ Self-employed and unpaid family workers

2006: 151 (138 wage and salary, 12 self-employed)
Projected 2016: 166 (153 wage and salary, 13 self-employed)

SOURCE: "Employment by Class of Worker, 2006 and Projected 2016," in "Occupational Employment," *Occupational Outlook Quarterly*, vol. 51, no. 3, Fall 2007, http://www.bls.gov/opub/ooq/2007/fall/art02.pdf (accessed February 11, 2008)

workers. In reality, self-employment is an option in nearly every type of occupation. Some workers choose self-employment as a career, while others use it to supplement full-time work or as a temporary source of income during times of layoff or job-hunting.

Regardless of the industry or the reason for becoming self-employed, self-employed workers appear to be generally more satisfied with their jobs than those who are employed by either private industry or the government. According to Dennis Jacobe in a 2006 Gallup Poll (*Most Small Business Owners Feel Successful*, The Gallup Organization, August 14, 2006, http://www.gallup.com/poll/24103/Most-Small-Business-Owners-Feel-Successful.aspx), 47% of self-employed workers feel they have been either extremely or very successful as small business owners. In addition, 87% of small business owners said they were satisfied with self-employment; just 12% said they were not. More than four out of five (83%) said that if they had to do it all over again, they would still become a small business owner. This poll suggested that self-employed people had a passion for their work. For more information about business opportunities and self-employment, see Chapter 9, "Business Opportunities."

FIGURE 5.19

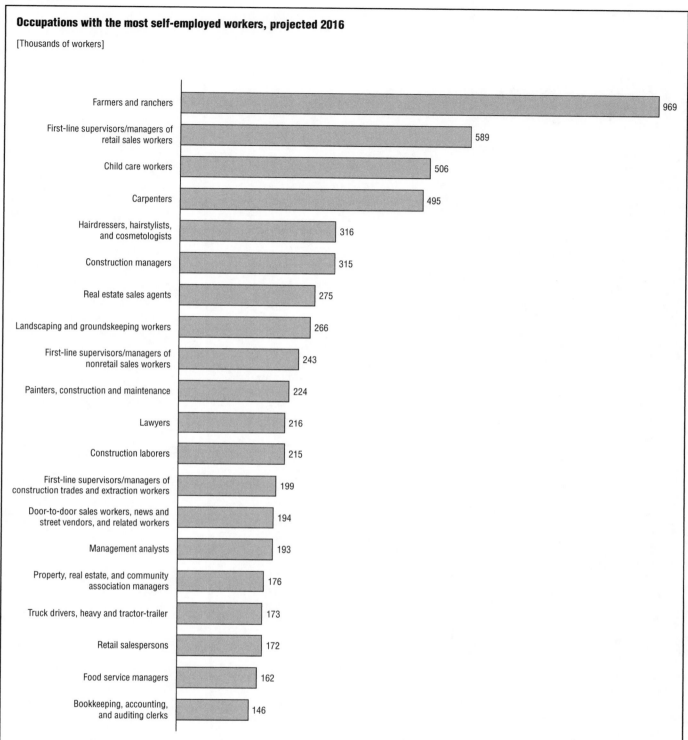

Occupations with the most self-employed workers, projected 2016

[Thousands of workers]

Occupation	Value
Farmers and ranchers	969
First-line supervisors/managers of retail sales workers	589
Child care workers	506
Carpenters	495
Hairdressers, hairstylists, and cosmetologists	316
Construction managers	315
Real estate sales agents	275
Landscaping and groundskeeping workers	266
First-line supervisors/managers of nonretail sales workers	243
Painters, construction and maintenance	224
Lawyers	216
Construction laborers	215
First-line supervisors/managers of construction trades and extraction workers	199
Door-to-door sales workers, news and street vendors, and related workers	194
Management analysts	193
Property, real estate, and community association managers	176
Truck drivers, heavy and tractor-trailer	173
Retail salespersons	172
Food service managers	162
Bookkeeping, accounting, and auditing clerks	146

SOURCE: "Occupations with the Most Self-Employed Workers, Projected 2016," in "Occupational Employment," *Occupational Outlook Quarterly*, vol. 51, no. 3, Fall 2007, http://www.bls.gov/opub/ooq/2007/fall/art02.pdf (accessed February 11, 2008)

CHAPTER 6
EARNINGS AND BENEFITS

EARNINGS

The federal government measures both the mean earnings (average) and the median earnings (one-half earn more than this figure, and one-half earn less than this figure) of the nation's workers. Individual income is the total amount brought in by an individual worker, and household income is the total amount earned by all members of a family, including earnings and money received from interest, pensions, and other sources.

Full-Time, Year-Round Workers

In 2006, according to statistics reported by Bruce H. Webster Jr. and Alemayehu Bishaw of the U.S. Census Bureau in *Income, Earnings, and Poverty Data from the 2006 American Community Survey* (August 2007, http://www.census2010.gov/prod/2007pubs/acs-08.pdf), the median earnings for full-time, year-round workers were $42,210 for men and $32,649 for women; women earned just 77.3% of what men earned. Asian workers earned the highest median salaries in 2006. Asian men earned a median of $50,159; Asian women earned a median of $38,613, 77% of what Asian men earned. Non-Hispanic white men earned a median of $47,814; non-Hispanic white women earned a median of $35,151, 73.5% of what non-Hispanic white men earned. African-American men earned a median of $34,480 in 2006; African-American women earned $30,398, 88.2% of what African-American men earned. Hispanics earned the lowest median salaries in 2006, but Hispanic women were closer in percentage to what Hispanic men earned than women of other races and ethnicities were to corresponding males of their same race or ethnicity. Hispanic men earned a median of $27,490; Hispanic women earned $24,738, 90% of what their male peers earned.

According to data reported by the U.S. Census Bureau in *Historical Income Tables* (March 2007, http://www.census.gov/hhes/www/income/histinc/p36ar.html), the median earnings of men aged fifteen and over working full-time, year-round, when converted to year 2005 dollars, have changed very little for more than three decades. In 1972 men had a median income equal to $42,617 in 2005 dollars. Wages dropped to a low of $40,958 in 1995, but had risen again to a high of $44,262 in 2001 before dropping again to below the 1972 level, at $42,188, in 2005. Women's earnings, on the other hand, have substantially increased. In constant 2005 dollars, women who worked full-time, year-round earned a median of only $24,479 in 1972. By 2005 full-time female workers earned a median of $33,256, down from a high of $33,619 in 2002.

Another way to examine incomes is to look at household incomes. Households in which two or more adults are working tend to have higher incomes than do single-adult households. In 2006 the median household income was $48,201. (See Table 6.1.) Married-couple households had a higher median income ($69,716) than did nonfamily households ($29,083). Family households headed by a single householder had substantially lower incomes than did married-couple households, especially when headed by a female. Family households headed by a single male had a median income of $47,078, and family households headed by a single female had a median income of only $31,818.

The race and ethnicity of a householder affected median household income as well. Asian householders had a substantially higher median income than any other group in 2006, at $64,238. Non-Hispanic white households had a median income of $52,423, Hispanic households had a median income of $37,781, and African-American households had a median income of just $31,969. (See Table 6.1.) Households of all races and ethnicities saw a slight rise in median incomes from 2005 to 2006 except for non-Hispanic white households, which experienced a slight decline in median income in 2006.

TABLE 6.1

Income and earnings by selected characteristics, 2006

[Income in 2006 dollars. Households and people as of March of the following year.]

Characteristic	2006 Number (thousands)	2006 Median income (dollars) Estimate
Households		
All households	16,011	48,201
Type of household		
Family households	78,425	59,894
Married-couple	58,945	69,716
Female householder, no husband present	14,416	31,818
Male householder, no wife present	5,063	47,078
Nonfamily households	37,587	29,083
Female householder	20,249	23,876
Male householder	17,338	35,614
Race* and Hispanic origin of householder		
White	94,705	50,673
White, not Hispanic	82,675	52,423
Black	14,354	31,969
Asian	4,454	64,238
Hispanic origin (any race)	12,973	37,781
Age of householder		
Under 65 years	92,282	54,726
15 to 24 years	6,662	30,937
25 to 34 years	19,435	49,164
35 to 44 years	22,779	60,405
45 to 54 years	24,140	64,874
55 to 64 years	19,266	54,592
65 years and older	23,729	27,798
Nativity of householder		
Native	100,603	49,074
Foreign born	15,408	43,943
Naturalized citizen	7,210	51,440
Not a citizen	8,198	39,497
Earnings of full-time, year-round workers		
Men with earnings	63,055	42,261
Women with earnings	44,663	32,515

*Federal surveys now give respondents the option of reporting more than one race. Therefore, two basic ways of defining a race group are possible. A group such as Asian may be defined as those who reported Asian and no other race (the race-alone or single-race concept) or as those who reported Asian regardless of whether they also reported another race (the race-alone-or-in-combination concept). This table shows data using the first approach (race alone). The use of the single-race population does not imply that it is the preferred method of presenting or analyzing data. The Census Bureau uses a variety of approaches.
About 2.6 percent of people reported more than one race in Census 2000. Data for American Indians and Alaska Natives, Native Hawaiians and other Pacific Islanders, and those reporting two or more races are not shown separately in this table.

SOURCE: Adapted from Carmen DeNavas-Walt, Bernadette D. Proctor, and Jessica Smith, "Table 1. Income and Earnings Summary Measures by Selected Characteristics: 2005 and 2006," in *Income, Poverty, and Health Insurance Coverage in the United States: 2006*, U.S. Census Bureau, August 2007, http://www.census.gov/prod/2007pubs/p60-233.pdf (accessed February 18, 2008)

Production and Nonsupervisory Earnings

According to data from the U.S. Bureau of Labor Statistics (BLS) in *Current Population Survey* (2008, ftp://ftp.bls.gov/pub/suppl/empsit.ceseeb2.txt), production workers and workers not in management positions on private, nonfarm payrolls worked an average of 33.8 hours per week in 2007 and earned a mean salary of $17.42 per hour. Hourly salaries and hours worked varied by industry.

Workers employed in professional and business service occupations worked an average of 34.8 hours per week at an hourly wage of $20.13. People employed in the private service-providing industry sector worked an average of 32.4 hours and earned less than the overall average—$17.10 per hour. Those in leisure and hospitality worked fewer hours per week (25.5) and earned only $10.41 per hour, well below the mean for all workers; the combination of their low wages and fewer hours meant that these workers earned much less than workers in other industries. Natural resources and mining workers and construction workers earned more than the total average earnings, bringing in, on average, $20.96 and $20.95 per hour, respectively. Workers in both categories also worked longer hours per week than the overall average (45.9 hours per week for those employed in natural resources and mining industries, and 39 for construction).

Occupations

Another way to look at earnings is to consider specific occupations. Someone working in a specific occupation may work in one of several industries. For example, a photographer might work at a university (in the education and health services industry), or in a photography studio (in the professional and business services industry). A janitor might work in a hospital (in the education and health services industry), in a manufacturing plant (in the manufacturing industry), or in a hotel (in the leisure and hospitality industry). However, the training and work experience requirements for the position, regardless of the industry in which it is located, are the same.

As reported by the BLS in *Employment and Earnings* (January 2008, http://www.bls.gov/cps/cpsaat39.pdf), full-time wage and salary workers earned a median of $695 per week in 2007, with men earning a median of $766 and women earning a median of $614. (See Table 6.2.) The highest paid occupations tended to be in management, business, and financial occupations and engineering occupations. These occupations almost always require advanced degrees. Chief executives, for example, earned the highest median weekly earnings of $1,882. Engineering managers ($1,713) and computer and information systems managers ($1,553) were also highly paid. All engineers made high median weekly earnings, especially aerospace engineers ($1,557), electrical and electronic engineers ($1,454), and chemical engineers ($1,410). Lawyers and judges also made high median weekly salaries ($1,591 and $1,728, respectively), as did pharmacists ($1,838) and physicians and surgeons ($1,475).

The lowest paid occupations were concentrated in the service occupations, particularly food preparation and service related occupations. These occupations require little, if any, education or training. In 2007 food preparation workers made a median of only $349 per week, counter attendants,

TABLE 6.2

Median weekly earnings of full-time wage and salary workers, by detailed occupation and sex, 2007

[Numbers in thousands; earnings in dollars.]

Occupation	2007					
	Both sexes		Men		Women	
	Number of workers	Median weekly earnings	Number of workers	Median weekly earnings	Number of workers	Median weekly earnings
Total, 16 years and over	107,339	$695	60,298	$766	47,041	$614
Management, professional, and related occupations	39,147	996	19,222	1,187	19,924	858
Management, business, and financial operations occupations	15,977	1,080	8,684	1,261	7,293	908
Management occupations	11,009	1,161	6,570	1,337	4,438	963
Chief executives	1,043	1,882	776	1,918	267	1,536
General and operations managers	893	1,221	644	1,332	249	987
Advertising and promotions managers	69	965	29	*	41	*
Marketing and sales managers	784	1,319	488	1,511	296	1,028
Public relations managers	60	1,145	29	*	30	*
Administrative services managers	97	1,057	69	1,068	28	*
Computer and information systems managers	444	1,553	321	1,596	123	1,363
Financial managers	1,070	1,078	495	1,452	575	909
Human resources managers	238	1,208	72	1,581	166	1,073
Industrial production managers	253	1,216	211	1,244	41	*
Purchasing managers	154	1,240	90	1,374	64	1,054
Transportation, storage, and distribution managers	252	845	208	836	43	*
Farm, ranch, and other agricultural managers	86	713	67	693	19	*
Construction managers	546	1,143	497	1,155	48	*
Education administrators	713	1,131	259	1,371	454	960
Engineering managers	116	1,713	107	1,748	9	*
Food service managers	646	645	338	731	308	584
Lodging managers	104	696	48	*	56	618
Medical and health services managers	448	1,136	122	1,414	326	1,063
Property, real estate, and community association managers	338	787	140	970	197	732
Social and community service managers	269	962	105	1,063	164	913
Managers, all other	2,296	1,180	1,399	1,307	897	1,006
Business and financial operations occupations	4,968	941	2,114	1,131	2,854	832
Wholesale and retail buyers, except farm products	157	750	77	794	81	737
Purchasing agents, except wholesale, retail, and farm products	260	854	112	992	148	753
Claims adjusters, appraisers, examiners, and investigators	270	809	106	898	164	743
Compliance officers, except agriculture, construction, health and safety, and transportation	125	936	62	1,124	63	747
Cost estimators	104	1,034	89	1,063	16	*
Human resources, training, and labor relations specialists	731	875	215	1,037	517	811
Logisticians	53	990	30	*	22	*
Management analysts	352	1,200	186	1,388	166	1,083
Other business operations specialists	195	834	59	1,026	136	772
Accountants and auditors	1,519	968	577	1,186	942	858
Appraisers and assessors of real estate	67	960	45	*	22	*
Budget analysts	53	1,124	20	*	33	*
Financial analysts	76	1,232	51	1,238	25	*
Personal financial advisors	260	1,204	171	1,377	89	1,047
Insurance underwriters	91	979	26	*	65	865
Loan counselors and officers	408	938	189	1,129	219	844
Tax examiners, collectors, and revenue agents	59	837	26	*	33	*
Tax preparers	52	761	21	*	32	*
Professional and related occupations	23,170	951	10,538	1,148	12,632	835
Computer and mathematical occupations	3,117	1,229	2,326	1,294	790	1,047
Computer scientists and systems analysts	712	1,173	511	1,243	201	1,041
Computer programmers	485	1,232	361	1,268	124	1,074
Computer software engineers	872	1,455	694	1,509	178	1,318
Computer support specialists	273	877	200	905	73	764
Database administrators	101	1,345	64	1,400	37	*
Network and computer systems administrators	205	1,180	178	1,204	27	*
Network systems and data communications analysts	328	1,039	237	1,181	91	853
Operations research analysts	85	1,182	47	*	38	*

cafeteria, food concession, and coffee shop workers made only $305 per week, waiters made $380 per week, dishwashers made $316 per week, and hosts and hostesses in restaurants made a median of $366 per week. (See Table 6.2.) Child care workers earned only $368 per week and personal and home care aides made just $380 per week. Agricultural workers were also paid very little, earning a median of $352 per week.

Although those working in managerial and professional specialties tended to earn the highest wages in 2007 and those in service occupations tended to earn the lowest wages, within each occupational grouping, many categories earned significantly more or less than the median wage. For example, among managerial occupations, chief executives had the highest weekly wages ($1,882), while lodging managers ($696) and food service managers ($645) earned

TABLE 6.2

Median weekly earnings of full-time wage and salary workers, by detailed occupation and sex, 2007 [CONTINUED]

[Numbers in thousands; earnings in dollars.]

Occupation	2007					
	Both sexes		Men		Women	
	Number of workers	Median weekly earnings	Number of workers	Median weekly earnings	Number of workers	Median weekly earnings
Architecture and engineering occupations	2,633	$1,213	2,249	$1,258	384	$981
Architects, except naval	160	1,151	120	1,296	40	*
Aerospace engineers	127	1,557	114	1,637	13	*
Chemical engineers	72	1,410	54	1,495	18	*
Civil engineers	330	1,337	295	1,358	35	*
Computer hardware engineers	66	1,325	63	1,352	3	*
Electrical and electronics engineers	325	1,454	292	1,483	32	*
Industrial engineers, including health and safety	163	1,223	135	1,250	28	*
Mechanical engineers	281	1,354	259	1,349	22	*
Engineers, all other	310	1,350	275	1,373	35	*
Drafters	161	823	126	885	35	*
Engineering technicians, except drafters	405	902	315	958	90	781
Surveying and mapping technicians	75	748	68	750	7	*
Life, physical, and social science occupations	1,152	1,053	683	1,151	469	939
Biological scientists	81	1,004	46	*	34	*
Medical scientists	145	1,098	78	1,374	66	856
Chemists and materials scientists	120	1,149	67	1,354	53	980
Environmental scientists and geoscientists	78	1,080	58	1,159	20	*
Physical scientists, all other	120	1,371	78	1,531	41	*
Market and survey researchers	122	1,062	54	1,160	68	1,035
Psychologists	100	1,170	38	*	63	1,152
Chemical technicians	57	785	37	*	21	*
Other life, physical, and social science technicians	117	749	76	833	41	*
Community and social services occupations	1,893	755	776	807	1,117	720
Counselors	577	760	202	833	375	724
Social workers	587	757	112	764	475	754
Miscellaneous community and social service specialists	272	680	103	788	169	636
Clergy	359	797	313	832	46	*
Religious workers, all other	62	668	30	*	32	*
Legal occupations	1,167	1,148	505	1,579	663	930
Lawyers	624	1,591	393	1,783	231	1,381
Judges, magistrates, and other judicial workers	67	1,728	41	*	26	*
Paralegals and legal assistants	285	797	34	*	251	789
Miscellaneous legal support workers	192	722	37	*	155	662
Education, training, and library occupations	6,500	841	1,810	1,007	4,690	784
Postsecondary teachers	860	1,131	491	1,239	370	962
Preschool and kindergarten teachers	488	567	15	1	473	561
Elementary and middle school teachers	2,595	863	514	938	2,081	847
Secondary school teachers	1,028	944	471	1,001	558	900
Special education teachers	323	881	58	860	265	886
Other teachers and instructors	335	766	147	987	188	685
Librarians	169	861	35	*	134	846
Teacher assistants	600	410	47	*	553	406
Arts, design, entertainment, sports, and media occupations	1,568	829	879	920	689	732
Artists and related workers	78	953	47	*	31	*
Designers	553	776	278	894	275	697
Producers and directors	93	1,008	64	988	29	*
Athletes, coaches, umpires, and related workers	119	773	94	798	25	*
News analysts, reporters and correspondents	63	943	36	*	27	*
Public relations specialists	110	851	39	*	70	804
Editors	134	931	75	979	59	804
Writers and authors	80	999	34	*	46	*
Broadcast and sound engineering technicians and radio operators	70	864	60	893	10	*
Photographers	61	660	35	*	26	*

the least. (See Table 6.2.) People working in sales and office occupations earned a median weekly wage of $598, less than the median earnings of all workers, but considerable variability existed. Sales representatives of securities, commodities, and financial services earned far more than others ($1,128). On the other hand, cashiers ($356), telemarketers ($407), and door-to-door sales workers and news and street vendors ($464) earned considerably below the median weekly wage for all workers in sales and office

occupations. Among office workers, tellers ($455) and stock clerks ($445) earned particularly low wages, while postal mail carriers ($896) earned relatively high wages.

The manufacturing industry is projected to lose jobs between 2006 and 2016, and considerable variability existed in the median wages of those working in production occupations. Although the median weekly wage of all workers in production was $581 in 2007, first-line

TABLE 6.2

Median weekly earnings of full-time wage and salary workers, by detailed occupation and sex, 2007 [CONTINUED]

[Numbers in thousands; earnings in dollars.]

Occupation	2007					
	Both sexes		Men		Women	
	Number of workers	Median weekly earnings	Number of workers	Median weekly earnings	Number of workers	Median weekly earnings
Healthcare practitioner and technical occupations	5,140	$920	1,310	$1,156	3,830	$875
Dietitians and nutritionists	76	734	6	*	70	720
Pharmacists	172	1,838	84	1,887	87	1,603
Physicians and surgeons	611	1,475	413	1,796	197	1,062
Physician assistants	71	1,211	22	*	48	*
Registered nurses	1,965	984	192	1,098	1,773	976
Occupational therapists	51	1,099	11	*	40	*
Physical therapists	139	1,143	60	1,247	79	1,096
Respiratory therapists	77	896	27	*	50	881
Speech-language pathologists	84	1,037	2	*	82	1,039
Therapists, all other	73	730	21	*	53	729
Clinical laboratory technologists and technicians	270	844	68	1,049	201	803
Dental hygienists	61	946	1	*	60	949
Diagnostic related technologists and technicians	226	916	83	1,050	144	845
Emergency medical technicians and paramedics	129	704	95	751	34	*
Health diagnosing and treating practitioner support technicians	341	579	68	687	273	538
Licensed practical and licensed vocational nurses	422	668	30	*	392	664
Medical records and health information technicians	72	507	4	*	68	509
Miscellaneous health technologists and technicians	99	688	33	*	66	681
Service occupations	14,716	454	7,371	515	7,345	406
Healthcare support occupations	2,187	454	261	522	1,926	447
Nursing, psychiatric, and home health aides	1,344	423	170	500	1,174	416
Dental assistants	169	508	14	*	155	508
Medical assistants and other healthcare support occupations	589	490	58	575	531	487
Protective service occupations	2,736	719	2,175	754	560	588
First-line supervisors/managers of police and detectives	124	1,067	105	1,084	20	*
First-line supervisors/managers of fire fighting and prevention work	59	1,197	53	1,119	6	*
Supervisors, protective service workers, all other	91	758	68	876	23	*
Fire fighters	266	901	252	919	14	*
Bailiffs, correctional officers, and jailers	437	648	304	686	132	578
Detectives and criminal investigators	134	1,066	104	1,121	30	*
Police and sheriff's patrol officers	655	891	568	907	86	791
Private detectives and investigators	64	696	46	*	17	*
Security guards and gaming surveillance officers	750	510	579	524	172	465
Lifeguards and other protective service workers	58	410	29	*	29	*
Food preparation and serving related occupations	4,107	385	2,070	403	2,037	363
Chefs and head cooks	290	518	236	535	53	482
First-line supervisors/managers of food preparation and serving workers	449	491	191	586	258	423
Cooks	1,263	365	815	377	448	341
Food preparation workers	322	349	124	367	198	335
Bartenders	212	479	108	551	104	404
Combined food preparation and serving workers, including fast food	145	340	46	*	99	358
Counter attendants, cafeteria, food concession, and coffee shop	91	305	36	*	55	299
Waiters and waitresses	865	380	274	415	592	360
Food servers, nonrestaurant	95	415	29	*	67	401
Dining room and cafeteria attendants and bartender helpers	156	356	89	370	67	345
Dishwashers	150	316	111	314	38	*
Hosts and hostesses, restaurant, lounge, and coffee shop	63	366	7	*	56	363

supervisors made quite a bit more, with a median of $824 per week. (See Table 6.2.) Computer control programmers and operators ($780) and tool and die makers ($918) also made fairly high median weekly wages. On the other hand, pressers of textiles, garment, and related materials made among the lowest wages of all workers, at $344 per week. Sewing machine operators ($361) and laundry and dry-cleaning workers ($380) also made very low median weekly wages. See the BLS publication *Occupational Outlook Handbook* (http://www.bls.gov/oco/home.htm) for detailed descriptions of each job.

Starting Salaries for New College Graduates

The National Association of Colleges and Employers (NACE) reported in *Salary Survey* (September 12, 2007, http://www.naceweb.org/press/display.asp?year=2007&

TABLE 6.2

Median weekly earnings of full-time wage and salary workers, by detailed occupation and sex, 2007 [CONTINUED]

[Numbers in thousands; earnings in dollars.]

| | 2007 | | | | | |
| | Both sexes | | Men | | Women | |
Occupation	Number of workers	Median weekly earnings	Number of workers	Median weekly earnings	Number of workers	Median weekly earnings
Building and grounds cleaning and maintenance occupations	3,520	$422	2,290	$472	1,230	$376
First-line supervisors/managers of housekeeping and janitorial work	180	586	126	646	54	481
First-line supervisors/managers of landscaping, lawn service, and groundskeeping workers	105	718	99	732	6	*
Janitors and building cleaners	1,444	434	1,028	475	416	388
Maids and housekeeping cleaners	849	366	132	439	717	357
Pest control workers	68	516	65	518	3	*
Grounds maintenance workers	874	420	840	421	34	*
Personal care and service occupations	2,166	434	574	578	1,593	402
First-line supervisors/managers of gaming workers	97	728	65	805	32	*
First-line supervisors/managers of personal service workers	50	605	20	*	30	*
Gaming services workers	88	627	51	655	36	*
Miscellaneous entertainment attendants and related workers	62	416	37	*	26	*
Hairdressers, hairstylists, and cosmetologists	309	425	31	*	278	409
Miscellaneous personal appearance workers	129	429	31	*	98	402
Baggage porters, bellhops, and concierges	53	522	44	*	9	*
Transportation attendants	96	595	25	*	71	557
Child care workers	445	368	38	*	408	360
Personal and home care aides	433	380	55	434	379	373
Recreation and fitness workers	164	523	68	626	96	513
Personal care and service workers, all other	51	489	24	*	28	*
Sales and office occupations	25,702	598	9,725	714	15,976	550
Sales and related occupations	10,448	643	5,773	791	4,675	493
First-line supervisors/managers of retail sales workers	2,352	647	1,349	746	1,004	538
First-line supervisors/managers of non-retail sales workers	865	928	587	990	278	768
Cashiers	1,459	356	385	409	1,074	344
Counter and rental clerks	95	504	50	567	45	*
Parts salespersons	122	598	101	638	21	*
Retail salespersons	2,034	513	1,193	638	841	409
Advertising sales agents	185	741	74	900	110	683
Insurance sales agents	357	747	168	959	189	644
Securities, commodities, and financial services sales agents	307	1,128	208	1,243	100	1,031
Travel agents	79	649	18	*	60	670
Sales representatives, services, all other	485	854	321	939	164	713
Sales representatives, wholesale and manufacturing	1,228	933	900	976	327	784
Real estate brokers and sales agents	504	851	241	1,027	263	701
Telemarketers	110	407	50	422	60	391
Door-to-door sales workers, news and street vendors, and related workers	55	464	26	*	29	*
Sales and related workers, all other	152	736	62	851	91	682
Office and administrative support occupations	15,253	581	3,952	619	11,301	570
First-line supervisors/managers of office and administrative support	1,396	711	406	803	990	675
Bill and account collectors	190	537	72	586	118	521
Billing and posting clerks and machine operators	365	560	39	*	327	560
Bookkeeping, accounting, and auditing clerks	964	606	105	666	859	601
Payroll and timekeeping clerks	156	652	14	*	142	636
Tellers	342	455	37	*	304	457
Court, municipal, and license clerks	92	623	17	*	74	626
Customer service representatives	1,570	541	485	608	1,085	521
Eligibility interviewers, government programs	68	661	14	*	54	619
File clerks	279	525	57	574	222	519
Hotel, motel, and resort desk clerks	97	406	33	*	64	396
Interviewers, except eligibility and loan	107	560	17	*	90	550
Loan interviewers and clerks	122	639	19	*	103	633
Order clerks	95	542	27	*	68	529
Receptionists and information clerks	1,019	482	79	503	940	480

prid=264) that starting salaries offered to new college graduates had increased over the previous year. The $53,051 average offer to computer science majors in 2007 represented a 4.5% increase over the 2006 aver-age. Economics graduates had average salary offers of $47,782, while finance graduates received average offers of $46,442. Management information systems graduates received average offers of $47,407, up 4.7%

TABLE 6.2

Median weekly earnings of full-time wage and salary workers, by detailed occupation and sex, 2007 [CONTINUED]

[Numbers in thousands; earnings in dollars.]

Occupation	2007 Both sexes		Men		Women	
	Number of workers	Median weekly earnings	Number of workers	Median weekly earnings	Number of workers	Median weekly earnings
Reservation and transportation ticket agents and travel clerks	130	$564	59	$562	71	$565
Information and record clerks, all other	87	597	7	*	80	586
Couriers and messengers	191	707	167	720	24	*
Dispatchers	265	602	122	649	143	551
Postal service clerks	151	831	75	812	76	850
Postal service mail carriers	315	896	209	929	105	799
Postal service mail sorters, processors, and processing machine operators	81	832	45	*	36	*
Production, planning, and expediting clerks	240	746	112	885	128	658
Shipping, receiving, and traffic clerks	468	508	318	514	150	500
Stock clerks and order fillers	1,067	445	684	448	383	441
Weighers, measurers, checkers, and samplers, recordkeeping	53	513	24	*	30	*
Secretaries and administrative assistants	2,668	599	90	694	2,578	597
Computer operators	145	595	74	628	71	562
Data entry keyers	381	519	80	511	302	521
Word processors and typists	180	585	16	*	164	586
Insurance claims and policy processing clerks	246	571	32	*	214	559
Mail clerks and mail machine operators, except postal service	101	516	50	509	51	523
Office clerks, general	748	556	123	584	625	550
Office and administrative support workers, all other	490	650	125	719	366	634
Natural resources, construction, and maintenance occupations	12,486	670	12,028	674	457	539
Farming, fishing, and forestry occupations	739	372	601	382	138	348
Graders and sorters, agricultural products	70	398	25	*	45	*
Miscellaneous agricultural workers	546	352	461	357	86	332
Logging workers	59	471	58	469	—	*
Construction and extraction occupations	7,227	646	7,071	648	156	573
First-line supervisors/managers of construction trades and extraction workers	678	901	663	906	15	*
Brickmasons, blockmasons, and stonemasons	170	609	165	608	4	*
Carpenters	1,182	615	1,162	615	20	*
Carpet, floor, and tile installers and finishers	153	511	148	515	5	*
Cement masons, concrete finishers, and terrazzo workers	86	527	83	530	3	*
Construction laborers	1,374	514	1,351	514	24	*
Operating engineers and other construction equipment operators	376	765	364	772	12	*
Drywall installers, ceiling tile installers, and tapers	189	511	179	509	10	*
Electricians	777	805	764	804	14	*
Painters, construction and maintenance	435	515	420	515	15	*
Pipelayers, plumbers, pipefitters, and steamfitters	584	721	579	720	5	*
Plasterers and stucco masons	63	513	63	513	—	—
Roofers	190	550	188	553	1	*
Sheet metal workers	123	790	118	786	6	*
Structural iron and steel workers	71	870	70	867	—	—
Helpers, construction trades	91	434	89	432	2	*
Construction and building inspectors	92	906	83	906	9	*
Highway maintenance workers	102	621	102	623	1	*
Mining machine operators	59	954	57	961	1	*
Other extraction workers	57	777	56	769	1	*
Installation, maintenance, and repair occupations	4,520	749	4,357	750	163	726
First-line supervisors/managers of mechanics, installers, and repairers	324	960	306	961	18	*
Computer, automated teller, and office machine repairers	251	751	217	777	34	*
Radio and telecommunications equipment installers and repairers	182	927	157	923	25	*
Security and fire alarm systems installers	59	739	59	739	—	—
Aircraft mechanics and service technicians	128	889	126	895	2	*

from the previous year, while marketing graduates' average offer of $39,269 was 5.6% higher than the year before.

NACE further indicated that almost all disciplines in engineering had increases in their average salaries in 2007. Chemical engineers received average starting salary offers of $59,218, up 5.2% from the year before. Civil engineers received average offers of $48,998, up 6.3% from 2006. Electrical engineers received average starting offers of $55,333, up 3.8% from the previous year. Mechanical engineering graduates received starting offers of $54,057 on average, up 4.3% from the previous year.

TABLE 6.2

Median weekly earnings of full-time wage and salary workers, by detailed occupation and sex, 2007 [CONTINUED]

[Numbers in thousands; earnings in dollars.]

	2007					
	Both sexes		**Men**		**Women**	
Occupation	**Number of workers**	**Median weekly earnings**	**Number of workers**	**Median weekly earnings**	**Number of workers**	**Median weekly earnings**
Automotive body and related repairers	119	$620	117	$623	2	*
Automotive service technicians and mechanics	670	655	667	656	3	*
Bus and truck mechanics and diesel engine specialists	332	698	328	697	4	*
Heavy vehicle and mobile equipment service technicians and mechanics	226	803	224	802	2	*
Miscellaneous vehicle and mobile equipment mechanics, installers, and repairers	70	508	70	506	—	—
Heating, air conditioning, and refrigeration mechanics and installers	345	728	342	729	3	*
Industrial and refractory machinery mechanics	393	798	381	798	12	*
Maintenance and repair workers, general	444	694	432	694	12	*
Maintenance workers, machinery	53	700	52	703	—	—
Millwrights	74	897	73	902	1	*
Electrical power-line installers and repairers	98	1,008	98	1,007	1	*
Telecommunications line installers and repairers	212	843	201	849	11	*
Coin, vending, and amusement machine servicers and repairers	50	685	43	*	7	*
Other installation, maintenance, and repair workers	134	618	124	620	10	*
Production, transportation, and material moving occupations	15,289	577	11,951	616	3,338	437
Production occupations	8,389	581	5,992	641	2,396	443
First-line supervisors/managers of production and operating workers	876	824	726	864	150	615
Electrical, electronics, and electromechanical assemblers	200	488	86	543	114	447
Miscellaneous assemblers and fabricators	951	524	588	587	362	460
Bakers	134	433	65	498	69	404
Butchers and other meat, poultry, and fish processing workers	240	495	183	558	57	406
Food batchmakers	74	493	33	*	41	*
Computer control programmers and operators	55	780	51	798	5	*
Cutting, punching, and press machine setters, operators, and tenders	120	563	101	577	19	*
Machinists	406	700	384	706	22	*
Molders and molding machine setters, operators, and tenders, metal	73	580	61	618	12	*
Tool and die makers	75	918	72	923	3	*
Welding, soldering, and brazing workers	536	607	499	618	37	*
Metalworkers and plastic workers, all other	422	551	299	588	123	48
Prepress technicians and workers	51	538	25	*	26	*
Printing machine operators	180	613	153	657	26	*
Laundry and dry-cleaning workers	176	380	78	496	98	340
Pressers, textile, garment, and related materials	50	344	17	*	33	
Sewing machine operators	226	361	47	*	179	359
Tailors, dressmakers, and sewers	54	453	20	*	34	*
Cabinetmakers and bench carpenters	67	598	61	607	6	*
Sawing machine setters, operators, and tenders, wood	54	483	49	*	5	*
Stationary engineers and boiler operators	88	752	86	757	1	*
Water and liquid waste treatment plant and system operators	74	722	69	731	5	*
Crushing, grinding, polishing, mixing, and blending workers	103	607	94	604	10	*
Cutting workers	84	527	63	546	21	*
Inspectors, testers, sorters, samplers, and weighers	687	625	419	735	268	506
Medical, dental, and ophthalmic laboratory technicians	77	504	38	*	38	*
Packaging and filling machine operators and tenders	264	430	126	493	138	396
Painting workers	168	576	153	590	16	*
Photographic process workers and processing machine operators	50	437	25	*	25	*
Production workers, all other	912	540	636	583	276	445

Liberal arts graduates enjoyed some of the biggest proportional increases in average starting salary offers, according to the NACE survey, although the amount of starting offers lagged behind offers to recent graduates of more technical disciplines. Every major liberal arts category saw an increase in average starting salary offers, including history majors, who averaged offers of $35,092, up 6.1% over the previous year; political science and government majors, who averaged offers of $35,261, up 6.5% over 2006; and sociology majors, who averaged offers of $32,161, up 3.4% over the previous year.

TABLE 6.2

Median weekly earnings of full-time wage and salary workers, by detailed occupation and sex, 2007 [CONTINUED]

[Numbers in thousands; earnings in dollars.]

Occupation	2007					
	Both sexes		Men		Women	
	Number of workers	Median weekly earnings	Number of workers	Median weekly earnings	Number of workers	Median weekly earnings
Transportation and material moving occupations	6,900	$570	5,959	$596	942	$424
Supervisors, transportation and material moving workers	203	811	164	836	39	*
Aircraft pilots and flight engineers	95	1,358	92	1,381	4	*
Bus drivers	365	507	187	540	178	476
Driver/sales workers and truck drivers	2,772	665	2,658	672	113	499
Taxi drivers and chauffeurs	217	501	189	518	28	*
Locomotive engineers and operators	54	1,157	51	1,184	2	*
Railroad conductors and yardmasters	51	912	49	*	2	*
Parking lot attendants	71	410	64	422	6	*
Service station attendants	63	404	57	411	6	*
Crane and tower operators	55	715	55	716	—	—
Industrial truck and tractor operators	532	519	503	522	29	*
Cleaners of vehicles and equipment	233	405	200	413	33	*
Laborers and freight, stock, and material movers, hand	1,428	474	1,195	486	233	418
Packers and packagers, hand	335	374	114	414	221	362
Refuse and recyclable material collectors	60	517	58	525	3	*

*Data are not shown where base is less than 50,000.

Note: Updated population controls are introduced annually with the release of January data. Dash indicates no data or data that do not meet publication criteria.

SOURCE: Adapted from "39. Median Weekly Earnings of Full-Time Wage and Salary Workers by Detailed Occupation and Sex," in *Employment and Earnings*, U.S. Department of Labor, Bureau of Labor Statistics, January 2008, http://www.bls.gov/cps/cpsaat39.pdf (accessed February 2, 2008)

EMPLOYEE BENEFITS

Government Employment

In 2008 the BLS stated in *Career Guide to Industries* ("State and Local Government, Except Education and Hospitals," http://www.bls.gov/oco/cg/cgs042.htm) that employer-provided benefits, such as health insurance, life insurance, and retirement benefits, were more commonly available to government employees than they were to workers employed in private industry. About three-fourths (73%) of employees of state and local governments had paid holidays in 1998 (still the most current statistics available from the BLS and published in *Employee Benefits in State and Local Governments, 1998*, December 2000, http://www.bls.gov/ncs/ebs/sp/ebbl0018.pdf). More than one-third (38%) of government workers were eligible for paid personal leave, and 96% had paid sick leave. Also as a benefit, 95% of state and local government employees were offered unpaid family leave. Most (89%) participated in employer-provided life insurance plans, and 86% had medical care plans, with 51% of the participants paying a monthly contribution to the health plan. Most government employees (98%) were provided with retirement income benefits.

Private Industry

According to data from the BLS in *National Compensation Survey: Employee Benefits in Private Industry in the United States* (August 2007, http://www.bls.gov/ncs/ebs/sp/ebsm0006.pdf), workers in goods-producing industries had greater access to benefits in March 2007 than did employees of service-producing industries. In addition, people who worked for companies that employed at least a hundred people often had greater access to a variety of benefits than did employees of small companies, especially retirement plans, health insurance, and disability benefits. Other benefits that workers in private industry typically received included paid holidays and vacations and life insurance plans, and occasionally child care resources, stock option plans, short-term disability plans, and long-term care insurance. These benefits are discussed in more detail below.

PAID HOLIDAYS AND VACATION DAYS. The number of paid holiday and vacation days that workers in private industry received varied by occupation, wages, size of workplace, union status, and industry. Over three-quarters (77%) of all workers received paid holidays and paid vacations, as reported by the BLS in the *National Compensation Survey*. On average, these workers received eight paid holidays per year. Workers whose wages were $15 per hour or higher averaged nine paid holidays, while workers with lower wages averaged only seven. Unionized workers received, on average, ten yearly paid holidays, compared with nonunion workers, who averaged only eight. The average number of vacation days workers were eligible for increased with length of service. After one year, as reported in the *National Compensation Survey*, workers were eligible for, on average, 8.9 vacation days, after five years they were eligible for 13.5 days, and after ten years they were eligible for 16.1 days. Workers in management and professional occupations were eligible for significantly more vacation days than workers in other occupations, as were workers who made $15 per hour or more and workers who worked in establishments with at least one hundred workers.

HEALTH INSURANCE. According to the *National Compensation Survey*, 71% of all private industry workers had access to employer-provided medical care plans and slightly more than half (52%) participated in such plans in March 2007. Medical care plans were the benefits most widely available to workers in private industry, followed closely by prescription drug coverage. (See Figure 6.1.) Nearly half of all workers (46%) had access to dental care, 29% had access to vision care, and 68% had access to prescription drug coverage. (See Table 6.3.) Workers in management and professional fields had more access to medical care (85%) than did workers in other fields, as did workers whose wages were $15 or more (87%), workers in goods-producing industries (85%), and workers in establishments with at least one hundred workers (84%).

Three-quarters (76%) of employees with single-coverage medical care and 87% of employees with family coverage were required to make a contribution toward their health insurance in March 2007. (See Table 6.4 and Table 6.5.) Employees with single coverage were required to pay, on average, 19% of their health insurance premiums, while those with family plans were required to pay, on average, 29% of their health insurance premiums. As shown in Table 6.4 and Table 6.5, employees with single coverage were required to pay an average of $81.37 per month, and those with family coverage were required to pay an average of $312.78 per month. These premiums were up from an average of $60.24 per month for single coverage and $228.98 per month for family coverage in 2003, figures reported by the BLS in *National Compensation Survey: Employee Benefits in Private Industry in the United States, 2002–2003* (January 2005, http://www.bls.gov/ncs/ebs/sp/ebbl0020.pdf).

Some employees in private industry had access to other health-care benefits in addition to health insurance in 2007. The *National Compensation Survey* found that 33% of all employees had access to health-care reimbursement accounts, a type of health-care plan in which employers set aside funds to reimburse employees for qualified medical expenses. (See Table 6.6.) Another 8% of all employees had access to health savings accounts, in which employees themselves could place pretax dollars into health-care accounts and then get reimbursed from that account for qualified medical expenses. Workers in management and professional occupations were much more likely than any other groups to have access to these accounts. More than half (55%) of all managers and professionals had access to health-care reimbursement accounts, compared with only 35% of sales and office workers and lesser proportions of the other major occupational groups. Likewise, managers

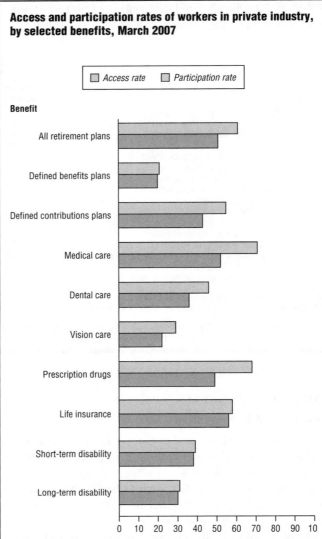

FIGURE 6.1

Access and participation rates of workers in private industry, by selected benefits, March 2007

Note: The access rate represents the percent of employees offered the benefit and the participation rate represents the percent of employees that receive the benefit.

SOURCE: "Chart 1. Access and Participation Rates of Workers by Selected Benefits, Private Industry, March 2007," in *National Compensation Survey: Employee Benefits in Private Industry in the United States, March 2007*, U.S. Department of Labor, Bureau of Labor Statistics, August 2007, http://www.bls.gov/ncs/ebs/sp/ebsm0006.pdf (accessed February 18, 2008)

and professionals (12%) as well as sales and office workers (11%) had more access to health savings accounts than did workers in other occupations. Workers that made at least $15 per hour were more likely to have access to both of these benefits than were workers who made less. Workers in larger establishments (one hundred workers or more) also had more access to these benefits than did workers in smaller establishments.

Other health-care benefits offered to some workers in private industry included wellness programs (25%), fitness centers (13%), and employee assistance programs (42%). (See Table 6.6.) Employees of establishments

TABLE 6.3

Percent of workers in private industry with access to and participating in health-care benefits, by selected characteristics, March 2007

[All workers = 100 percent]

Characteristics	Medical care			Dental care			Vision care			Outpatient prescription drug coverage		
	Access	Partici-pation	Take-up rate[a]	Access	Partici-pation	Take-up rate[a]	Access	Partici-pation	Take-up rate[a]	Access	Partici-pation	Take-up rate[a]
All workers	**71**	**52**	**73**	**46**	**36**	**77**	**29**	**22**	**76**	**68**	**49**	**73**
Worker characteristics												
Management, professional, and related	85	67	78	62	51	82	39	30	77	82	64	78
Service	46	28	61	28	20	70	20	14	72	44	27	62
Sales and office	71	48	68	47	33	70	27	19	73	67	46	68
Natural resources, construction, and maintenance	76	61	80	43	36	85	31	26	84	72	58	80
Production, transportation, and material moving	78	60	77	49	38	79	30	24	79	75	57	77
Full time	85	64	75	56	44	79	35	27	78	81	61	75
Part time	24	12	51	16	9	56	11	7	63	23	12	51
Union	88	78	88	68	62	90	53	47	88	85	75	88
Nonunion	69	49	71	44	33	74	26	19	74	66	46	71
Average wage less than $15 per hour[b]	57	37	64	34	23	67	20	14	70	54	35	64
Average wage $15 per hour or higher[b]	87	70	80	61	51	83	39	31	80	84	67	80
Establishment characteristics												
Goods producing	85	68	81	54	45	84	33	27	82	81	66	81
Service providing	67	47	70	44	33	75	28	21	75	64	45	70
1 to 99 workers	59	42	71	30	24	78	19	14	73	55	39	71
100 workers or more	84	62	75	64	49	76	40	31	78	81	60	74
Geographic areas												
Metropolitan areas	72	52	73	47	36	77	29	22	76	68	50	73
Nonmetropolitan areas	66	48	73	41	32	77	26	21	79	64	46	72
New England	68	47	69	51	38	75	23	16	67	65	45	68
Middle Atlantic	72	54	74	46	36	77	34	25	75	67	50	75
East North Central	72	53	74	45	35	78	25	20	78	70	52	74
West North Central	67	52	77	43	36	82	20	17	81	66	50	77
South Atlantic	72	52	71	44	33	73	27	20	72	69	49	72
East South Central	75	57	75	52	42	80	39	33	85	73	55	75
West South Central	66	46	69	39	29	75	21	15	75	61	42	69
Mountain	70	48	69	44	32	73	28	21	77	68	47	69
Pacific	72	54	75	54	43	79	39	31	78	68	51	75

[a]The take-up rate is an estimate of the percentage of workers with access to a plan who participate in the plan, rounded for presentation.
[b]The wage breakout is based on the average wage for each occupation surveyed, which may include workers both above and below the threshold.

SOURCE: "Table 5. Healthcare Benefits: Access, Participation, and Take-Up Rates, Private Industry Workers, National Compensation Survey, March 2007," in *National Compensation Survey: Employee Benefits in Private Industry in the United States, March 2007*, U.S. Department of Labor, Bureau of Labor Statistics, August 2007, http://www.bls.gov/ncs/ebs/sp/ebsm0006.pdf (accessed February 18, 2008)

with one hundred workers or more were much more likely to have access to these benefits than other employees, as were employees with wages of $15 per hour or more.

RETIREMENT BENEFITS. Six out of every ten workers (61%) in private industry had access to retirement benefits in March 2007, according to the *National Compensation Survey*. Half of all workers (51%) participated in these plans; 84% of all workers with access to a retirement plan took part in it. (See Table 6.7.)

Retirement plans may be one of two types: defined benefit or defined contribution. Defined benefit plans promise a specified monthly benefit at retirement. Most benefit plans of this type are protected by federal insurance provided through the Pension Benefit Guaranty Corpora-

tion. Defined contribution plans, on the other hand, do not promise a specific amount of benefits at an employee's retirement. Instead, the employer or the employee, or more commonly both, contribute a set amount of money (usually a percentage of annual salary) to the employee's retirement account. These contributions are generally invested in stock, real estate, or other investments. The balance in the account on retirement is available to the employee. Defined contribution plans include 401(k) plans, 403(b) plans, and employee stock ownership plans. Defined contribution plans were much more commonly available to workers in private industry than were defined benefit plans in 2007. (See Figure 6.1.)

In 2007 one in five workers in private industry (21%) had access to a defined benefit plan; almost all took part in these plans, because they generally require no

TABLE 6.4

Single coverage medical plans in private industry, by employer and employee premiums, March 2007

[All workers with single coverage medical plans = 100 percent]

Characteristics	Total		Employee contribution not required		Employee contribution required		
	Percent of participating employees	Average flat monthly employer premium	Percent of participating employees	Average flat monthly employer premium	Percent of participating employees	Average flat monthly employer premium	Average flat monthly employee contribution
All workers with single coverage medical plans	100	$293.25	24	$382.19	76	$265.74	$81.37
Worker characteristics							
Management, professional, and related	100	293.74	21	355.26	79	277.73	79.97
Service	100	272.50	18	395.85	82	246.32	88.89
Sales and office	100	281.24	21	353.90	79	262.06	83.63
Natural resources, construction, and maintenance	100	350.37	38	467.49	62	278.37	82.21
Production, transportation, and material moving	100	286.82	26	365.77	74	258.43	75.38
Full time	100	293.71	24	381.90	76	266.38	80.67
Part time	100	285.50	23	387.22	77	254.81	93.04
Union	100	408.46	50	479.57	50	337.51	62.45
Nonunion	100	272.12	19	334.72	81	257.62	83.51
Average wage less than $15 per hour*	100	264.97	18	334.58	82	249.33	84.74
Average wage $15 per hour or higher*	100	310.99	27	402.53	73	277.24	79.00
Establishment characteristics							
Goods producing	100	316.48	29	423.72	71	272.53	76.48
Service providing	100	284.66	22	361.53	78	263.46	83.00
1 to 99 workers	100	295.65	31	388.57	69	253.71	89.89
100 workers or more	100	291.49	18	374.16	82	273.16	76.10
Geographic areas							
Metropolitan areas	100	297.17	24	391.33	76	267.20	81.33
Nonmetropolitan areas	100	270.98	21	321.56	79	257.78	81.56
New England	100	306.88	16	478.99	84	273.42	96.82
Middle Atlantic	100	310.74	27	392.86	73	280.16	79.79
East North Central	100	301.64	23	407.53	77	269.43	81.06
West North Central	100	303.72	25	399.77	75	271.89	77.38
South Atlantic	100	268.39	19	323.38	81	255.49	82.96
East South Central	100	245.03	16	307.96	84	232.61	84.61
West South Central	100	293.21	22	350.70	78	277.24	78.48
Mountain	100	297.90	23	418.44	77	262.47	85.42
Pacific	100	303.50	32	387.57	68	263.44	75.65

*The wage breakout is based on the average wage for each occupation surveyed, which may include workers both above and below the threshold.
Note: Because of rounding, sums of individual items may not equal totals.

SOURCE: "Table 11. Medical Plans, Single Coverage: Employer and Employee Premiums by Employee Contribution Requirement, Private Industry Workers, National Compensation Survey, March 2007," in *National Compensation Survey: Employee Benefits in Private Industry in the United States, March 2007*, U.S. Department of Labor, Bureau of Labor Statistics, August 2007, http://www.bls.gov/ncs/ebs/sp/ebsm0006.pdf (accessed February 18, 2008).

contribution from the employee. (See Table 6.7.) Over half (55%) of all workers had access to a defined contribution plan; 43% of all workers participated in such a plan. Only 77% of all workers with access to a defined contribution plan took part in it.

As with other benefits, managers and professionals were the most likely workers to have access to retirement benefits (76% of them did); service workers were least likely to have such access (36% of them did). (See Table 6.7.) Unionized workers were much more likely than nonunion workers to have access to retirement benefits (84% and 58%, respectively). Workers who earned $15 per hour or more were more likely than lower-paid workers to have retirement benefits (76% and 47%, respectively). Workers in establishments with one hundred or more workers were more likely than workers in smaller establishments to have access to retirement benefits (78% and 45%, respectively).

Although women have increasingly entered the workforce since the 1970s, elderly women continue to have lower retirement income than do men. As reported by the U.S. Government Accountability Office in *Retirement Security: Women Face Challenges in Ensuring Financial Security in Retirement* (October 2007, http://www.gao.gov/new.items/d08105.pdf), this is largely due to their lower labor force participation and lower average lifetime earnings. Therefore, women have less income from pensions and Social Security, both income-dependent sources of retirement benefits. This lower income is particularly problematic for divorced women and widowed women.

TABLE 6.5

Family coverage medical plans in private industry, by employer and employee premiums, March 2007

[All workers with family coverage medical plans = 100 percent]

Characteristics	Total		Employee contribution not required		Employee contribution required		
	Percent of participating employees	Average flat monthly employer premium	Percent of participating employees	Average flat monthly employer premium	Percent of participating employees	Average flat monthly employer premium	Average flat monthly employee contribution
All workers with family coverage medical plans	**100**	**$664.04**	**13**	**$814.44**	**87**	**$642.02**	**$312.78**
Worker characteristics							
Management, professional, and related	100	702.15	9	810.82	91	691.43	313.42
Service	100	576.28	8	678.24	92	567.06	342.92
Sales and office	100	645.71	9	795.13	91	630.42	333.44
Natural resources, construction, and maintenance	100	659.83	26	839.20	74	595.82	314.33
Production, transportation, and material moving	100	683.19	18	844.44	82	648.82	263.68
Full time	100	666.82	13	823.89	87	643.76	311.94
Part time	100	614.21	12	637.67	88	610.93	327.75
Union	100	790.21	43	832.68	57	758.15	211.91
Nonunion	100	641.65	7	795.63	93	629.33	323.80
Average wage less than $15 per hour*	100	602.29	8	705.18	92	593.33	326.84
Average wage $15 per hour or higher*	100	702.52	16	849.05	84	675.14	303.21
Establishment characteristics							
Goods producing	100	706.84	20	869.49	80	666.51	267.46
Service providing	100	648.36	10	775.06	90	634.02	327.58
1 to 99 workers	100	608.18	15	804.48	85	572.25	359.49
100 workers or more	100	704.14	11	824.65	89	689.50	280.99
Geographic areas							
Metropolitan areas	100	670.64	13	815.33	87	648.13	315.15
Nonmetropolitan areas	100	626.35	9	806.67	91	608.87	299.92
New England	100	717.53	9	889.88	91	700.81	319.38
Middle Atlantic	100	711.96	17	792.19	83	695.66	299.81
East North Central	100	723.92	17	898.43	83	687.79	285.19
West North Central	100	658.46	15	790.69	85	635.56	294.00
South Atlantic	100	623.01	7	833.53	93	607.34	334.43
East South Central	100	584.50	6	816.51	94	568.80	294.46
West South Central	100	638.59	6	721.43	94	633.45	334.41
Mountain	100	620.32	11	809.18	89	596.74	359.24
Pacific	100	644.94	19	752.05	81	620.60	312.25

*The wage breakout is based on the average wage for each occupation surveyed, which may include workers both above and below the threshold.
Note: Because of rounding, sums of individual items may not equal totals.

SOURCE: "Table 12. Medical Plans, Family Coverage: Employer and Employee Premiums by Employee Contribution Requirement, Private Industry Workers, National Compensation Survey, March 2007," in *National Compensation Survey: Employee Benefits in Private Industry in the United States, March 2007*, U.S. Department of Labor, Bureau of Labor Statistics, August 2007, http://www.bls.gov/ncs/ebs/sp/ebsm0006.pdf (accessed February 18, 2008)

EMPLOYEE CONTRIBUTIONS. In most defined contribution retirement plans, such as the 401(k), employee contributions are made with pretax dollars. This means the employee's taxable income is reduced by the amount of the contribution. However, taxes are deferred, not eliminated. When the employee starts withdrawing funds from the plan, taxes must be paid on the pretax contributions, any employer-matching funds, and any earnings on these contributions.

All of these plans require a basic employee contribution, which may be matched by the employer. However, not all employers make matching contributions. Many plans allow an additional contribution by the employee in excess of the maximum amount matched

by the employer. This is called a voluntary employee contribution.

Employee savings, thrift, and retirement benefit plans are expected to come under closer public and government scrutiny in the wake of individual and corporate losses caused by stock market fluctuations in the early 2000s. During the strong market years of the mid- to late-1990s, some industry leaders and politicians believed that even government-mandated programs such as Social Security should rely more heavily on private-market investment at the discretion of the individual worker. As the stock market dropped in value at the start of the decade, particularly following the terrorist attacks in New York City and Washington, D.C., in September

TABLE 6.6

Percent of workers in private industry with access to selected health benefits, March 2007

[All workers = 100 percent]

Characteristics	Health savings accounts	Health-care reimbursement accounts	Wellness programs	Fitness centers	Employee assistance programs
All workers	**8**	**33**	**25**	**13**	**42**
Worker characteristics					
Management, professional, and related	12	55	42	25	60
Service	2	18	13	9	26
Sales and office	11	35	24	11	45
Natural resources, construction, and maintenance	3	19	16	5	27
Production, transportation, and material moving	6	27	23	10	41
Full time	9	38	28	14	46
Part time	4	17	15	8	29
Union	3	37	37	11	64
Nonunion	8	33	24	13	39
Average wage less than $15 per hour*	6	23	15	8	31
Average wage $15 per hour or higher*	10	45	36	19	54
Establishment characteristics					
Goods producing	7	31	25	13	39
Service providing	8	34	25	13	43
1 to 99 workers	4	17	11	4	21
100 workers or more	11	51	40	22	65
Geographic areas					
Metropolitan areas	8	34	26	13	43
Nonmetropolitan areas	5	26	18	12	34
New England	8	37	27	18	42
Middle Atlantic	5	31	25	14	39
East North Central	8	35	29	15	42
West North Central	7	40	26	16	42
South Atlantic	10	32	22	9	46
East South Central	8	25	20	16	41
West South Central	7	33	21	10	40
Mountain	8	36	22	11	39
Pacific	8	31	27	12	42

*The wage breakout is based on the average wage for each occupation surveyed, which may include workers both above and below the threshold.

SOURCE: "Table 6. Selected Health Benefits: Access, Private Industry Workers, National Compensation Survey, March 2007," in *National Compensation Survey: Employee Benefits in Private Industry in the United States, March 2007*, U.S. Department of Labor, Bureau of Labor Statistics, August 2007, http://www.bls.gov/ncs/ebs/sp/ebsm0006.pdf (accessed February 18, 2008).

2001, opponents of privatizing Social Security argued that individual workers should not have to shoulder increased risk in the investment of their own Social Security funds.

Laws related to employee retirement plans changed following the 2001 accounting scandal and subsequent bankruptcy of Enron Corporation, which left employee 401(k) accounts ravaged. Many Enron employees, with management's encouragement, had heavily invested their retirement savings in their own company. A large number of current and former Enron employees lost their entire retirement savings when the company collapsed. In the aftermath of the Enron scandal, Congress began to discuss restricting the percentage of an employee's 401(k) that can be invested in the employee's own company. Congress passed a Pension Protection Act in 2006 that made employer retirement savings plans less vulnerable. The legislation included provisions addressing employee retirement income security, the tax ramifications of sav-

ings plans, benefit accrual standards, and health care affordability.

Social Security

The Social Security Act of 1935 created the Old-Age and Survivors Insurance Program, which provided retirement benefits to workers aged sixty-five and older. It financed these benefits through a payroll tax, paid in part by employers and in part by employees. By January 2007, according to the Employee Benefit Research Institute (EBRI) in "The Basics of Social Security" (May 2007, http://www.ebri.org/pdf/publications/facts/0507fact.pdf), retired workers received an average monthly Social Security benefit of $1,044. A retired couple, both receiving benefits, averaged $1,713 per month.

The EBRI indicated that the aging of the U.S. population and the expected retirement of many baby-boomers in the coming two decades will put a severe strain on Social Security funds. Using intermediate cost assumptions, the

TABLE 6.7

Percent of workers in private industry with access to and participating in retirement benefits, by selected characteristics, March 2007

[All workers = 100 percent]

Characteristics	All retirement benefits[a]			Defined benefit			Defined contribution		
	Access	Participation	Take-up rate[b]	Access	Participation	Take-up rate[b]	Access	Participation	Take-up rate[b]
All workers	**61**	**51**	**84**	**21**	**20**	**95**	**55**	**43**	**77**
Worker characteristics									
Management, professional, and related	76	69	91	29	28	97	71	60	84
Service	36	25	69	8	7	94	32	20	63
Sales and office	64	54	84	19	17	93	60	47	78
Natural resources, construction, and maintenance	61	51	84	26	25	97	51	40	77
Production, transportation, and material moving	65	54	83	26	25	96	56	41	74
Full time	70	60	85	24	23	96	64	50	79
Part time	31	23	73	10	9	90	27	18	65
Union	84	81	96	69	67	97	49	41	85
Nonunion	58	47	82	15	15	95	56	43	76
Average wage less than $15 per hour[c]	47	36	75	11	10	92	44	30	70
Average wage $15 per hour or higher[c]	76	69	90	33	32	97	69	57	83
Establishment characteristics									
Goods producing	70	61	86	29	28	98	62	49	79
Service providing	58	48	83	19	18	94	53	41	77
1 to 99 workers	45	37	82	9	9	96	42	33	79
100 workers or more	78	66	85	34	32	95	70	53	76
Geographic areas									
Metropolitan areas	61	52	85	22	21	95	56	43	78
Nonmetropolitan areas	57	44	78	14	14	96	53	38	72
New England	57	50	88	21	20	96	53	44	83
Middle Atlantic	62	55	90	27	26	97	53	44	83
East North Central	64	56	87	25	24	96	56	45	80
West North Central	63	55	87	21	20	96	56	45	81
South Atlantic	62	50	80	17	17	96	59	44	75
East South Central	66	46	71	14	13	92	64	42	66
West South Central	55	44	80	17	16	95	51	38	74
Mountain	63	50	79	18	16	92	60	44	74
Pacific	57	48	84	21	20	95	49	38	77

[a]Includes defined benefit pension plans and defined contribution retirement plans. The total is less than the sum of the individual items because many employees participated in both types of plans.
[b]The take-up rate is an estimate of the percentage of workers with access to a plan who participate in the plan, rounded for presentation.
[c]The wage breakout is based on the average wage for each occupation surveyed, which may include workers both above and below the threshold.

SOURCE: "Table 1. Retirement Benefits: Access, Participation, and Take-Up Rates, Private Industry Workers, National Compensation Survey, March 2007," in *National Compensation Survey: Employee Benefits in Private Industry in the United States, March 2007*, U.S. Department of Labor, Bureau of Labor Statistics, August 2007, http://www.bls.gov/ncs/ebs/sp/ebsm0006.pdf (accessed February 18, 2008)

government estimates that the trust funds that finance Social Security benefits (through a combination of taxes and interest income) will become bankrupt by 2041.

Many proposals have been put forth to keep the Social Security trust fund solvent. The proposals all would cut benefits for future retirees, especially for those born later, according to the EBRI in "Estimating the Value of Changes in OASI Benefits under Social Security Reforms" (June 2006, http://www.ebri.org/publications/notes/index.cfm?fa=notesDisp&content_id=3643). For example, benefit cuts for people born in 1962 might range from $300 annually for those with the smallest benefits to about $3,000 annually for those entitled to the largest benefits. However, workers born in 1997 could see reductions in annual benefits ranging from $2,200 to $10,370. Therefore, many retirees in the future will not be able to maintain their standard of living without saving additional

amounts of money themselves to supplement their reduced Social Security benefits. This prospect makes retirement benefits offered by employers as part of the employment package even more valuable.

Americans are very uncomfortable with the crisis facing the Social Security system, as it puts their overall quality of life in retirement years at risk. Lydia Saad of the Gallup Poll reported in "State of the Union: Both Good and Bad" (January 24, 2008, http://www.gallup.com/poll/103918/Americans-State-Union-Ratings-All-Bad.aspx) that less than a third of people surveyed (31%) in January 2008 were satisfied with the state of the nation's Social Security and Medicare (health insurance for seniors) systems. Additional Gallup data from 2005 (http://www.gallup.com/poll/1693/Social-Security.aspx) indicated that 45% of Americans agreed that immediate changes were needed to ensure the long-term future of the Social Security system. Another third (36%) believed changes were needed within the next decade, and nearly two in ten (19%) either had no opinion or did not think major changes were needed before 2015. More than half of poll respondents from April and May 2005 (54%) opposed a proposal that would cut Social Security benefits for middle and high income workers even if benefits for lower income workers and those born before 1950 were not affected. Nearly four in ten (38%) favored this idea.

CHAPTER 7
JOB PLACEMENT

CHOOSING A CAREER

There are many reasons individuals may select one career over another. Career counselors often urge people to consider what they are passionate about. Career seekers might consider what skills they use in activities they engage in during their free time, and they can then explore occupations that use these skills.

Another way to explore potential careers is to take a career aptitude test. Many job centers or school advising centers have these tests on hand to help students and job searchers explore their interests. There are also many examples available online, including one at Career Explorer (http://www.careerexplorer.net/aptitude.asp), Live Career (http://www.livecareer.com/?cobrand=CAEO), and Job Diagnosis (http://www.jobdiagnosis.com/).

Once a person has a sense of the kind of occupation he or she would like to do, other things should be taken under consideration when deciding on a career. The education and training requirements for this occupation, the opportunities for advancement, job prospects, potential earnings and benefits, levels of stress in an occupation, and other considerations may go into deciding on a career path.

Education and Training Requirements

All jobs require some kind of training, even those that primarily use simple, everyday skills. Many people acquire these most basic job skills during the process of growing up and through compulsory education. Additional on-the-job training is often sufficient for success in a first part-time job. Most careers, however, require more education and training than can be provided through basic life experience and new employee orientation programs.

Free career training for some fields may be available through vocational courses in public schools, local branches of state employment offices, or apprenticeship programs. Some occupations require a few months of training, while others may take many years of education and be very costly. Physicians, for instance, may spend as many as fifteen years and many tens of thousands of dollars to learn a specialty in medicine.

Colleges, schools, and training institutes readily reply to requests for information about their programs. Professional and trade associations have lists of schools that offer career preparation in their fields. Information on financial aid for study or training is available from a variety of sources—high school guidance counselors, college financial aid officers, banks and credit unions, the Internet, and state and federal governments. Directories and guides to sources of student financial aid can be found in guidance offices and public libraries. Some federal government Web sources include:

- Free Application for Federal Student Aid (FAFSA) provides information on applying for federal aid (http://www.fafsa.ed.gov/).

- *Funding Education Beyond High School: The Guide to Federal Student Aid*, a publication of the U.S. Department of Education, provides descriptions of federal financial aid opportunities, including grants, loans, and work-study programs (http://www.studentaid.ed.gov/students/publications/student_guide/index.html).

- The U.S. Department of Education provides information on state education and financial aid offices in its *Education Resource Organizations Directory*, available online at http://wdcrobcolp01.ed.gov/Programs/EROD/org_list_by_territory.cfm

Working Conditions

Individuals should research prospective jobs and take into consideration their common working conditions when making a career choice. The *Occupational Outlook Handbook*, published by the U.S Department of Labor's Bureau of Labor Statistics (BLS), is available at http://

www.bls.gov/oco/ and provides detailed information on hundreds of jobs. Some jobs are very stressful. Louise Jaggs in Skillsoft ("IT Pros More Likely to Suffer from Stress, Says New Survey," May 2006, http://www.skillsoft.com/EMEA/news/19-May-06.asp) reports that a survey in 2006 found the top ten most stressful professions included, in order from most stressful to least stressful, positions in information technology, medicine, engineering, sales and marketing, education, finance, human resources, operations, production, and clerical. Work stresses included a high workload, feeling undervalued, and deadlines. Other studies, such as the Institute of Medicine's "Economic Influences and Socioeconomic Status," published in *Reducing Suicide: A National Imperative* (2002, http://www.nap.edu/openbook.php?record_id=10398&page=205), have found that some professions are more at risk for suicide than others, notably physicians and dentists. These are important considerations when choosing a career path.

Sources of Career Information

The first step in securing a job—whether it is a part-time first job for a fourteen-year-old, or a mid-career change of fields for a successful business executive—is to research the job market. What jobs are available? What are the educational or experiential requirements needed for employment? Will a move to another part of the country be necessary to secure a job doing a particular kind of work? There are several ways to begin to gather this type of career information.

PERSONAL CONTACTS. Families and friends can be extremely helpful in providing career information. Although they may not always have the information needed, they may know other knowledgeable people and be able to put the job seeker in touch with them. These contacts can lead to an "information interview," which usually means talking to someone who can provide information about a company or career. This person should have the experience to describe how he or she trained for the job, how promotions were received, and the likes or dislikes of the job. Not only can the person advise what to do, he or she can advise what not to do.

LIBRARIES AND CAREER CENTERS. Libraries offer a great deal of information about careers and job training. Job seekers can begin by searching the catalog under "vocations" or "careers" and then looking under specific fields of work that match areas of interest. For instance, those who like working with animals can find descriptions about the work of veterinarians and veterinary assistants, zoologists, animal trainers, breeders, groomers, and others whose occupations involve working with animals. Trade publications and magazines describe and discuss many kinds of work in various fields.

School career centers often offer individual counseling and testing, guest speakers, field trips, and career days.

Information in career guidance materials should be current. It is important for the job seeker to find a number of sources, because one resource might glamorize an occupation, overstate the earnings, or exaggerate the demand for workers in the field.

THE INTERNET. The Internet provides much of the same job information that is available through libraries, career centers, and guidance offices. No single network or resource, however, will contain all the desired information. As in a library search, one must look through various lists by field or discipline or by using keyword searches.

A good place to start an Internet search for career information is at the previously mentioned Web site of the BLS, where job seekers can find the most current edition of the *Occupational Outlook Handbook*. This resource contains specific information and statistics on occupations from aircraft mechanics to zoologists. Topics covered range from the type of education or training required, to working conditions, earnings, prospects for career openings and advancement, and a description of what workers do on the job.

Since October 2003 the U.S. Department of Education has operated the Career Voyages Web site (http://www.careervoyages.gov/). Information focuses on in-demand occupations within select industries that have projected high growth, including advanced manufacturing, the aerospace industry, the automotive industry, construction, the energy industry, financial services, health care, homeland security, hospitality, information technology, retail, and transportation. In addition, the site highlights such emerging industries as biotechnology, geospatial technology, and nanotechnology. Career Voyages gears information to students (including a special section directed at those still in elementary school) and their parents and career counselors, as well as toward people looking to change their careers. It offers advice on how to begin a job search, how to qualify for a particular career, which industries and occupations are growing, and how to pay for education and training.

COUNSELORS. Counselors are professionals trained to help clients assess their own strengths and weaknesses, evaluate their goals and values, and determine what they want in a career. Counselors can be found in:

- High school guidance offices
- Placement offices in private vocational or technical schools
- College career planning and placement offices
- Vocational rehabilitation agencies
- Counseling service offices offered by community organizations
- Private counseling agencies
- State employment service offices

TABLE 7.1

Unemployed jobseekers by sex, reason for unemployment, and active job search methods used, 2007

| | Thousands of persons | | Methods used as a percent of total jobseekers | | | | | | | |
Sex and reason	Total unemployed	Total jobseekers	Employer directly	Sent out resumes or filled out applications	Placed or answered ads	Friends or relatives	Public employment agency	Private employment agency	Other	Average number of methods used
Total, 16 years and over	7,078	6,102	57.4	50.7	16.0	21.7	17.7	7.6	12.9	1.84
Job losers and persons who completed temporary jobs*	3,515	2,539	59.4	49.8	19.3	26.4	23.6	10.6	14.4	2.04
Job leavers	793	793	61.8	51.8	17.3	20.8	15.8	7.4	12.2	1.88
Reentrants	2,142	2,142	54.6	50.9	13.2	18.1	13.6	5.4	12.7	1.69
New entrants	627	627	53.1	52.3	9.8	16.8	9.9	3.3	8.2	1.54
Men, 16 years and over	3,882	3,266	58.3	48.5	15.7	23.2	17.8	7.8	13.1	1.85
Job losers and persons who completed temporary jobs*	2,175	1,559	60.3	47.5	18.4	27.7	22.8	10.3	14.7	2.02
Job leavers	408	408	62.9	50.9	15.9	21.0	14.3	7.1	12.4	1.85
Reentrants	956	956	55.3	47.5	13.4	18.8	13.7	5.4	12.9	1.67
New entrants	343	343	52.0	52.8	9.9	17.7	10.4	3.7	7.7	1.54
Women, 16 years and over	3,196	2,836	56.3	53.3	16.2	20.0	17.6	7.4	12.6	1.84
Job losers and persons who completed temporary jobs*	1,340	980	58.0	53.4	20.8	24.2	25.0	11.0	13.9	2.07
Job leavers	385	385	60.5	52.7	18.8	20.7	17.3	7.7	12.0	1.91
Reentrants	1,186	1,186	54.0	53.7	13.1	17.4	13.6	5.4	12.6	1.70
New entrants	285	285	54.5	51.7	9.8	15.9	9.3	2.8	8.8	1.53

*Data on the number of jobseekers and the job search methods used exclude persons on temporary layoff.
Note: The jobseekers total is less than the total unemployed because it does not include persons on temporary layoff. The percent using each method will always total more than 100 because many jobseekers use more than one method. Updated population controls are introduced annually with the release of January data.

SOURCE: "34. Unemployed Jobseekers by Sex, Reason for Unemployment, and Active Jobsearch Methods Used," in *Employment and Earnings*, U.S. Department of Labor, Bureau of Labor Statistics, January 2008, http://www.bls.gov/cps/cpsaat34.pdf (accessed February 2, 2008)

ORGANIZATIONS. Professional societies, trade associations, labor unions, business firms, and educational institutions offer a variety of free or inexpensive career materials. Such reference books as *Guide to American Directories* and the *Encyclopedia of Associations*, found at local libraries, are useful resources. Trade organizations are particularly useful sources of information if one already has a job and is seeking another or fears being "downsized" by one's present employer.

JOB SEARCH METHODS

How do people search for employment? *Employment and Earnings*, an annual publication by the BLS, has found that unemployed workers use a variety of methods to find new jobs. In 2007 most job seekers tried an average of 1.84 different techniques. (See Table 7.1.) Over half of unemployed workers (57.4%) approached an employer directly, and half (50.7%) sent out résumés or filled out applications. Other methods included seeking help from friends or relatives (21.7%), contacting a public employment agency (17.7%), placing or answering an employment advertisement (16%), and using a private employment agency (7.6%). Women (53.3%) were somewhat more likely than men (48.5%) to send out résumés or fill out applications, while men favored contacting the employer directly (58.3%) slightly more

than women did (56.3%). Men (23.2%) were also more likely than women (20%) to solicit job leads from friends or relatives. New entrants in the labor market were more likely than other job seekers to send out résumés and fill out applications (52.3%) but less likely than other job seekers to use the other job seeking methods.

Successfully finding a job starts with knowing where and how to look for one. Most job seekers are familiar with the "Help Wanted" advertisements in the local newspaper. Although hundreds of jobs may be listed in the classified ads, however, this is not necessarily the most effective resource for job-hunting. Table 7.2 provides a list of sources of job listings, which are discussed in more detail below.

Networking

A good place to start a job search is by networking. Many jobs are never advertised—the only way to know about the opening is to ask family, friends, and acquaintances if they know of any jobs in your field. One should not be afraid to ask friends or relatives if they know of an available job. Many people get jobs through personal contacts. Often, a friend or family member will not personally know of available jobs but will be able to provide an introduction to someone else who does—the definition of networking.

TABLE 7.2

Where to learn about job openings

- Personal contacts
- School career planning and placement offices
- Employers
- Classified ads:
  - National and local newspapers
  - Professional journals
  - Trade magazines
- Internet resources
- Professional associations
- Labor unions
- State employment service offices
- Federal government
- Community agencies
- Private employment agencies and career consultants
- Internships

SOURCE: "Where to Learn about Job Openings," in *Occupational Outlook Handbook, 2008–09 Edition*, U.S. Department of Labor, Bureau of Labor Statistics, December 2007, http://www.bls.gov/oco/oco20041.htm (accessed February 18, 2008)

Networking is useful to job-hunters at any stage of career building. A young person's first job often results from a peer connection or a referral from a teacher or parent. Later on, word-of-mouth recommendations from professional peers may open doors to interviews, although they generally do not have significant influence on actual hiring decisions.

Internet Networks and Resources

Many people find that the Internet is a valuable source of job listings and job search resources and techniques. Internet resources are available whenever a job seeker has time to access them. No single network or online resource, though, will contain all of the information on employment or career opportunities, so the job seeker should be prepared to search a bit. Some jobs boards will provide national listings, and all kinds of jobs; others will be local listings, or contain jobs in only one field. Job listings may be posted by field or discipline, so searchers should begin by using keywords related to their field.

A good place to start the job search is at *CareerOne-Stop* (http://www.careeronestop.org/). This Web site, run by the U.S. Department of Labor, provides information on preparing résumés and using the Internet for job searches. It also discusses trends in the U.S. job market. On this site there are links to state job banks, private sector job banks, and veteran and government job banks. Job seekers also can post their résumés on the site for potential employers. Another valuable Internet source for careers is *O-Net Online* (http://online.onetcenter.org/). Like *CareerOne-Stop*, *O-Net Online* is run in collaboration with the Department of Labor and, according to its Web site, "serves as the nation's primary source of occupational information, pro-

viding comprehensive information on key attributes and characteristics of workers and occupations."

Internet job search resources also include such popular Web sites as Monster (http://www.monster.com) and HotJobs (http://hotjobs.yahoo.com). These sites provide job listings, résumé assistance, links to career advice, and a variety of other tools for job seekers. In addition to these Web sites, newspapers in many cities publish help wanted ads online, so job seekers in other areas can browse them remotely.

Classified Ads

"Help Wanted" advertisements may provide leads to prospective jobs. The listings do not contain all of the job openings available in a particular area, however, and they usually do not provide very much pertinent information about the available positions. Ads generally offer little or no description of the jobs, working conditions, or pay. Some advertisements do not identify the employer. They may instead offer only a post office box to which a résumé should be sent, which makes follow-up inquiries very difficult. It also makes it difficult for the job-hunter to learn anything useful about the company. Furthermore, some advertisements refer job seekers to employment agencies rather than to actual employers. Those looking for employment by searching classified advertisements should keep the following things in mind:

- Classified ads can be useful resources, but they should not be the only source of prospective job information.

- Ads should be answered promptly; openings may be filled even before the ad stops appearing in the paper.

- The Sunday edition of a newspaper usually includes the most listings, but some jobs appear only in week-day editions; searchers should read the classified ads daily for the best exposure.

- Ads that emphasize "no experience necessary" are often for jobs characterized by low wages, poor working conditions, or commission work.

- It is useful to keep track of ads responded to; good records should include both the date of the ad and the date of response to it, and the specific skills, educational background, and personal qualifications required for each advertised position.

Employment Services

States operate employment services and workforce agencies in coordination with the U.S. Employment Service of the U.S. Department of Labor. These are local offices with free resources to help job hunters find positions and to help employers find qualified workers. Telephone listings under "Job Service" or "Employment" in the state government telephone listings will provide contact information for the nearest offices. As public access to the Internet becomes more widespread, government-funded employment service delivery is increasingly Web-based rather than located in a full-service office building. Web links to state career and employment agencies are located on the Career Voyages Web site at http://www.careervoyages.gov/links-bystate.cfm.

Private employment agencies can also be helpful, but they are in business to make money. Most agencies operate on a commission basis, with the fee dependent upon a percentage of the salary paid to a successful applicant. Either the newly hired employee or the hiring company will have to pay a sizable fee. Job seekers should find out the exact cost and who is responsible for paying the fees before using the service.

College Career Planning and Placement Offices

College placement offices assist in job placement for their students and alumni. They set up appointments and provide facilities for interviews with recruiters. Placement offices usually list part-time, temporary, and summer jobs offered on campus. They also list jobs in regional business, nonprofit, and government organizations. Students can receive career counseling, testing, and job search advice and can also use career resource libraries maintained by placement offices. Access to these resources is usually included in tuition fees.

Community Agencies

Many nonprofit organizations, including churches, synagogues, and vocational rehabilitation agencies, offer counseling, career development, and job placement services. These are often targeted to a particular group, such as women, youth, minorities, ex-offenders, or older workers.

Employers

Job seekers who would like to work for a specific employer can approach that employer even if the company is not currently advertising job openings. Unadvertised job openings abound, and if candidates restrict themselves to just the advertised openings, they will miss many opportunities. To begin accessing this market, job seekers should research prospective companies in business directories, yellow pages, and online; "cold call" the prospective employer by telephoning or inquiring in person for potential job openings; and begin networking. When individuals search out unadvertised job openings, they have an advantage—not only will they face less competition for the jobs they find, but they will show the prospective employer their initiative.

APPLYING FOR A JOB

A job seeker must become qualified to work in a particular field, whether through education or experience, or a combination of the two. When it is time to seek a first job or a new position, the prospective employee should learn as much as possible about potential employers. Using this background of knowledge and experience, a job seeker should then prepare a good résumé. This will be his or her introduction to a potential employer. Finally, when an effective résumé results in an interview, the job seeker should be prepared to meet possible new employers with courteous manners, a good appearance, and sound interview skills.

Résumés and Application Forms

Sending a résumé (summary of a job applicant's previous employment, education, and skills) and filling out an application form are two ways to provide employers with written evidence of one's qualifications. Some employers prefer that prospective employees present a résumé, while others require a completed application form instead of (or in addition to) a résumé.

There are many ways to organize a résumé. Books on the topic are available in local libraries and bookstores. The Internet is also a good source for finding résumé-writing techniques. Résumé writers should be sure to include any information about their education, experience, or activities that relates to the position being sought. Basic information that should be listed on a résumé includes contact information; any schooling and other training, such as degrees received and any coursework that is relevant to the position; extracurricular activities, especially if they relate to the desired position; volunteer work—even unpaid work counts as experience; awards or other kinds of special recognition; any computer skills or other technological skills; and references. If a company supplies an application form, it should be filled out completely and correctly.

Cover Letters

A cover letter is sent with a résumé or application form as a way to introduce the job seeker to prospective employers. It should capture the employer's attention, follow a business-letter format, and include the following information:

- The name and address of the specific person to whom the letter is addressed
- The reason for the applicant's interest in the company and the type of job the applicant is seeking
- A brief list of qualifications for the position, including education, job experience, and unpaid experience, if applicable
- Any special skills
- References (if requested)
- A request for an interview
- Home and work phone number

TABLE 7.3

Job interview tips

Preparation

- Learn about the organization.
- Have a specific job or jobs in mind.
- Review your qualifications for the job.
- Be ready to briefly describe your experience, showing how it relates it the job.
- Be ready to answer broad questions, such as "Why should I hire you?" "Why do you want this job?" "What are your strengths and weaknesses?"
- Practice an interview with a friend or relative.

Personal appearance:

- Be well groomed.
- Dress appropriately.
- Do not chew gum or smoke.

The interview:

- Be early.
- Learn the name of your interviewer and greet him or her with a firm handshake.
- Use good manners with everyone you meet.
- Relax and answer each question concisely.
- Use proper English—avoid slang.
- Be cooperative and enthusiastic.
- Use body language to show interest—use eye contact and don't slouch.
- Ask questions about the position and the organization, but avoid questions whose answers can easily be found on the company Web site.
- Also avoid asking questions about salary and benefits unless a job offer is made.
- Thank the interviewer when you leave and shake hands.
- Send a short thank you note.

Information to bring to an interview:

- Social Security card.
- Government-issued identification (driver's license).
- Resume or application. Although not all employers require a resume, you should be able to furnish the interviewer information about your education, training, and previous employment.
- References. Employers typically require three references. Get permission before using anyone as a reference. Make sure that they will give you a good reference. Try to avoid using relatives as references.
- Transcripts. Employers may require an official copy of transcripts to verify grades, coursework, dates of attendance, and highest grade completed or degree awarded.

SOURCE: "Job Interview Tips," in *Occupational Outlook Handbook, 2008–09 Edition*, U.S. Department of Labor, Bureau of Labor Statistics, December 2007, http://www.bls.gov/oco/oco20045.htm (accessed February 18, 2008)

Interviewing

An interview showcases qualifications to an employer. Table 7.3 provides some helpful hints about interviewing. Personal appearance and the information presented at an interview are very important, but being prepared is perhaps the most important aspect of interviewing. Adequate preparation shows that the candidate is knowledgeable and confident and helps the interviewee feel more at ease with answering questions and taking any tests required. Job candidates should learn all they can about the position they are interviewing for as well as about the company itself. They should also be prepared to answer basic questions describing their interest in the position and how hiring them would be of benefit to the company.

For every interview, a job candidate should be well groomed and appear polished and confident. It is always better to be overdressed than underdressed. One rule of thumb offered to potential interviewees is to research the dress policy of a company, and wear an outfit that is at the formal end of the company's usual range of attire.

Candidates interviewing for a new position in their present company may be well served by dressing as if they have achieved their new position. Job candidates should never smoke, chew gum, or accept an alcoholic beverage at an interview.

Whether the position is offered or not, it is important that the job seeker follow through with a brief note of thanks to the interviewer. The note can also be another opportunity for the job candidate to "sell" his or her strong qualities. This is a courtesy that leaves a positive impression on a potential employer. If another job becomes available, the interviewer may remember the gracious gesture and approach the candidate about the position.

Testing

Many employers require prospective employees to take tests that measure skills, drug or alcohol use, or psychological traits in order to be considered for positions at their companies. Such tests are closely regulated by state and federal laws, including the Americans with Disabilities Act. Tests must directly relate to the skills required for the particular job in question and must be given to all applicants for the position.

EVALUATING A JOB OFFER

When a job is offered, the job seeker must carefully evaluate the opportunity. There are many issues to be considered, including the salary, hours, responsibilities, and location of the job. Prospective employees should also consider the stability of the organization, the opportunities for training and advancement, benefits associated with the position, and the culture and business philosophy under which the enterprise operates. Information about large businesses, agencies, or organizations is generally available on company Web sites or in annual reports or company newsletters. In addition, in order to help job candidates become more acquainted with the company, employers often provide company background information, including its history, its corporate philosophy, its size, and the range of its products or services. Print resources for company information include Dun & Bradstreet's *Million Dollar Directory, Standard and Poor's Register of Corporations, Directors and Executives*, and *Ward's Business Directory of U.S. Private and Public Companies*. Internet databases that offer business and financial information are numerous, and the most comprehensive of these can be accessed through a library or school subscription.

When evaluating a job offer, a candidate should consider the likelihood of feeling satisfied in that job in the long term. Job satisfaction is often linked with earnings and benefits, as well as opportunities for advancement. It is also important to consider the work itself, the hours of the job, and whether overtime will be required

TABLE 7.4

Public opinion poll on job satisfaction, August 2007

NOW I'LL READ A LIST OF JOB CHARACTERISTICS. FOR EACH, PLEASE TELL ME HOW SATISFIED OR DISSATISFIED YOU ARE WITH YOUR CURRENT JOB IN THIS REGARD. FIRST, ARE YOU COMPLETELY SATISFIED, SOMEWHAT SATISFIED, SOMEWHAT DISSATISFIED, OR COMPLETELY DISSATISFIED WITH [RANDOM ORDER]?

[Asked of adults who are employed full- or part-time]

(2007 Aug. 13–16)	Completely satisfied	Total satisfied	Total dissatisfied
	%	%	%
Your relations with coworkers	74	94	2
The physical safety conditions of your workplace	73	92	8
The flexibility of your hours	68	90	9
Your boss or immediate supervisor	60	84	9
Your job security	56	87	12
The amount of vacation time you receive	55	79	16
The amount of work that is required of you	54	88	11
The recognition you receive at work for your work accomplishments	47	81	17
Your chances for promotion	39	68	21
The health insurance benefits your employer offers	36	64	23
The amount of on-the-job stress in your job	32	75	23
The retirement plan your employer offers	32	62	23
The amount of money you earn	29	75	25

SOURCE: Joseph Carroll, "Now I'll Read a List of Job Characteristics. For Each, Please Tell Me How Satisfied or Dissatisfied You Are with Your Current Job in This Regard. First, Are You Completely Satisfied, Somewhat Satisfied, Somewhat Dissatisfied, or Completely Dissatisfied with [RANDOM ORDER]," in *U.S. Workers Remain Largely Satisfied with Their Jobs*, The Gallup Organization, November 27, 2007, http://www.gallup.com/poll/102898/US-Workers-Remain-Largely-Satisfied-Their-Jobs.aspx (accessed February 18, 2008). Copyright © 2008 by The Gallup Organization. Reproduced by permission of The Gallup Organization.

FIGURE 7.1

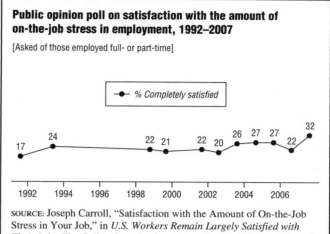

Public opinion poll on satisfaction with the amount of on-the-job stress in employment, 1992–2007

[Asked of those employed full- or part-time]

SOURCE: Joseph Carroll, "Satisfaction with the Amount of On-the-Job Stress in Your Job," in *U.S. Workers Remain Largely Satisfied with Their Jobs*, The Gallup Organization, November 27, 2007, http://www.gallup.com/poll/102898/US-Workers-Remain-Largely-Satisfied-Their-Jobs.aspx (accessed February 18, 2008). Copyright © 2008 by The Gallup Organization. Reproduced by permission of The Gallup Organization.

2007, http://www.gallup.com/poll/102898/US-Workers-Remain-Largely-Satisfied-Their-Jobs.aspx) that almost half of all workers said they were completely satisfied, with most of the rest of workers surveyed at least somewhat satisfied; only 6% of workers were dissatisfied. As shown in Table 7.4, employees expressed most satisfaction with relations with their coworkers (94%) and their physical safety on the job (92%). Workers were also very satisfied with the flexibility of their hours (90%), the amount of work required of them (88%), and their job security (87%).

Workers have become more satisfied in recent years with two important aspects of their jobs: flexibility of hours and on-the-job stress. Although on-the-job stress is one of the lowest-rated items, the one-third (32%) of workers surveyed in 2007 that said they were completely satisfied with the amount of stress in their jobs is the highest since 1992. (See Figure 7.1.) Workers have also become much more satisfied with the flexibility of their hours, perhaps because companies are becoming more open to flexible work arrangements. In 2007, 68% of workers said they were satisfied with this aspect of their employment; fifteen years earlier, just 39% said they were satisfied with the flexibility of their work hours. (See Figure 2.2 from Chapter 2.)

and if such overtime is exempt from overtime pay (as in salaried positions). Benefits—such as health insurance, retirement benefits, and holidays and vacation days—are important as well.

Job Satisfaction

Worker satisfaction often depends on such factors as relationships with coworkers, flexibility of hours, one's boss, job security, amount of vacation and paid holidays, the salary and benefits package, recognition at work, opportunity for advancement, and the amount of on-the-job stress. An August 2007 Gallup Poll revealed that most American workers are satisfied with their jobs. Joseph Carroll reports in *U.S. Workers Remain Largely Satisfied with Their Jobs* (The Gallup Organization, November 27,

CHAPTER 8
WORKERS' RIGHTS

Over the past century, federal, state, and local governments have created a body of laws, rules, and regulations to protect the rights of workers. These laws cover many aspects of work. A helpful source of information on the topic is *Your Rights in the Workplace* by Barbara Kate Repa (Nolo, 2005). Minimum wages and maximum hours, family and medical leave, unemployment benefits, on-the-job safety, protection from discrimination and harassment, the right to unionize, employer testing, and privacy rights are discussed below.

WAGES AND HOURS

Passed in 1938, the Fair Labor Standards Act (FLSA-52 Stat. 1060) is the most important wage and hour law in the United States. It applies to all businesses involved in interstate commerce and establishes rules covering minimum hourly wages, overtime pay, and the work of children. Many states also have statutes that set higher standards than the FLSA. Employers must abide by the more stringent rules.

A federal minimum wage of $0.25 per hour was instituted by the FLSA in 1938. The minimum wage had increased by 400% to $1.25 by the mid-1960s. It doubled again by the late 1970s to $2.65, and grew in small increments during the 1980s and early 1990s to $4.75 by October 1996. The minimum wage was increased to $5.15 per hour on September 1, 1997, and then to $5.85 per hour on July 24, 2007. As reported by the U.S. Department of Labor (DOL) in "Wages: Minimum Wage" (http://www.dol.gov/dol/topic/wages/minimumwage.htm), the minimum wage legislation also set future minimum wage increases, including a rise to $6.55 in July 2008 and an increase to $7.25 per hour in July 2009.

With a few minor exceptions, the FLSA requires that workers earning an hourly wage be paid overtime pay of at least one and one-half times the regular pay rate for all hours worked in a work week after the first forty hours.

Employees who customarily and regularly receive tips totaling at least $30 per month can be paid at the lower direct wage of $2.13 if that amount plus the tips will equal at least the federal minimum wage of $5.85.

The FLSA also regulates the work hours and wages of children. Individuals under the age of sixteen may work only under certain conditions. Youths fourteen and fifteen years old may work outside of school hours in various nonmanufacturing, nonmining, nonhazardous jobs. They may work up to three hours on a school day or eight hours on a nonschool day for a total of eighteen hours in a school week and forty hours in a nonschool week. In addition, work must be performed between the hours of 7:00 AM and 7:00 PM, except from June 1 through Labor Day, when evening hours are extended to 9:00 PM.

Employers may pay youth under twenty years of age a minimum wage that is lower than the national rate—$4.25 per hour during their first ninety consecutive calendar days of employment. Full-time students employed in retail or service stores, agriculture, or colleges and universities can be paid at 85% of the national minimum wage, or $4.98 per hour, and are limited to working eight hours in one day or twenty hours in a week when school is in session and forty hours per week when school is not in session. Students at least sixteen years old who are enrolled in vocational education classes can be paid at 75% of minimum wage in jobs related to their course of study.

When the minimum wage increased by seventy cents per hour in July 2007, it was the first minimum wage increase in a decade, the longest time since minimum wage legislation was enacted in 1938 that the wage had not been adjusted for inflation. In *Poverty in America: One Nation Pulling Apart* (July 2007, http://www.povertyinamerica.psu.edu/2007/07/), Amy K. Glasmeier of Pennsylvania State University argued that the minimum wage would need to increase to at least

$9.00 per hour to have a positive impact on the living standards of the nation's lowest-paid workers. According to Glasmeier, the seventy-cent increase merely offset the rising costs of necessities like housing, transportation, and health care. She cited a 2006 Congressional Research Service Report that found that if the minimum wage was linked to the dollar's real purchasing power, it would have reached $9.05 per hour before the minimum wage increase in July 2007. The real purchasing power of the minimum wage in 2007, Glasmeier estimated, was actually at a fifty-year low.

As of January 1, 2008, most states had set minimum wage rates higher than the federal minimum wage. These states included Alaska, Arizona, Arkansas, California, Colorado, Connecticut, Delaware, Florida, Hawaii, Illinois, Iowa, Maine, Maryland, Massachusetts, Michigan, Minnesota, Missouri, Montana, Nevada, New Hampshire, New Jersey, New Mexico, New York, North Carolina, Ohio, Oregon, Pennsylvania, Rhode Island, Vermont, Washington, West Virginia, Wisconsin, and the District of Columbia. The 2008 federal minimum wage rate increase matched or exceeded some of these state rates. In "Minimum Wage Laws in the States, January 1, 2008" (December 2007, http://www.dol.gov/esa/minwage/america.htm), the DOL reported that Washington at $8.07 had the highest minimum wage of any state, followed closely by California and Massachusetts, both at $8.00 an hour. A local ordinance in San Francisco set the highest minimum wage standard in the nation at $9.36 per hour, effective January 1, 2008.

FAMILY AND MEDICAL LEAVE

The Family and Medical Leave Act (FMLA), enacted in 1993, gives employees the right to take unpaid leave up to twelve weeks for certain circumstances while protecting their jobs. This leave can be used for an employee's own health situation, for the birth or adoption of a child (either parent), or to care for an immediate family member with a serious health condition.

The most recent survey, conducted by the BLS in 2000, found that 16.5% of all employees had taken a leave for family or medical reasons during the previous eighteen months, about the same percentage as a previous survey had found in 1995. However, the reasons for taking leave under the act had shifted considerably. Although six out of ten employees (61.4%) taking leave in 1995 had done so for their own health, by 2000 that percentage was down to 47.2%. (See Table 8.1.) Instead, higher proportions of employees taking leave were doing so because of maternity or disability (4.6% in 1995 and 7.8% in 2000), to care for a newborn or a newly adopted child or newly placed foster child (14.3% in 1995 and 17.9% in 2000), to care for an ill spouse (3.6% in 1995 and 5.9% in 2000), or to care for an ill parent (7.6% in 1995 and 11.4% in 2000). This shift might reflect a growing awareness in the years since the FMLA passed of the types of leave available under the act.

TABLE 8.1

Reasons for taking family or medical leave, 1995 and 2000

	Percent distribution	
Reason for taking leave	1995	2000
Own health	61.4	47.2
Maternity or disability	4.6	7.8
Care for newborn, newly adopted child, or newly placed foster child	14.3	17.9
Care for ill child	8.5	9.8
Care for ill spouse	3.6	5.9
Care for ill parent	7.6	11.4

SOURCE: Jane Waldfogel, "Reason for Taking Leave," in "Family and Medical Leave: Evidence from the 2000 Surveys," *Monthly Labor Review*, vol. 124, no. 9, September 2001, http://www.bls.gov/opub/mlr/2001/09/art2full.pdf (accessed February 21, 2008)

UNEMPLOYMENT

The Social Security Act of 1935 (49 Stat. 620), which passed during the Great Depression when unprecedented numbers of Americans were out of work, created a federal unemployment compensation system. Shortly afterward the federal government empowered states to create their own unemployment systems, which every state subsequently implemented. Along with meeting minimum federal standards, each state must determine who is eligible for benefits, how much money unemployed workers will receive, and how long the benefits will last. Unemployment insurance benefits are paid entirely by taxes imposed on employers, except in three states (Alaska, New Jersey, and Pennsylvania), where the employees also contribute to the benefits.

Benefits

Unemployment insurance pays benefits to qualified workers who are unemployed and looking for work. The benefit amount is calculated as a percentage of an individual's earnings over a previous period totaling fifty-two weeks. Most states pay a maximum of twenty-six weeks of benefits. People may be disqualified from receiving benefits for various reasons, such as voluntarily leaving work without good cause or being fired for misconduct. Another reason is the refusal of suitable work without good cause. "Good cause" must be connected with the job, rather than with the individual's personal life. Also, with few exceptions, workers are not eligible for benefits if their unemployment is caused by a labor dispute. Therefore, the insured unemployment rate is lower than the total unemployment rate. The insured unemployment rate for the week ending February 23, 2008, was 2.1%; the average number of people receiving benefits each week in the four weeks preceding that date was 2.8 million people, according to the DOL in "Unemployment Insurance Weekly Claims Report" (March 6, 2008, http://workforcesecurity.doleta.gov/press/2008/030608.asp).

ON-THE-JOB SAFETY

In 1970 Congress passed the Occupational Safety and Health Act (P.L. 91-596). This law set up a comprehensive national policy to guarantee workers a safe and healthy workplace. A branch of the DOL, the Occupational Safety and Health Administration (OSHA), enforces this statute. Under the law, employers must furnish employment that is "free from recognized hazards" that are "likely to cause death or serious physical harm." OSHA has established hundreds of detailed occupational safety and health standards that regulate specific workplace hazards so employers will know what is required of them. Things covered include personal protective equipment, machine protections, structural protections, fire protection, and protection against hazardous materials, such as flammable gases.

Although OSHA has established many required standards, it also issues nonbinding regulations. For example, in April 1998 OSHA recommended that retail outlets, such as convenience stores with a history of crime, use bulletproof glass or employ at least two clerks at night. It also suggested that such stores keep a minimum amount of cash on hand, use drop safes (a cashier can put money into but cannot take the money out of such a safe) and security cameras, be well lit, and train workers how to behave during an armed robbery.

OSHA also gives workers the right to information about the kinds of hazards to which they are exposed in the workplace. Workers may be entitled to recover damages if they are harmed by unsafe and unhealthy workplace conditions. In certain rare circumstances, workers can walk off the job rather than expose themselves to an imminently dangerous situation.

For young people, workplace safety is covered by FLSA, in addition to the OSHA regulations covering all workers. FLSA prohibits employing minors under age eighteen to work at seventeen hazardous nonfarm jobs. The prohibited jobs include driving a motor vehicle, being an outside helper on a motor vehicle, operating various power-driven machines, and performing roofing operations. Limited exemptions are provided for apprentices and student-learners under specified conditions.

Occupational Injuries, Illnesses, and Fatalities

In 2006, according to statistics published by the BLS (November 8, 2007 http://www.bls.gov/news.release/osh2.t20.htm), the most common type of workplace injury by far was sprains, strains, and tears, with a rate of 51.1 per 10,000 full-time workers. Twelve of every 10,000 full-time workers suffered from cuts, lacerations, and punctures, 11 of every 10,000 suffered from bruises or contusions, and 10 out of every 10,000 suffered from fractures. Less common injuries included burns from heat or chemicals, carpal tunnel syndrome, amputations, and tendonitis. The BLS

reported in November 2007 (http://www.bls.gov/news.release/osh2.t11.htm) that fractures and carpal tunnel syndrome required the most days away from work in 2006, at medians of twenty-eight and twenty-seven, respectively.

The industry with the highest number of cases of injury or illness in the workplace in 2006 as reported by the BLS in *Workplace Injuries and Illnesses in 2006* (October 16, 2007, http://www.bls.gov/news.release/pdf/osh.pdf) was transportation and warehousing, where the incidence was 6.5 cases per 100 full-time workers. Other industries with high rates of worker injury or illness in 2006 included agriculture, forestry, fishing and hunting, and manufacturing, both with 6 cases per 100 full-time workers, and construction, with 5.9 cases per 100 workers.

In 2006 there were 2.3 cases per 100 workers in private industry of occupational injury or illness that were severe enough to warrant days away from work, job transfer, or job restrictions, as reported by the BLS in *Workplace Injuries and Illnesses in 2006*. A job transfer or restriction could involve shorter work hours, a temporary job change, or a temporary restriction of job duties. The number of such cases varied by the type of industry and occupation. In 2006 transportation and warehousing had the highest rate of these injuries, at 4.3 per 100 full-time workers; finance and insurance had the lowest rate of these injuries, at approximately 0.4 per 100 full-time workers. (See Figure 8.1.)

According to the BLS in *National Census of Fatal Occupational Injuries in 2006* (August 9, 2007, http://www.bls.gov/news.release/pdf/cfoi.pdf) there were 5,703 fatal injuries in the workplace in 2006, down slightly from the 5,734 fatalities recorded in 2005. This was a rate of 3.9 fatalities per 100,000 workers.

The most common fatal work-related event in 2006 was a fatal highway incident; in 2006, 1,329 workers died in highway incidents, accounting for almost one in four fatal work injuries. (See Figure 8.2.) However, these fatalities were down 7.5% in 2006 from the year before. Falls accounted for 809 fatalities, up 5% from 770 in 2005. Being struck by an object accounted for 583 fatalities, while homicides accounted for 516 fatalities. Both of these fatal events were down from the previous year.

Occupations with the ten highest fatality rates in 2006 are shown in Figure 8.3. Fishers and fishing workers had the highest work-related fatality rate, at 141.7 per 100,000 workers. Aircraft pilots and flight engineers (87.8 per 100,000 workers), logging workers (82.1 per 100,000 workers), and structural iron and steel workers (61 per 100,000 workers) also had very high fatality rates. The top ten most dangerous occupations also included refuse and recyclable material collectors (41.8 per 100,000 workers), farmers and ranchers (37.1 per 100,000 workers), electrical power-line installers and repairers (34.9 per 100,000

FIGURE 8.1

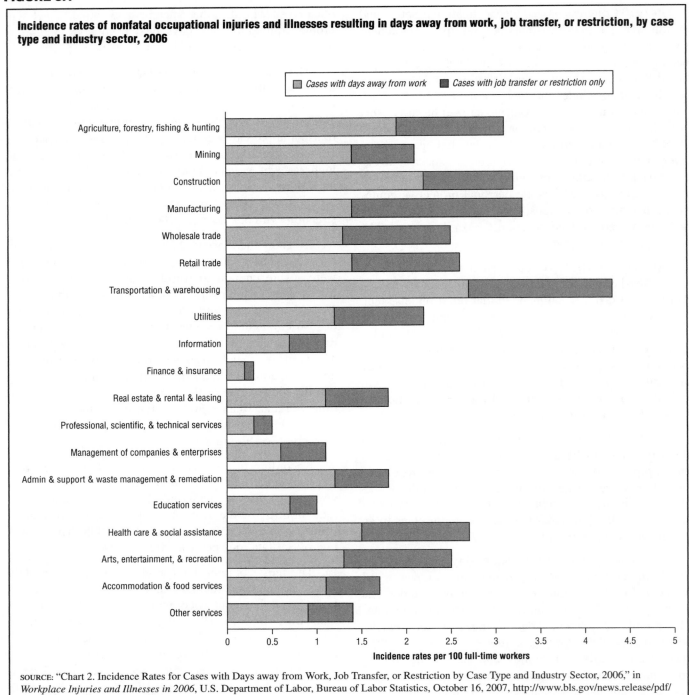

Incidence rates of nonfatal occupational injuries and illnesses resulting in days away from work, job transfer, or restriction, by case type and industry sector, 2006

☐ Cases with days away from work ■ Cases with job transfer or restriction only

Incidence rates per 100 full-time workers

SOURCE: "Chart 2. Incidence Rates for Cases with Days away from Work, Job Transfer, or Restriction by Case Type and Industry Sector, 2006," in *Workplace Injuries and Illnesses in 2006*, U.S. Department of Labor, Bureau of Labor Statistics, October 16, 2007, http://www.bls.gov/news.release/pdf/osh.pdf (accessed February 3, 2008)

workers), roofers (33.9 per 100,000 workers), drivers and truck drivers (27.1 per 100,000 workers), and other agricultural workers (21.7 per 100,000 workers).

COMPENSATION FOR WORK-RELATED INJURIES AND ILLNESSES. If a person is injured on the job or becomes ill because of the work environment, he or she will likely come in contact with the workers' compensation program, which is familiarly known as "workers' comp."

Workers' comp is an insurance program that pays compensation to injured workers for their lost wage-earning capability. It also pays workers' medical and rehabilitation expenses and provides benefits for dependents of workers who are killed on the job.

This program is financed primarily by insurance premiums paid by employers. Both workers and employers benefit from this program. Workers receive compensation

FIGURE 8.2

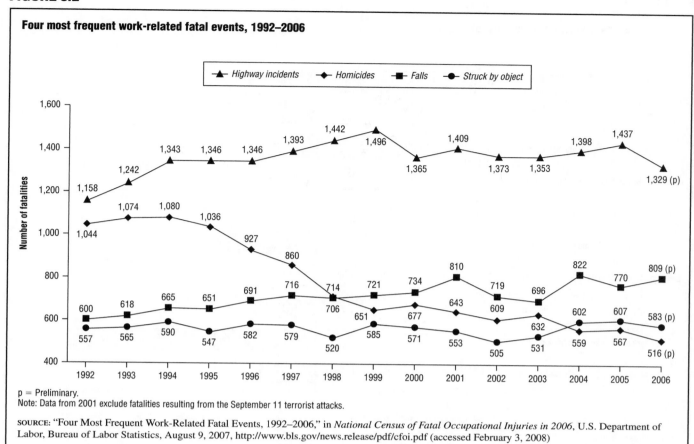

Four most frequent work-related fatal events, 1992–2006

Legend: Highway incidents, Homicides, Falls, Struck by object

p = Preliminary.
Note: Data from 2001 exclude fatalities resulting from the September 11 terrorist attacks.

SOURCE: "Four Most Frequent Work-Related Fatal Events, 1992–2006," in *National Census of Fatal Occupational Injuries in 2006*, U.S. Department of Labor, Bureau of Labor Statistics, August 9, 2007, http://www.bls.gov/news.release/pdf/cfoi.pdf (accessed February 3, 2008)

in the event they are injured and unable to work. Employers benefit because the program makes the costs of workers' compensation a predictable business expense that can be included in production costs. Each state administers its own workers' comp program.

For workers' comp to apply, there must be an "injury by accident." Generally, the accident must occur when the person is working. The injured worker and the workers' comp insurance company, or state insurance fund, try to reach a settlement. If they cannot, there is an appeal process. Many states have a payment schedule that specifies definite amounts for particular injuries. In most cases, workers' comp will pay a worker a weekly amount equal to a percentage of his or her average weekly pay, up to a maximum set by law.

Workplace Crime

In 2005 more than nine out of ten of all workplaces (92.1%) reported there were no violent incidents during the previous year. (See Table 8.2.) However, 5.3% of all workplaces did experience at least one incident of workplace violence in the twelve months prior to the survey. The largest workplaces were particularly at risk; half of all workplaces with a thousand employees or more (49.9%) had experienced some workplace violence during the past

year. The largest establishments in private industry reported higher percentages of coworker violence (33.1%) compared with customer or client violence (24.2%) and incidents involving domestic violence (24.1%). However, in large government workplaces, customer or client violence was most frequently reported (38%), followed by coworker violence (27.1%) and incidents involving domestic violence (19.2%).

Nearly three-quarters of American workplaces (72.1%) have at least one form of security in place. (See Table 8.3.) Types of security include electronic surveillance systems (burglar alarms, surveillance cameras, and motion detectors), physical security (secured entries and locked doors), and security staff. However, security measures are almost universal in the largest workplaces (99% have at least one form of security in place), which are at greatest risk for violence. Nine out of ten of these large establishments (90.6%) had physical security in place along with either an electronic surveillance system or security staff.

DISCRIMINATION AND HARASSMENT

Federal law prohibits employers from discriminating against employees or prospective employees on the basis of sex, race, religion, national origin, or disability. Furthermore,

FIGURE 8.3

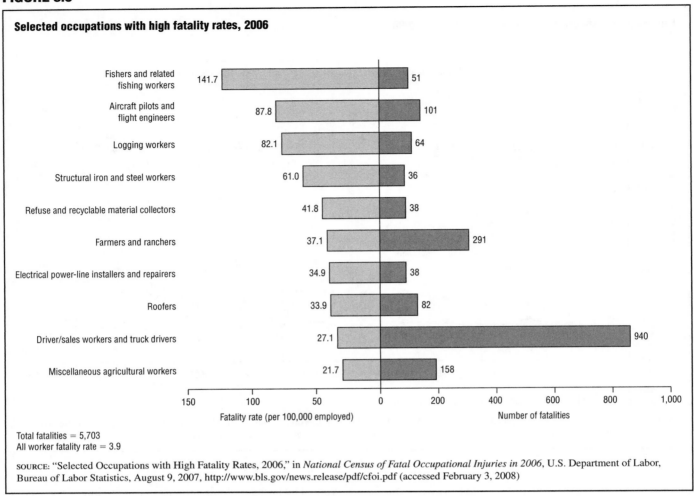

Selected occupations with high fatality rates, 2006

Total fatalities = 5,703
All worker fatality rate = 3.9

SOURCE: "Selected Occupations with High Fatality Rates, 2006," in *National Census of Fatal Occupational Injuries in 2006*, U.S. Department of Labor, Bureau of Labor Statistics, August 9, 2007, http://www.bls.gov/news.release/pdf/cfoi.pdf (accessed February 3, 2008)

employers are required to ensure that workers are not subjected to sexual harassment.

Discrimination

There are many national laws protecting employees from discrimination in the workplace with respect to hiring, compensation, terms, conditions, and privileges of employment. These laws cover employees in all types of businesses, from very large to very small. They also apply to employment agencies and labor organizations. State and local laws extend the coverage of the federal statutes in different ways. Some state laws extend federal protections to employers who are not covered by those statutes because of their small size, for example. Other states protect against discrimination based on factors not covered by federal law, such as sexual preference.

Although sometimes discrimination complaints are filed with the Equal Employment Opportunity Commission (EEOC), many other incidents of workplace discrimination in the workplace are never brought to the attention of the EEOC. Instead, as described in the Level Playing Field Institute survey *The Cost of Employee*

Turnover Due Solely to Unfairness in the Workplace (2006, http://www.lpfi.org/docs/cl-executive-summary.pdf), victims suffer silently or leave their places of employment.

GENDER DISCRIMINATION. The Equal Pay Act of 1963 (P.L. 88-38) establishes that employers cannot pay lower wages to an employee based on gender. Equal pay must be paid to workers for equal work if the jobs they perform require "equal skill, effort, and responsibility and are performed under similar working conditions."

In fiscal year (FY) 2007, 24,826 cases were filed with the EEOC alleging sex-based discrimination, as reported in *Enforcement Statistics and Litigation* (February 26, 2008, http://www.eeoc.gov/stats/sex.html). That same year, the EEOC resolved 21,982 charges. Of those, 2,900 (13.2%) were settled, with payments totaling $135.4 million to the charging parties. The percent of cases settled was up substantially since 1997, when only 4.1% were settled. In 2007 another 1,299 (5.9%) of the claims were found to have reasonable cause; 439 (2%) of these were charges with reasonable cause closed after successful conciliation, and 860 (3.9%) of them were charges with reasonable cause closed after unsuccessful conciliation. Another

TABLE 8.2

Percent of establishments that have experienced an incident of workplace violence in the past 12 months, by type of incident, industry, and size, 2005

Industry[a] and size class	Total establishments	Total	Percent of establishments						
			Type of incident					No incident	Data not available
			Any incidents	Criminal	Customer or client	Co-worker	Domestic violence		
Total all ownerships									
Total all sizes	7,361,560	100.0	5.3	2.2	2.2	2.3	0.9	92.1	2.6
1–10	4,976,870	100.0	2.4	1.4	1.0	0.6	0.1	95.6	2.0
11–49	1,813,590	100.0	9.1	3.5	3.9	4.6	2.0	87.8	3.1
50–249	489,480	100.0	16.0	4.7	6.4	8.1	2.9	77.8	6.2
250–999	68,350	100.0	28.8	6.8	12.2	16.8	9.0	63.9	7.3
1,000+	13,280	100.0	49.9	17.2	28.3	34.1	24.1	43.8	6.2
Private industry[b]									
Total all sizes	7,144,950	100.0	4.8	2.1	1.9	2.1	0.8	92.5	2.7
1–10	4,890,830	100.0	2.2	1.4	0.9	0.5	—	95.7	2.0
11–49	1,748,090	100.0	8.6	3.5	3.6	4.4	2.0	88.2	3.2
50–249	439,730	100.0	15.2	4.6	5.4	8.1	2.8	78.0	6.9
250–999	56,760	100.0	26.6	6.3	9.6	16.9	9.1	64.9	8.5
1,000+	9,540	100.0	46.8	15.2	24.2	33.1	24.1	45.3	8.0
Goods producing									
Total all sizes	1,211,150	100.0	3.4	1.0	0.1	2.2	0.4	94.4	2.2
1–10	805,970	100.0	—	—	—	—	—	95.9	3.0
11–49	296,810	100.0	5.7	—	—	4.8	—	93.7	0.6
50–249	90,800	100.0	11.6	1.5	0.5	9.3	1.5	87.7	0.8
250–999	15,190	100.0	26.1	2.7	1.4	22.3	7.6	71.6	2.2
1,000+	2,390	100.0	43.9	5.4	3.8	39.7	17.2	46.4	9.6
Service providing									
Total all sizes	5,933,800	100.0	5.1	2.4	2.3	2.1	0.9	92.1	2.7
1–10	4,084,870	100.0	2.5	1.4	1.1	0.6	—	95.7	1.8
11–49	1,451,290	100.0	9.2	4.1	4.3	4.4	2.3	87.1	3.7
50–249	348,930	100.0	16.1	5.4	6.6	7.8	3.2	75.4	8.5
250–999	41,570	100.0	26.8	7.6	12.6	14.9	9.6	62.4	10.8
1,000+	7,150	100.0	47.6	18.3	31.0	30.9	26.4	44.9	7.4
State government									
Total all sizes	63,260	100.0	32.2	8.7	15.4	17.7	5.5	65.3	2.4
1–10	30,680	100.0	25.6	9.9	13.2	11.9	—	74.3	—
11–49	16,180	100.0	40.0	—	11.6	24.8	7.0	54.0	—
50–249	10,560	100.0	28.9	7.5	18.7	16.6	4.9	67.7	3.4
250–999	4,380	100.0	47.0	9.6	29.2	23.1	10.5	50.2	2.7
1,000+	1,450	100.0	65.5	24.8	40.7	51.7	31.7	30.3	4.1
Local government									
Total all sizes	153,360	100.0	14.7	3.7	10.3	4.3	2.1	85.1	0.2
1–10	55,360	100.0	4.8	0.8	2.3	3.3	1.1	95.2	—
11–49	49,310	100.0	15.5	4.4	12.7	2.3	0.8	84.0	—
50–249	39,190	100.0	21.8	5.1	14.9	5.6	2.9	78.1	—
250–999	7,210	100.0	35.0	9.4	22.5	12.5	7.6	64.6	0.4
1,000+	2,290	100.0	53.7	21.0	38.0	27.1	19.2	46.3	—

[a]*North American Industry Classification System*—United States, 2002.
[b]Excludes farms with fewer than 11 employees.
Notes: Survey respondents were asked to provide data for the 12 months prior to completing the survey. The 12-month period could fall from September 2004 to June 2006.
Because of rounding, data exclusion of nonclassifiable responses, omission of questionnaire response, and questions where more than one response is allowed, data do not sum to the totals. Dashes indicate data that do not meet publication guidelines

SOURCE: "Table 1. Percent of Establishments That Have Experienced an Incident of Workplace Violence in the 12 Months Prior to the Survey by Selected Type of Incident, Industry, and Size Class, 2005," in *Survey of Workplace Violence Prevention, 2005*, U.S. Department of Labor, Bureau of Labor Statistics, October 27, 2006, http://www.bls.gov/iif/oshwc/osnr0026.pdf (accessed February 5, 2008).

1,443 cases (6.6%) were withdrawn by the charging party on receipt of desired benefits ("withdrawals with benefits"). In other words, in FY 2007 over 4,600 cases of discrimination based on gender were found to have reasonable cause or were settled or withdrawn after the employer admitted culpability and submitted to a monetary settlement.

RACIAL DISCRIMINATION. The Civil Rights Act of 1964 (P.L. 88-352) makes it unlawful for an employer to discriminate against individuals on the basis of race, color, religion, national origin, or sex. This law was amended in 1978 (P.L. 95-555), making it unlawful for an employer to discriminate on the basis of pregnancy, childbirth, or a related medical condition. This law not only applies to

TABLE 8.3

Percent of establishments and employment, by type of security and size of establishment, 2005

	All size classes	1–10 workers	11–49 workers	50–249 workers	259–999 workers	1,000+ workers
Establishments						
At least one form of security	72.1	64.9	84.7	94.0	97.0	99.0
Electronic surveillance only	14.5	14.9	14.9	10.4	3.1	1.3
Security staff only	0.9	1.0	0.8	0.6	0.6	0.2
Physical security only	17.2	18.1	16.8	10.9	3.6	6.2
Physical security and either electronic surveillance or security staff	38.4	29.9	50.6	70.8	88.1	90.6
No security	26.6	33.4	14.6	5.6	2.8	0.8
Employment						
At least one form of security	90.8	69.8	86.5	94.4	97.2	99.2
Electronic surveillance only	8.7	14.3	14.8	9.2	2.9	1.2
Security staff only	0.7	1.2	0.9	0.7	1.0	0.1
Physical security only	10.2	18.2	16.3	10.0	3.4	3.4
Physical security and either electronic surveillance or security staff	69.8	35.1	52.9	73.1	88.4	93.6
No security	8.8	29.2	12.9	5.3	2.5	0.6

SOURCE: "Table A. Percent of Establishments and Employment by Type of Security and Size of Establishment, 2005," in *Survey of Workplace Violence Prevention, 2005*, U.S. Department of Labor, Bureau of Labor Statistics, October 27, 2006, http://www.bls.gov/iif/oshwc/osnr0026.pdf (accessed February 5, 2008)

hiring but also to promotion and termination. In 1997 the Supreme Court ruled in *Robinson v. Shell Oil Company* (No. 95-1376) that the Civil Rights Act of 1964 protected workers from retaliation for filing complaints about discrimination on the job. This ruling included forbidding retaliation in the form of a bad job recommendation after the worker is no longer employed.

In FY 2007 the EEOC received 30,510 charges alleging race-based discrimination. (See Table 8.4.) That same year the EEOC resolved 25,882 charges. Of those, 2,945 (11.4%) were settled, up from only 3.3% in FY 1997, with payments totaling $67.7 million to the charging parties. Another 998 (3.9%) of the claims were found to have reasonable cause; 285 (1.1%) of these were charges with reasonable cause closed after successful conciliation and 713 (2.8%) of them were charges with reasonable cause closed after unsuccessful conciliation. Another 1,235 cases (4.8%) were withdrawn by the charging party on receipt of desired benefits ("withdrawals with benefits"). Therefore, in FY 2007 nearly 3,200 cases of racial discrimination were found to have reasonable cause or were settled or withdrawn with benefits.

AGE DISCRIMINATION. The Age Discrimination in Employment Act of 1967 (P.L. 90-202) makes it unlawful for an employer to discriminate against individuals aged forty or older with respect to hiring, compensation, and employment on the basis of age.

In fiscal year 2007 the EEOC received 19,103 charges alleging age-based discrimination. (See Table 8.5.) That same year the EEOC resolved 16,134 charges. Of those, 1,795 (11.1%) were settled, a percentage that had risen gradually for ten years. Payments totaled $66.8 million to the charging parties. Another 625 (3.9%) of the

claims were found to have reasonable cause; 186 (1.2%) of these were charges with reasonable cause closed after successful conciliation, and 439 (2.7%) of them were charges with reasonable cause closed after unsuccessful conciliation. Another 958 cases (5.9%) were withdrawn by the charging party on receipt of desired benefits ("withdrawals with benefits"). Nearly 3,400 cases of age discrimination were found to have reasonable cause or were settled or withdrawn with benefits in FY 2007.

DISCRIMINATION AGAINST PEOPLE WITH DISABILITIES. The Americans with Disabilities Act of 1990 (ADA; P.L. 101-336) makes it unlawful for an employer to discriminate in hiring, compensating, or employing individuals with disabilities. This law applies to companies that have fifteen or more employees. The law requires reasonable accommodation for disabled applicants and employees. For example, if an employee cannot fit his or her wheelchair through the entrance to the workplace, the employer may be required to alter that entrance or provide a different work area. The ADA affected approximately fifty million Americans in 2008, according to the ADA Web site (http://www.ada.gov/).

In fiscal year 2007 the EEOC received 17,734 charges alleging discrimination based on disability. (See Table 8.6.) That same year the EEOC resolved 15,708 charges. Of those, 2,037 (13%) were settled, and payments totaled $54.4 million to the charging parties. Another 837 (5.3%) of the claims were found to have reasonable cause; 322 (2%) of these were charges with reasonable cause closed after successful conciliation, and 515 (3.3%) of them were charges with reasonable cause closed after unsuccessful conciliation. Another 1,005 cases (6.4%) were withdrawn by the charging party on receipt of desired benefits ("with-

TABLE 8.4

Race-based charges filed and resolved under Title VII of the Civil Rights Act of 1964, fiscal years 1997–2007

	FY 1997	FY 1998	FY 1999	FY 2000	FY 2001	FY 2002	FY 2003	FY 2004	FY 2005	FY 2006	FY 2007
Receipts	29,199	28,820	28,819	28,945	28,912	29,910	28,526	27,696	26,740	27,238	30,510
Resolutions	36,419	35,716	35,094	33,188	32,077	33,199	30,702	29,631	27,411	25,992	25,882
Resolutions by type											
Settlements	1,206	1,460	2,138	2,802	2,549	3,059	2,890	2,927	2,801	3,039	2,945
	3.3%	4.1%	6.1%	8.4%	7.9%	9.2%	9.4%	9.9%	10.2%	11.7%	11.4%
Withdrawals with benefits	912	823	1,036	1,150	1,203	1,200	1,125	1,088	1,167	1,177	1,235
	2.5%	2.3%	3.0%	3.5%	3.8%	3.6%	3.7%	3.7%	4.3%	4.5%	4.8%
Administrative closures	8,395	7,871	7,213	5,727	5,626	5,043	4,759	4,261	3,674	3,436	3,931
	23.1%	22.0%	20.6%	17.3%	17.5%	15.2%	15.5%	14.4%	13.4%	13.2%	15.2%
No reasonable cause	24,988	24,515	23,148	21,319	20,302	21,853	20,506	20,166	18,608	17,324	16,773
	68.6%	68.6%	66.0%	64.2%	63.3%	65.8%	66.8%	68.1%	67.9%	66.7%	64.8%
Reasonable cause	918	1,047	1,559	2,190	2,397	2,044	1,422	1,189	1,161	1,016	998
	2.5%	2.9%	4.4%	6.6%	7.5%	6.2%	4.6%	4.0%	4.2%	3.9%	3.9%
Successful conciliations	248	287	382	529	691	580	392	330	377	292	285
	0.7%	0.8%	1.1%	1.6%	2.2%	1.7%	1.3%	1.1%	1.4%	1.1%	1.1%
Unsuccessful conciliations	670	760	1,177	1,661	1,706	1,464	1,030	859	784	724	713
	1.8%	2.1%	3.4%	5.0%	5.3%	4.4%	3.4%	2.9%	2.9%	2.8%	2.8%
Merit resolutions	3,036	3,330	4,733	6,142	6,149	6,303	5,437	5,204	5,129	5,232	5,178
	8.3%	9.3%	13.5%	18.5%	19.2%	19.0%	17.7%	17.6%	18.7%	20.1%	20.0%
Monetary benefits (millions)*	$41.8	$32.2	$53.2	$61.7	$86.5	$81.1	$69.6	$61.1	$76.5	$61.4	$67.7

*Does not include monetary benefits obtained through litigation. FY = Fiscal year.
Notes: The total of individual percentages may not always sum to 100% due to rounding. Equal Employment Opportunity Commission (EEOC) total workload includes charges carried over from previous fiscal years, new charge receipts and charges transferred to EEOC from Fair Employment Practice Agencies (FEPAs). Resolution of charges each year may therefore exceed receipts for that year because workload being resolved is drawn from a combination of pending, new receipts and Fair Employment Practices Act (FEPA) transfer charges rather than from new charges only.

SOURCE: "Race-Based Charges, FY 1997–FY2007," in *Enforcement Statistics and Litigation*, U.S. Equal Employment Opportunity Commission, February 26, 2008, http://www.eeoc.gov/stats/race.html (accessed February 28, 2008)

TABLE 8.5

Age discrimination charged filed with the Equal Employment Opportunity Commission, fiscal years 1997–2007

	FY 1997	FY 1998	FY 1999	FY 2000	FY 2001	FY 2002	FY 2003	FY 2004	FY 2005	FY 2006	FY 2007
Receipts	15,785	15,191	14,141	16,008	17,405	19,921	19,124	17,837	16,585	16,548	19,103
Resolutions	18,279	15,995	15,448	14,672	15,155	18,673	17,352	15,792	14,076	14,146	16,134
Resolutions by type											
Settlements	642	755	816	1,156	1,006	1,222	1,285	1,377	1,326	1,417	1,795
	3.5%	4.7%	5.3%	7.9%	6.6%	6.5%	7.4%	8.7%	9.4%	10.0%	11.1%
Withdrawals with benefits	762	580	578	560	551	671	710	787	764	767	958
	4.2%	3.6%	3.7%	3.8%	3.6%	3.6%	4.1%	5.0%	5.4%	5.4%	5.9%
Administrative closures	4,986	4,175	3,601	3,232	3,963	6,254	2,824	3,550	2,537	2,639	2,754
	27.3%	26.1%	23.3%	22.0%	26.1%	33.5%	16.3%	22.5%	18.0%	18.7%	17.1%
No reasonable cause	11,163	9,863	9,172	8,517	8,388	9,725	11,976	9,563	8,866	8,746	10,002
	61.1%	61.7%	59.4%	58.0%	55.3%	52.1%	69.0%	60.6%	63.0%	61.8%	62.0%
Reasonable cause	726	622	1,281	1,207	1,247	801	557	515	583	612	625
	4.0%	3.9%	8.3%	8.2%	8.2%	4.3%	3.2%	3.3%	4.1%	4.3%	3.9%
Successful conciliations	74	119	184	241	409	208	166	139	169	177	186
	0.4%	0.7%	1.2%	1.6%	2.7%	1.1%	1.0%	0.9%	1.2%	1.3%	1.2%
Unsuccessful conciliations	652	503	1,097	966	838	593	391	376	414	435	439
	3.6%	3.1%	7.1%	6.6%	5.5%	3.2%	2.3%	2.4%	2.9%	3.1%	2.7%
Merit resolutions	2,130	1,957	2,675	2,923	2,804	2,694	2,552	2,679	2,673	2,796	3,378
	11.7%	12.2%	17.3%	19.9%	18.5%	14.4%	14.7%	17.0%	19.0%	19.8%	20.9%
Monetary benefits (millions)*	$44.3	$34.7	$38.6	$45.2	$53.7	$55.7	$48.9	$69.0	$77.7	$51.5	$66.8

*Does not include monetary benefits obtained through litigation. FY = Fiscal year.
Notes: The total of individual percentages may not always sum to 100% due to rounding. Equal Employment Opportunity Commission (EEOC) total workload includes charges carried over from previous fiscal years, new charge receipts and charges transferred to EEOC from Fair Employment Practice Agencies (FEPAs). Resolution of charges each year may therefore exceed receipts for that year because workload being resolved is drawn from a combination of pending, new receipts and Fair Employment Practices Act (FEPA) transfer charges rather than from new charges only.

SOURCE: "Age Discrimination in Employment Act (ADEA) Charges, FY 1997–FY 2007," in *Enforcement Statistics and Litigation*, U.S. Equal Employment Opportunity Commission, February 26, 2008, http://www.eeoc.gov/stats/adea.html (accessed February 28, 2008)

TABLE 8.6

Disabilities-based charges filed under the Americans with Disabilities Act (ADA) of 1990, fiscal years 1997–2007

	FY 1997	FY 1998	FY 1999	FY 2000	FY 2001	FY 2002	FY 2003	FY 2004	FY 2005	FY 2006	FY 2007	Cumulative total 7/26/92–9/30/07
Receipts	18,108	17,806	17,007	15,864	16,470	15,964	15,377	15,376	14,893	15,575	17,734	253,199
Resolutions	24,200	23,324	22,152	20,475	19,084	18,804	16,915	16,949	15,357	15,045	15,708	267,477
Resolutions by type												
Settlements	1,000	1,154	1,433	1,852	1,722	1,705	1,748	1,800	1,685	1,812	2,037	20,695
	4.1%	4.9%	6.5%	9.0%	9.0%	9.1%	10.3%	10.6%	11.0%	12.0%	13.0%	8.2%
Withdrawals with benefits	888	816	867	862	834	833	750	814	846	866	1,005	13,478
	3.7%	3.5%	3.9%	4.2%	4.4%	4.4%	4.4%	4.8%	5.5%	5.8%	6.4%	5.4%
Administrative closures	7,336	6,461	5,434	4,209	3,662	3,335	2,995	3,083	2,691	2,452	2,861	68,017
	30.3%	27.7%	24.5%	20.6%	19.2%	17.7%	17.7%	18.2%	17.5%	16.3%	18.2%	27.0%
No reasonable cause	13,916	13,458	12,753	11,431	10,332	11,346	10,251	10,318	9,268	9,077	8,968	148,708
	57.5%	57.7%	57.6%	55.8%	54.1%	60.3%	60.6%	60.9%	60.4%	60.3%	57.1%	59.1%
Reasonable cause	1,060	1,435	1,665	2,121	2,534	1,585	1,171	934	867	850	837	16,591
	4.4%	6.2%	7.5%	10.4%	13.3%	8.4%	6.9%	5.5%	5.6%	5.6%	5.3%	6.6%
Successful	385	535	518	663	741	644	487	357	338	330	322	5,852
	1.6%	2.3%	2.3%	3.2%	3.9%	3.4%	2.9%	2.1%	2.2%	2.2%	2.0%	2.3%
Unsuccessful	675	900	1,147	1,458	1,793	941	684	577	529	520	515	10,739
	2.8%	3.9%	5.2%	7.1%	9.4%	5.0%	4.0%	3.4%	3.4%	3.5%	3.3%	4.3%
Merit resolutions	2,948	3,405	3,965	4,835	5,090	4,123	3,669	3,548	3,398	3,528	3,879	50,764
	12.2%	14.7%	17.9%	23.6%	26.7%	21.9%	21.7%	20.9%	22.1%	23.4%	24.7%	20.2%
Monetary benefits(millions)	$41.3	$53.7	$55.8	$54.4	$47.9	$50.0	$45.3	$47.7	$44.8	$48.8	$54.4	$677.0

*Does not include monetary benefits obtained through litigation. FY = Fiscal year.

Notes: The total of individual percentages may not always sum to 100% due to rounding. Equal Employment Opportunity Commission (EEOC) total workload includes charges carried over from previous fiscal years, new charge receipts and charges transferred to EEOC from Fair Employment Practice Agencies (FEPAs). Resolution of charges each year may therefore exceed receipts for that year because workload being resolved is drawn from a combination of pending, new receipts and Fair Employment Practices Act (FEPA) transfer charges rather than from new charges only.

SOURCE: "Americans with Disabilities Act of 1990 (ADA) Charges, FY 1997–FY 2007," in *Enforcement Statistics and Litigation*, U.S. Equal Employment Opportunity Commission, February 26, 2008, http://www.eeoc.gov/stats/ada-charges.html (accessed February 28, 2008).

drawals with benefits"). Nearly 3,900 cases of discrimination based on disability were found to have reasonable cause or were settled or withdrawn with benefits in FY 2007.

In November 1999 Congress supplemented the provisions of the ADA with the Ticket to Work and Work Incentives Improvement Act (TWWIIA) to give Americans with disabilities both the incentive and the means to seek employment. In part this provides assurance to disabled workers that they will not lose their medical insurance if their income or savings exceed certain levels.

Sexual Harassment

Workers have the right to be free from sexual harassment—unwelcome sexual advances or conduct—from supervisors and coworkers, as well as from customers and clients. There are two main forms of sexual harassment. One is demanding sexual favors in return for job benefits over which the individual has some control, such as promotions. This is known as quid pro quo sexual harassment. Another type is "hostile work environment" sexual harassment. When individuals use obscene language, post lewd pictures, make unwelcome sexual advances, or talk about sex in an offensive manner, they are creating a hostile work environment.

Sexual harassment is a violation of the 1964 Civil Rights Act, as amended in 1972 (P.L. 92-261). Under the Civil Rights Act of 1991 (P.L. 102-166), victims of sexual harassment are entitled to damages for pain and suffering, as well as to any lost pay resulting from the harassment. The EEOC defines sexual harassment as unwelcome sexual advances, requests for sexual favors, and other verbal or physical conduct of a sexual nature.

In fiscal year 2007 the EEOC received 12,510 charges alleging sexual harassment; 84% of them were from women. (See Table 8.7.) That same year the EEOC resolved 11,592 charges. Of those, 1,571 (13.6%) were settled. Payments totaled $49.9 million to the charging parties. Another 767 (6.6%) of the claims were found to have reasonable cause; 282 (2.4%) of these were charges with reasonable cause closed after successful conciliation, and 485 (4.2%) of them were charges with reasonable cause closed after unsuccessful conciliation. Another 1,177 cases (10.2%) were withdrawn by the charging party on receipt of desired benefits ("withdrawals with benefits"). Over 3,500 cases of sexual harassment brought before the EEOC or state or local Fair Employment Practices agencies were found to have reasonable cause or were settled or withdrawn with benefits in FY 2007.

TABLE 8.7

Sexual harassment charges filed with the Equal Employment Opportunity Commission and state and local Fair Employment Practices agencies, fiscal years 1997–2007

[Chart represents the total number of charge receipts filed and resolved under Title VII alleging sexual harassment discrimination as an issue. Data reflect charges filed with EEOC and the state and local fair employment practices agencies around the country that have a work sharing agreement with the commission.]

	FY 1997	FY 1998	FY 1999	FY 2000	FY 2001	FY 2002	FY 2003	FY 2004	FY 2005	FY 2006	FY 2007
Receipts	15,889	15,618	15,222	15,836	15,475	14,396	13,566	13,136	12,679	12,025	12,510
% of charges filed by males	11.6%	12.9%	12.1%	13.6%	13.7%	14.9%	14.7%	15.1%	14.3%	15.4%	16.0%
Resolutions	17,333	17,115	16,524	16,726	16,383	15,792	14,534	13,786	12,859	11,936	11,592
Resolutions by type											
Settlements	1,178	1,218	1,361	1,676	1,568	1,692	1,783	1,646	1,471	1,458	1,571
	6.8%	7.1%	8.2%	10.0%	9.6%	10.7%	12.3%	11.9%	11.4%	12.2%	13.6%
Withdrawals with benefits	1,267	1,311	1,299	1,389	1,454	1,235	1,300	1,138	1,146	1,175	1,177
	7.3%	7.7%	7.9%	8.3%	8.9%	7.8%	8.9%	8.3%	8.9%	9.8%	10.2%
Administrative closures	6,908	6,296	5,412	4,632	4,306	3,957	3,600	3,256	2,808	2,838	2,804
	39.9%	36.8%	32.8%	27.7%	26.3%	25.1%	24.8%	23.6%	21.8%	23.8%	24.2%
No reasonable cause	7,172	7,243	7,272	7,370	7,309	7,445	6,703	6,708	6,364	5,668	5,273
	41.4%	42.3%	44.0%	44.1%	44.6%	47.1%	46.1%	48.7%	49.5%	47.5%	45.5%
Reasonable cause	808	1,047	1,180	1,659	1,746	1,463	1,148	1,037	1,070	797	767
	4.7%	6.1%	7.1%	9.9%	10.7%	9.3%	7.9%	7.5%	8.3%	6.7%	6.6%
Successful conciliations	298	357	383	524	551	455	350	311	324	253	282
	1.7%	2.1%	2.3%	3.1%	3.4%	2.9%	2.4%	2.3%	2.5%	2.1%	2.4%
Unsuccessful conciliations	510	690	797	1,135	1,195	1,008	798	726	746	544	485
	2.9%	4.0%	4.8%	6.8%	7.3%	6.4%	5.5%	5.3%	5.8%	4.6%	4.2%
Merit resolutions	3,253	3,576	3,840	4,724	4,768	4,390	4,231	3,821	3,687	3,430	3,515
	18.8%	20.9%	23.2%	28.2%	29.1%	27.8%	29.1%	27.7%	28.7%	28.7%	30.3%
Monetary benefits (millions)*	$49.5	$34.3	$50.3	$54.6	$53.0	$50.3	$50.0	$37.1	$47.9	$48.8	$49.9

*Does not include monetary benefits obtained through litigation. FY = Fiscal year.
Notes: The total of individual percentages may not always sum to 100% due to rounding. Equal Employment Opportunity Commission (EEOC) total workload includes charges carried over from previous fiscal years, new charge receipts and charges transferred to EEOC from Fair Employment Practice Agencies (FEPAs). Resolution of charges each year may therefore exceed receipts for that year because workload being resolved is drawn from a combination of pending, new receipts and FEPA transfer charges rather than from new charges only.

SOURCE: "Sexual Harassment Charges, EEOC and FEPAS Combined: FY1997–FY2007," in *Enforcement Statistics and Litigation*, U.S. Equal Employment Opportunity Commission, February 26, 2008, http://www.eeoc.gov/stats/harass.html (accessed February 28, 2008)

THE RIGHT TO JOIN A UNION

The National Labor Relations Act of 1935 (49 Stat. 449) guarantees nonsupervisory employees the right to organize a union, to choose their own representatives, and to bargain collectively with their employer for higher pay, better benefits, improved working conditions, and more relaxed work rules. Workers have the right to join a union if one exists or to help organize one if one does not exist. The law prohibits employers from punishing employees who exercise their right to join a union and participate in union activities. Workers in a company who want to form a union must ask a federal or state agency, such as the National Labor Relations Board, to hold an election to determine if a majority of workers want to be represented by a union.

In certain organizations workers may be required to join a union after they are hired; such workplaces are called union shops. Twenty-two states have enacted right-to-work laws that prohibit union shops, and most are located in the South and Midwest. A list of right-to-work states compiled by the DOL as of January 2008 (http://www.dol.gov/esa/programs/whd/state/righttowork .htm) included: Alabama, Arizona, Arkansas, Florida, Georgia, Idaho, Iowa, Kansas, Louisiana, Mississippi, Nebraska, Nevada, North Carolina, North Dakota, Oklahoma, South Carolina, South Dakota, Tennessee, Texas, Utah, Virginia, and Wyoming. This means that to get or hold a job in these states, workers do not have to join a union if one exists. Closed shops, in which only union members in good standing can be hired, were outlawed by the Taft-Hartley Act in 1947.

By law all workers in a bargaining unit are entitled to the benefits gained through union collective bargaining, whether they are union members or not. Nonunion workers employed by a unionized company get the same benefits as union members, even if they do not join the union.

Although unions historically developed in order to represent the interests of the working class, they also have a growing presence in professional specialties. The Union of American Physicians and Dentists was formed in California in 1972 and by 2008 totaled 3,000 members. Their initiative to organize was driven partly by policies that made it possible for patients to sue for malpractice under state laws, but their efforts also provide doctors with representation in contract negotiations and in disputes with such entities as hospital administrations, HMOs, insurance companies, and medical boards.

EMPLOYER TESTING

Employers may administer various tests to potential or current employees in order to determine their fitness to perform the duties of a position. For example, as testing technologies improved and became widely available during the 1980s and '90s, many companies introduced testing for the use of drugs or began administering polygraph (lie detector) exams and psychological tests.

Drug and Alcohol Testing

Growing concern over the impact of drug and alcohol abuse in the workplace has led to an increase in the number of employers who test for drug and alcohol abuse. These tests are performed on employees and, increasingly, on job applicants. Workers in some jobs, such as airline pilots, are required by law to submit to drug and alcohol testing, but an increasing number of employers are requiring employees to submit to testing as a condition of employment.

Some programs use mandatory and random testing. Others test only on the basis of reasonable suspicion. Workers in jobs that are particularly related to safety or security concerns are more likely to be tested. The Omnibus Transportation Employee Testing Act of 1991 requires certain employers to have drug-free workplace programs that include drug and alcohol testing of workers in "safety-sensitive" positions, such as those who operate airplanes, buses, and large trucks.

What happens to job applicants or employees who refuse to take drug tests? That depends on where they work and any applicable state law. In many cases refusal to take the test is grounds for not getting a job or being fired.

If a job applicant takes the test and tests positive, he or she may not get the job. If a worker tests positive on a random drug test, treatment and counseling sponsored by the company may be given or employment may be terminated.

These tests have led to controversy throughout the country because many people think the tests invade personal privacy. By 2006 some states (California, Florida, Georgia, Illinois, and South Carolina) required state contractors to have drug-free workplace programs in place. Another twenty states, however, regulated drug-testing procedures to protect the rights of employees. Some states ban or restrict random drug testing, while others required that a second, confirmatory drug test be given if the first one was positive. Some states required that the results of these tests be kept confidential, while others limited the type of discipline employers can mete out to employees who fail drug tests. The National Conference of State Legislatures provides comparative information on state drug-testing laws online in "State Statute Chart on Drug Testing in the Workplace" (January 2006, http://www.ncsl.org/programs/employ/drugtest.htm).

Polygraph Exams

At one time it was popular among many employers to use polygraph tests on their employees. Workers often resented these tests, and their aversion eventually led a number of states to pass laws limiting their use. In 1988 Congress passed the Employee Polygraph Protection Act (P.L. 100-347), which prohibits most private employers from using lie detector tests either for pre-employment screening or during the course of employment. In most circumstances employers are prohibited from requiring or requesting any employee or job applicant to take a lie detector test. Employers are also prevented from discharging, disciplining, or discriminating against an employee or prospective employee for refusing to take a test or for exercising other rights under this act.

Still, many employers may administer these tests. Federal, state, and local governments are exempt from the Employee Polygraph Protection Act, and the law does not apply to tests given by the federal government to certain private individuals engaged in national security–related activities. Furthermore, the act permits polygraph tests to be administered in the private sector to certain prospective employees of security service firms and pharmaceutical manufacturers, distributors, and dispensers.

The act also permits polygraph testing of certain employees who are reasonably suspected of involvement in a workplace incident, such as theft or embezzlement, that resulted in economic loss to the employer. Some restrictions may apply in these cases, and state or local law or collective bargaining agreements may be more restrictive.

Where polygraph tests are permitted, they are subject to numerous strict standards concerning the conduct and length of the test. People who take polygraph tests have a number of specific rights, including the right to a written notice before testing, the right to refuse or discontinue a test, and the right not to have test results disclosed to unauthorized individuals.

In cases where employers cannot legally administer polygraph testing, they may instead be able to administer what is known as honesty testing. This form of testing is typically a written true or false test that offers choices of alternatives of behavior in given circumstances. There are no wrong answers, but evaluators believe they can use the results to determine patterns of behavior and, therefore, predict who is at high risk for dishonest behavior. Honesty testing has opponents, including some labor unions and others that are concerned about where to draw the line regarding privacy. On the other hand, such methods sustain interest from employers, who wish to make the best hiring decisions and minimize, in some cases, company theft. Employers may also request information such as applicants' credit reports or criminal records.

Psychological Testing

Concerned about the high costs and legal problems that can result from hiring the wrong person for the job, some employers administer psychological tests to prospective employees and to employees who are under consideration for promotions. According to David W. Arnold and Alan J. Thiemann of the Association of Personnel Test Publishers in "To Test or Not to Test: The Status of Psychological Testing under the ADA" (1992, http://eric.ed.gov/ERIC-Docs/data/ericdocs2sql/content_storage_01/0000019b/80/13/57/7b.pdf), these tests do not violate requirements of the ADA if they are used only to assess personality traits, behavior, or attitudes and are not designed to uncover a mental or psychological disorder. For instance, employers may administer personality tests to determine a prospective employee's suitability for a particular job, especially when the job is a sensitive position in the public trust, such as a police officer or firefighter.

In "Employment Tests and Selection Procedures" (February 2008, http://www.eeoc.gov/policy/docs/factemployment_procedures.html) the EEOC warns employers wishing to use psychological testing that these tests should be administered without regard to race, ethnicity, sex, religion, age, or disability; that the tests should be used for very specific, job-related results; and that employers and managers should not use psychological testing casually—the effectiveness and limitations of specific tests should be thoroughly understood and appreciated before they are administered or scored.

PRIVACY RIGHTS

Employees whose jobs involve computers, telephones, and other communications equipment are guaranteed few rights to privacy while at work. The Electronic Communications Privacy Act of 1986 (ECPA), which prohibits the intentional interception of electronic communications, nevertheless allows employers to monitor their workers while on the job. In *Fraser v. Nationwide Mutual Insurance Co.* (3rd Cir. 2003), the court ruled that a company is permitted to review e-mail stored on its own computers. In the court's opinion, the ECPA outlawed *interception* of communications, but stored e-mails were exempt and could be legally reviewed by employers. According to the Privacy Rights Clearinghouse in "Fact Sheet 18: Online Privacy" (April 2008, http://www.privacyrights.org/fs/fs18-cyb.htm), "If the e-mail system is owned by an employer, the employer may inspect the contents of employee e-mail on the system. Therefore, any e-mail sent from a business location is probably not private."

In fact, according to the American Management Association and the ePolicy Institute in *2007 Electronic Monitoring & Surveillance Survey* (February 28, 2008, http://press.amanet.org/press-releases/177/2007-electronic-monitoring-surveillance-survey/), many companies are now monitoring, recording, and videotaping their employees. Two-thirds of all surveyed employers (66%) monitored employees' Internet connections, and 65% of the companies reported using software to block inappropriate sites. Nearly half (43%) of the companies had systems in place to store employees' computer files and e-mail for subsequent review, while 45% tracked content, keystrokes, and time spent at the keyboard. According to the survey, more than a quarter (28%) of all employers had fired workers for misusing e-mail, including inappropriate or offensive language or excessive personal use. Almost one-third (30%) had fired employees for misusing the Internet, including viewing inappropriate or offensive content or excessive personal use.

Compared with the rates of surveillance for Internet use, companies monitored employees' phone use to a much lesser extent. Only 6% of companies in the *2007 Electronic Monitoring & Surveillance Survey* confirmed that they had fired employees for misusing the telephone, although 45% monitored time spent on the phone and the numbers called, and 16% recorded some or all employees' phone conversations. As of 2007, with few federal or state statutes addressing worker privacy, many companies were adopting policies that informed workers their communications and on-the-job activities would be monitored and that they should have no expectation of privacy while at work.

CHAPTER 9
BUSINESS OPPORTUNITIES

Starting or acquiring a business has long been valued as part of the American dream. For many Americans, this dream is a reality, whether the business is a part-time venture with annual receipts of less than $25,000 or a corporate entity with receipts of millions of dollars per year. For the purpose of discussing the present and future of self-ownership business opportunities in the United States, the material in this chapter will focus primarily on what has been published about small business and home-based business from a variety of sources, including the U.S. Census Bureau (http://www.census.gov/) and the U.S. Small Business Administration (SBA; http://www.sba.gov/).

In its efforts to estimate the number of small businesses in the country, the U.S. Census Bureau counts Schedule C businesses (individual proprietorship or self-employed individuals), partnerships, and Subchapter S corporations (usually small corporations in which the profits pass through to the owners without being taxed first). It does not count the large number of small businesses incorporated as standard corporations.

Every five years, in years ending in "2" and "7," the U.S. Census Bureau surveys business enterprises and publishes an Economic Census that compiles and analyzes a wide variety of statistical data about business and industry. The entire report is published in stages, starting two years after the designated census date. The most recent reports available are taken from the Economic Census of 2002, and these reports provide the most accurate data available concerning the state of small business at the turn of the twenty-first century.

STARTING A BUSINESS
How Many Americans Are Beginning Small Businesses?

Self-employment is on the rise. In 2005, 10.1% of all workers were self-employed. (See Table 9.1.) This was a 13.1% increase since 1995. The self-employment rate of some groups is rising faster than others. Asians and Native Americans had a self-employment rate of 10.6% in 2005, a 60.6% increase since 1995. African-Americans, while having a relatively low self-employment rate of 4.5% in 2005, are increasing their numbers quickly; the number of self-employed African-Americans increased by 26.6% between 1995 and 2005. Hispanics increased their self-employment rate by 95.7% over the course of that decade; by 2005, 6.7% of Hispanics were self-employed. Although women had a lower self-employment rate than did men in 2005 (7.2% and 12.7%, respectively), their rate rose faster in the 1995–2005 period than did men's (13.3% and 12.9%, respectively).

According to the SBA, more than five hundred thousand businesses started (called employer births) each year between 1990 and 2006. (See Table 9.2.) In the years between 1990 and 2006, the highest number of business starts in one year occurred in 2005, with 653,100 small business starts that year, followed closely by 2006, which saw 649,700 small business starts.

Why Start a Business?

In the *Characteristics of Business Owners Survey* conducted by the U.S. Census Bureau in 1992 (http://www.census.gov/prod/3/97pubs/cbo-9201.pdf), business owners were queried on the reasons for embarking on their own business ventures. These particular statistics were not updated in the 1997 or 2002 surveys. The 1992 survey revealed that one-fifth (21.3%) of business owners reported that they became an owner to have a primary source of income, while one-fourth (25.6%) wanted to have a secondary source of income. Another one-fifth (21.5%) wanted to be their own boss. Less than 3% said their primary reason was to bring a new idea to the marketplace. Approximately 8% wanted to have more freedom to meet family responsibilities.

TABLE 9.1

Self-employment demographics, 1995–2005

	Self-employment rate, 2005	Percent change 1995–2005
Total	**10.1**	**13.1**
Female	7.2	13.3
Male	12.7	12.9
Asian/American Indian	10.6	60.6
Black	4.5	26.6
White	10.9	8.7
Multiple race	9.3	NA
Hispanic origin	6.7	95.7
Veteran status	15.1	−22.3

NA = Not available.

Notes: Self-employment (incorporated and unincorporated) was the primary occupation during the year. Self-employment figures presented here differ from the published monthly annual averages. Asian/American Indian = Asian, Pacific, Hawaiian, American Indian and Aleut Eskimo. The rate is the self-employment divided by the number of individuals that had any job during the year.

SOURCE: "Table 1.3. Self-Employment Demographics, 1995–2005," in *The Small Business Economy 2007*, U.S. Small Business Administration, Office of Advocacy, December 2007, http://www.sba.gov/advo/research/sb_econ2007.pdf (accessed February 21, 2008)

TABLE 9.2

Business turnover, 1990–2006

Year	Employer births	Employer terminations	Business bankruptcies
2006	649,700 e.	564,900 e.	19,695
2005	653,100 e.	543,700 e.	39,201
2004	628,917	541,047	34,317
2003	612,296	540,658	35,037
2002	569,750	586,890	38,540
2001	585,140	553,291	40,099
2000	574,300	542,831	35,472
1999	579,609	544,487	37,884
1998	589,982	540,601	44,367
1997	590,644	530,003	54,027
1996	597,792	512,402	53,549
1995	594,369	497,246	51,959
1994	570,587	503,563	52,374
1993	564,504	492,651	62,304
1992	544,596	521,606	70,643
1991	541,141	546,518	71,549
1990	584,892	531,400	64,853

Note: e. = estimate.

SOURCE: Adapted from "Table A.2. Business Turnover, 1985–2006," in *The Small Business Economy 2007*, U.S. Small Business Administration, Office of Advocacy, December 2007, http://www.sba.gov/advo/research/sb_econ2007.pdf (accessed February 21, 2008)

The SBA, in "Is Entrepreneurship for You?" (http://www.sba.gov/smallbusinessplanner/plan/getready/SERV_SBPLANNER_ISENTFORU.html), suggests that potential entrepreneurs assess their strengths and weaknesses as they prepare to start a small business in order to minimize the risks involved. The organization suggests answering questions such as: Are you a self starter? Are you able to get along with people with different personalities? Are you able to make decisions quickly and under pressure? Do you have the ability to commit to long workdays and workweeks? Are you able to plan? Are you organized? Do you have the emotional stamina and drive to shoulder all the responsibility for your business's success or failure? Are you prepared for the business's effects on your family life? After honestly considering these questions, a potential small business owner may decide to move forward, or not.

Business Plan

All entrepreneurs need a business plan. This document should be a work-in-progress and be updated periodically as the business grows and changes. In "Write a Business Plan" (http://www.sba.gov/smallbusinessplanner/plan/writeabusinessplan/SERV_ESSENTIAL.html), the SBA outlines essential elements of the process:

- Executive Summary: Although this section appears first in a business plan, it should be the last section written. This section provides both an overview of the entire plan and a history of the company. It illustrates where the company is and where the owner wants to take it.

- A Market Analysis: This section should give an overview of the industry the business is in, the outlook of the industry, the business's target market, any marketing test results, and an overview of the competition.

- Company Description: This is a summary of the business, and how different parts of the business fit together. What is the nature of the business? Why will it be successful?

- Organization and Management: Here is a description of the structure of the business, its ownership, and profiles of all managers and anyone sitting on a board of directors. This section should include a description of the salaries and benefits of any paid managers or board members.

- Marketing and Sales Strategies: What is the business's marketing strategy? This part includes a strategy for growing the business, distributing the product, and communicating with customers. This section should be very detailed, including whether or not salespeople will be employed, how they will be recruited and what they will be paid, and what specific sales activities the business will conduct.

- Service or Product Line: This section should include a detailed description of the service or product provided and its benefits to customers. It should also include a summary of any plans to develop new products.

- Funding Request: This section should detail any funding needed to start or expand the business. It should include current funding requirements, funding requirements for the next five years, long-range financial strategies, and how funds will be used.

- Financials: If a business is already established, this section should include historical data on the company's finances for the past five years, including income, balance sheets, and cash flow statements. Start-ups as well as established businesses will need to provide prospective financial data for the next five years. Each year's documents should include expected income statements, balance sheets, cash flow statements, and capital expenditures.

What Type of Business?

STRUCTURE. Most small businesses begin as sole proprietorships. In this type of business structure, one person owns the business, usually the person who has the responsibility for its day-to-day operations. Sole proprietors own all of the business's assets and all of its profits, but they also have complete responsibility for its debts. Basically, the owner and the business are one and the same. This is the easiest and least expensive way to organize a business that is just starting out, and this structure gives the owner unlimited control over the business and its profits. However, sole proprietors put both their businesses and personal assets at risk.

In partnerships, two or more people own a single business. Just like in sole proprietorships, the law does not distinguish between the business and its owners. If deciding to set up a business as a partnership, the owners should have a legal agreement that specifies how decisions will be made, profits shared, disputes resolved, and other partners admitted or bought out. Although a business with more than one owner has increased ability to raise funds, each partner is legally liable for the actions of other partners.

Corporations are considered to be a separate entity from the business's owners and therefore can be taxed, sued, and can enter into contracts separately from its owners, called its shareholders. Corporations are chartered by the state in which they are headquartered. This type of structure is more complicated to set up than sole proprietorships or partnerships, but shareholders have only limited liability for the debts of the corporation.

A limited liability company (LLC) is a hybrid business structure that can be set up in most states. It provides both the limited liability protection of incorporation and the flexibility of a partnership. The owners are members of the LLC. This business structure is more costly to set up than sole proprietorships or partnerships, as papers must be filed at the time of setup. The limited liability is time limited, although it can be extended at its expiration.

SIZE. Most business start-ups are very small. The U.S. Census Bureau, in *Nonemployer Statistics, 2005* (June 21, 2007, http://www.census.gov/epcd/nonemployer/2005/ us/US000.HTM), found that in 2005 there were almost 20.4 million nonemployer businesses in the United States, meaning they had no paid employees. The leading sector for nonemployer businesses in 2005, with approximately 2.9 million, was "other services," which included those employed in machinery repair, administering religious activities, personal care services, death care services, pet care services, photofinishing services, temporary parking services, and dating services. Closely following this sector, with almost 2.9 million businesses, was "professional, technical, and scientific services," including legal advice and representation, accounting and payroll services, architectural and engineering services, computer services, consulting services, research services, and veterinary services, among others. Other leading sectors included construction (2.5 million) and real estate and rental/leasing (2.4 million).

A 2003 analysis of 24.1 million full- and part-time business enterprises conducted by Patrick O'Rourke in *Useful Business Statistics* for BizStats ("Number of Business by Annual Revenue," http://www.bizstats.com/) revealed that 57.9% had annual revenues of less than $25,000. The proportion of businesses reporting revenues of less than $25,000 was 67.6% among sole proprietorships, which is the largest category of small business owners.

BUSINESS START-UP TYPES. Prospective entrepreneurs may decide to either start a business or buy an existing business. New start-ups can be particularly risky and difficult. Owners must create business plans, attract investors or attain other financing, and deal with the legal issues involved with new start-ups. However, people who choose to start a business have complete control over the entire process.

Buying an existing business may be appealing to entrepreneurs because there will be a drastic reduction in the time and energy needed to start the business, and cash flow may start immediately. If the business has been successful in the past, it may be easier to obtain financing. However, the large initial cost of purchasing an existing business may be a distinct disadvantage.

One way to become a small business owner is to buy a franchise. This is a legal relationship between the owner of a trademark or trade name and an individual who will use that trademark in a business. The franchise governs how the business will be run. Usually a franchisee sells goods or services provided by the franchiser. Franchising has distinct advantages to a prospective entrepreneur: The franchiser provides business expertise in the form of business and marketing plans, training, and the like to the small business owner, while the franchisee brings the energy and drive needed to build a successful small business. Entrepreneurs who choose to go this route will have less control over their businesses than they would if they bought existing businesses or began businesses of their own.

Safest and Riskiest Businesses

O'Rourke, in *Useful Business Statistics* for BizStats ("The Safest and Riskiest Small Business"), analyzes 120 categories of sole proprietorships and provides an overview of the safest and riskiest small businesses as of 2002, based on which categories had the highest number of sole proprietorships with profits. Four health care–related businesses appeared among the top ten safest businesses to start: optometrists had a 93% likelihood of profitability; dentists, 91.8%; mental health practitioners, 87.8%; and physicians, 87.1%. Also among the top ten were two construction-related categories: special trade contractors, with an 88.2% chance of profitability, and residential building construction, with 85.9%. Sole proprietorships experiencing less than 50% profitability and therefore were considered high risk included health and personal care stores (49.5%); videotape and disc rental stores (48.4%); computer and electronic products manufacturing (35.4%); and scenic and sightseeing transportation (33.8%).

Data from the Bureau of Labor Statistics (BLS) can also help evaluate the risk inherent in a proposed business. The BLS estimates that, overall, 81.2% of businesses begun in 1999 survived their first year. (See Table 9.3.) Businesses in certain sectors were more likely than others to survive. Businesses in education and health services were most likely to survive their first year (85.6%) as well as the subsequent four years, with manufacturing (84.2% survived their first year) and financial activities (84.1% survived their first year) also having high survival rates. Sectors that had lower than average survival rates included construction (80.7% survived their first year) and information services (80.8% survived their first year).

Perceptions of Success

A 2006 Gallup Poll found that despite the difficulties facing small business owners, most feel successful and say they would do it over again. When asked, "Overall, how successful do you feel you have been as a small business owner?" eight percent replied they had been extremely successful and another 39% said they had been very successful. (See Figure 9.1.) Nearly half (45%) answered that they had been at least somewhat successful. Only 7% said they had been not too successful or not at all successful.

In addition, according to Dennis Jacobe in the same Gallup Poll (*Most Small Business Owners Feel Successful*, The Gallup Organization, August 14, 2006, http://www.gallup.com/poll/24103/Most-Small-Business-Owners-Feel-Successful.aspx), 56% of small business owners surveyed

TABLE 9.3

Survival rates of new businesses, by sector and years since birth, 1999–2002

NAICS* supersector	First year (1999)	Second year (2000)	Third year (2001)	Fourth year (2002)
National	81.2	81.0	82.6	81.7
Natural resources and mining	82.3	84.5	85.4	83.4
Construction	80.7	81.5	81.5	79.5
Manufacturing	84.2	81.6	83.0	83.2
Trade, transportation, and utilities	82.6	80.9	81.9	81.7
Information	80.8	77.8	78.7	76.2
Financial activities	84.1	82.7	84.2	84.1
Professional and business services	82.3	81.2	82.5	80.3
Education and health services	85.6	85.1	87.5	86.9
Leisure and hospitality	81.2	80.1	82.5	81.6
Other services	80.7	80.3	82.3	82.3

*North American Industry Classification System.

SOURCE: Amy E. Knaup, "Table 1. Survival Rates of Previous Year's Survivors, by Sector and Years Since Birth, 1999–2002," in "Survival and Longevity in the Business Employment Dynamics Data," *Monthly Labor Review*, vol. 128, no. 5, May 2005, http://www.bls.gov/opub/mlr/2005/05/ressum.pdf (accessed February 28, 2008)

FIGURE 9.1

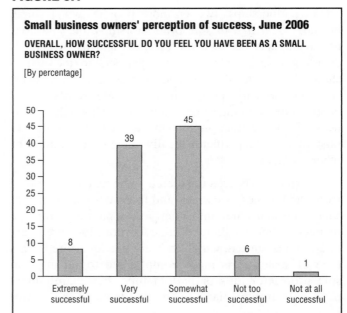

Small business owners' perception of success, June 2006

OVERALL, HOW SUCCESSFUL DO YOU FEEL YOU HAVE BEEN AS A SMALL BUSINESS OWNER?

[By percentage]

SOURCE: Dennis Jacobe, "Overall, How Successful Do You Feel You Have Been As a Small Business Owner?" in *Most Small Business Owners Feel Successful*, The Gallup Organization, August 14, 2006, http://www.gallup.com/poll/24103/Most-Small-Business-Owners-Feel-Successful.aspx (accessed February 18, 2008). Copyright © 2008 by The Gallup Organization. Reproduced by permission of The Gallup Organization.

said they were extremely or very satisfied with being a small business owner, and only 12% said they were not too satisfied or not at all satisfied. Four out of five (83%) said they would become a small business owner all over again if given a chance to do something else.

BUSINESS FAILURES AND TERMINATIONS

Business Bankruptcies

Bankruptcy is one measure of business failure. According to statistics from the SBA, between 1990 and 2006 the largest number of business bankruptcies occurred in 1991, when 71,549 businesses filed for bankruptcy. (See Table 9.2.) Since that time, the number of business bankruptcies has declined markedly. In 2006 the number of business bankruptcies was down drastically from the year before; in 2005, 39,201 businesses went bankrupt, while in 2006, only 19,695 businesses met this end.

Table 9.4 offers a state-by-state analysis of business bankruptcies in 2005 and 2006. Only two states, Connecticut and Delaware, saw a rise in business bankruptcies between 2005 and 2006. Some states saw especially dramatic decreases in bankruptcies, including California, which dropped from 4,236 in 2005 to 2,098 in 2006, a 50.5% decrease; Georgia, which dropped from 2,232 in 2005 to 1,148 in 2006, a 48.6% decrease; Minnesota, which dropped from 1,721 in 2005 to 381 in 2006, a 77.9% decrease; Ohio, which dropped from 2,099 in 2005 to 957 in 2006, a 54.4% decrease; Oklahoma, which dropped from 944 in 2005 to 236 in 2006, a 75% decrease; Oregon, which dropped from 1,160 in 2005 to 301 in 2006, a 74.1% decrease; and Utah, which dropped from 449 in 2006 to only 148 in 2006, a 67% decrease.

Business Closures

Business owners may also choose to terminate their businesses without declaring bankruptcy, and it should be noted that business owners may decide to terminate a business for a variety of reasons, including success that leads to a sale of the business, retirement, or merely the decision to pursue another line of work—in other words, a business closure does not mean the business was a failure. In 2005 nationwide, 543,700 businesses closed; in 2006, 564,900 businesses closed. Table 9.4 offers a state-by-state analysis of employer firm terminations for those years. Some states saw a decline in the number of businesses closed, including Alaska, California, Delaware, the District of Columbia, Illinois, Indiana, Kansas, Louisiana, Maryland, Michigan, Minnesota, Missouri, Nevada, New Mexico, New York, North Dakota, Oregon, Pennsylvania, Tennessee, Texas, Utah, Virginia, Washington, and Wisconsin. Arizona saw a dramatic rise in the number of business closures, from 18,249 in 2005 to 52,375 in 2006, a 187% increase.

DEMOGRAPHICS OF SMALL BUSINESSES

O'Rourke, in *Useful Business Statistics* for BizStats ("Industry Sales by Type of Firm [Sole Proprietorship]"), provides a view of the spectrum of the 17.6 million sole proprietorships operating in the United States during 2003 by number within broad business type

category and by monetary receipts. When taken together, these businesses had receipts totaling $969.3 billion in 2003. Broad categories include professional, scientific, and technical services; health care and social assistance; information; wholesale trade; retail trade; accommodation and food services; construction; manufacturing; transportation and warehousing; finance and insurance; real estate and rental industries; other services; and agriculture, forestry, and fishing.

The most numerous sole proprietorships in 2003 were special trade construction contractors, with nearly 1.8 million businesses; administrative and support services operators, with 1.4 million sole proprietorships; personal and laundry services operators (1.1. million); and nonstore retailers, operating more than one million businesses. Businesses with the most receipts included special trade contractors ($101.1 billion), residential building construction ($38 billion), investment advice and other investment activities ($37.8 billion), administrative and support services ($36.1 billion), and real estate agents, brokers, managers, and appraisers ($34 billion).

Nonemployer Businesses

The U.S. Census Bureau, in *Nonemployer Statistics, 2005*, reported that nearly 20.4 million businesses in the United States were operated that year by the owners alone with no other workers. (Sole proprietorships, discussed above, are businesses with a single owner that can have few or many employees.) As defined by the Census Bureau, nonemployer businesses have no paid employees, have annual receipts of at least $1,000, and are subject to federal income taxes. The 2005 national total represented a growth of about 4.6% over the 19.5 million nonemployer businesses counted the previous year.

Nonemployer Statistics, 2005 reported that these businesses accounted for over $951 billion in receipts during 2005. Sectors that provided the largest shares of receipts among nonemployer businesses in 2005 included real estate and rental and leasing ($207.7 billion, or 21.8%); construction ($153.8 billion, or 16.2%); professional, scientific, and technical services ($118.6 billion, or 12.5%); and retail trade ($83.6 billion, or 8.8%). The lowest receipts for nonemployer businesses were in utilities, with $671.3 million.

Home-based Businesses

A home-based business, as defined by the SBA, is "a business that is conducted out of a residence with no other headquarters location." According to researcher Harry B. R. Beale of Microeconomic Applications Inc. in *Home-Based Business and Government Regulation* for the SBA (February 2004, http://www.sba.gov/advo/research/rs235tot.pdf), home-based businesses make up about half of all U.S. businesses. More than two-thirds of

TABLE 9.4

Business turnover by state, 2005–06

	Firm births		Firm terminations		Business bankruptcies	
	2005	2006	2005	2006	2005	2006
U.S. total	653,100 e.	649,700 e.	543,700 e.	564,900 e.	39.201	19.695
Alabama	10,575	10,096	10,168	11,128	331	219
Alaska	1,982	1,904	2,294	2,239	83	45
Arizona	21,339	21,555	18,249	52,375	525	261
Arkansas	7,591	9,551	7,021	7,289	426	276
California	121,482	115,684	151,944	149,212	4,236	2,098
Colorado	26,610	22,708	14,035	24,158	1,120	435
Connecticut	9,220	9,516	11,131	11,214	156	219
Delaware	3,299	3,153	3,355	3,295	218	244
District of Columbia	4,316	4,232	3,952	3,111	46	27
Florida	84,890	79,870	58,737	64,423	1,622	991
Georgia	29,804	31,677	29,315	29,787	2,232	1,148
Hawaii	3,763	3,813	3,794	3,789	81	25
Idaho	9,312	9,159	6,334	6,713	141	56
Illinois	30,445	30,230	32,846	33,426	1,042	669
Indiana	14,545	14,653	16,504	13,851	758	376
Iowa	6,004	5,877	6,802	7,248	455	208
Kansas	7,095	6,973	7,330	7,000	410	158
Kentucky	9,617	8,973	8,515	10,230	409	200
Louisiana	9,393	11,034	9,123	8,972	718	476
Maine	4,251	4,497	4,711	4,769	144	85
Maryland	22,083	21,535	21,769	20,745	760	333
Massachusetts	19,723	17,800	18,878	22,376	406	253
Michigan	24,642	23,508	26,971	21,268	1,071	753
Minnesota	12,555	13,739	15,302	14,403	1,721	381
Mississippi	6,071	6,862	6,823	7,898	200	187
Missouri	17,239	15,805	20,109	18,124	438	284
Montana	4,768	4,727	4,394	4,469	129	39
Nebraska	5,127	4,820	4,982	5,117	296	182
Nevada	11,299	10,743	8,485	8,423	333	178
New Hampshire	4,758	4,703	5,406	5,481	586	218
New Jersey	33,022	36,258	32,751	32,959	765	493
New Mexico	5,272	5,536	5,670	5,274	828	95
New York	62,045	61,718	62,667	61,190	2,112	1,201
North Carolina	25,906	26,729	22,867	23,165	612	403
North Dakota	1,893	1,821	2,512	2,181	95	32
Ohio	22,542	22,213	23,429	25,412	2,099	957
Oklahoma	8,609	9,962	7,231	7,829	944	236
Oregon	14,445	15,085	14,804	14,039	1,160	301
Pennsylvania	36,609	34,928	36,989	35,805	1,356	742
Rhode Island	3,677	3,739	4,164	4,572	136	48
South Carolina	12,341	12,373	10,681	11,661	176	82
South Dakota	2,102	2,003	2,354	2,449	196	47
Tennessee	17,484	17,207	17,135	16,395	574	397
Texas	55,858	58,943	55,039	54,479	3,590	2,081
Utah	11,536	13,379	11,871	11,190	449	148
Vermont	1,911	1,957	2,346	2,365	78	36
Virginia	25,061	23,686	21,359	20,972	476	283
Washington	30,353	32,726	40,944	36,331	786	401
West Virginia	3,493	3,823	4,869	4,854	282	114
Wisconsin	13,656	13,371	13,397	13,060	820	307
Wyoming	2,632	2,570	2,689	2,773	84	40

Notes: State birth and termination totals do not add to the U.S. figure as firms can be in more than one state. U.S. estimates are based on U.S. Census Bureau and Department of Labor, Employment and Training Administration data. Some terminations reflected in the state data may result in successor firms not listed as new firms. Data for total bankruptcies include territories.
e. = estimate.

SOURCE: "Table A.5. Business Turnover by State, 2005–2006," in *The Small Business Economy 2007*, U.S. Small Business Administration, Office of Advocacy, December 2007, http://www.sba.gov/advo/research/sb_econ2007.pdf (accessed February 21, 2008).

sole proprietorships, partnerships, and S corporations are based in owners' homes.

The BLS, in *Work at Home in 2004* (September 22, 2005, http://www.bls.gov/news.release/pdf/homey.pdf), found that in 2004 approximately seven million Americans had home-based businesses. About 1.7 million (23.8%) were in professional or business services, 1.1 million (15.6%) were in construction, and one million were in wholesale and retail trade (14.5%). Smaller numbers of people were employed in education and health services (885,000, or 12.7%), financial activities (848,000, or 12.2%), leisure and hospitality (452,000, or 6.5%), manufacturing (271,000, or 3.9%), transportation and utilities (181,000, or 1%), and information services (181,000, or 1%).

According to Beale, most home-based business owners work alone. Nine out of ten home-based businesses have no employees; 7.2% have between one and five employees; 1% report having five to nineteen employees; and 0.2% have twenty employees or more. In addition, most of these businesses are quite small in terms of receipts. Most (77%) have gross receipts less than $25,000, and 96% have gross receipts less than $50,000. Only 3.5% report receipts of $100,000 or more.

The 1999 U.S. Small Business Advocacy report *Home-based Business: The Hidden Economy* by Joanne H. Pratt (http://www.sba.gov/advo/research/rs194tot.pdf) gathered information from 125,000 businesses and remains the most extensive consideration of the demographics of home-based business in the United States. Included in the sample were businesses owned by women (33%); by non-Hispanic white men (59%); by African-Americans (3%); by Hispanics (4%); and by "other minorities," mainly Asian and Pacific Islanders and Native Americans or Alaska Natives (4%).

Based on 24.8 million nonfarm business tax forms filed in 1998, the SBA report estimated that the number of home-based businesses had increased between 11% and 33% (from nine million to ten–twelve million) between 1992 and 1999. Among home-based businesses, 90% were sole proprietorships; only 2.1% were franchises. More than 86% of home-based businesses were run by the founder, compared with 72% of businesses run by the founder that were not based in homes. According to Pratt in the SBA report *The Impact of Location on Net Income: A Comparison of Homebased and Non-Homebased Sole Proprietors*, May 2006, http://www.sba.gov/advo/research/rs275tot.pdf), home-based sole proprietors earned, on average, less than nonhome-based sole proprietors, although they generated $102 billion in 2002.

Minority Businesses

According to a report within the U.S. Census Bureau's 2002 Survey of Business Owners (*Characteristics of Businesses: 2002*, September 2006, http://www.census.gov/csd/sbo/cbsummaryoffindings.htm), most business owners in the United States were white, non-Hispanic individuals. Only 6.8% of business owners were of Hispanic origin, even though, as reported in the Census Bureau's national population estimates (May 17, 2007, http://www.census.gov/popest/national/asrh/NC-EST2006-srh.html), the U.S. population was 11.1% Hispanic. African-Americans represented only 5.2% of business owners, while 11.6% of the U.S. population was African-American. Only 0.9% of business owners were Native American or Alaska Native, compared with 1.3% of the U.S. population. Among minority groups, only Asian-Americans, who represented 4.8% of business

owners, were overrepresented in comparison with their presence in the U.S. population (4.4%). Minorities were even more underrepresented among business owners who owned firms with paid employees.

Impact of the Internet

The ability of consultants, graphic designers, writers, editors, and others to provide their services via the Internet, and of employees to perform some or all of their work from home, has created a new business category: telecommuting. It has been difficult to determine the exact number of telecommuters in the United States, but various estimates indicate that within the first decade of the twenty-first century, tens of millions of Americans worked exclusively via telecommuting. In 2003, according to data from the BLS in *Computer and Internet Use at Work in 2003* (August 10, 2005, http://www.bls.gov/news.release/pdf/ciuaw.pdf), 55.5% of American workers reported using a computer during their job, with approximately 40% of employed Americans using the Internet as part of their job.

Pratt, writing again for the SBA in *E-Biz: Strategies for Small Business Success* (October 2002, http://www.sba.gov/advo/research/rs220tot.pdf), reported that e-mail is the most frequently used feature of the Internet among business owners. Thirty-six percent of women and 38% of men say they use e-mail very frequently. More than half of both men and women characterized their e-mail use as either occasional or somewhat frequent. Less than 10% of business owners said they never used e-mail. After e-mail, the most common reason that business owners said they used the Internet was to transmit files or documents; 22% of women and 25% of men reported that they use the Internet for this purpose very frequently.

For most other business-related activities, including conducting fact-finding research, selling products or services, purchasing products or services, and seeking business opportunities, Internet usage was generally rated as occasional or somewhat frequent, if at all, by business owners surveyed by the SBA. The Internet capabilities least likely to be used by business owners included conducting online meetings (more than 80% said "never") and recruiting or hiring employees.

WEB-BASED BUSINESSES. According to Plunkett Research Inc. (http://www.plunkettresearch.com/Industries/AdvertisingandBranding/advertisingandbrandingtrends/tabid/84/Default.aspx), in December 2007 there were ninety million home and business broadband Internet connections in the United States. Broadband connections enable the rapid transmission and use of text and graphics from the Internet. With this expanding popularity of high speed connections and use of the Internet, businesses that cater to Internet users and to people or companies running a business over the Internet—known as e-commerce—have grown. Examples of goods and services available to help Internet users include Web-hosting Internet sites (which provide storage, connectivity, and services needed to manage the files of a Web site), Internet software, virtual assistants (where services such as accounting, meeting organization, secretarial, and even some administration are provided to an existing business), e-mail marketing, and Web-site design. Because some of these services can be provided using home-based computer systems, Web-based businesses designed to serve Internet users have become very popular as a part-time occupation for homemakers or as a full-time, home-based occupation.

Maintaining an Internet site is not a complex undertaking. If the site is popular and is visited by many people, it provides an attractive forum for advertisers, which increases revenue for the site owner/business owner. In 2007 online advertising revenues on Internet sites in the United States generated close to $25 billion, according to Plunkett Research. Furthermore, retail sales over the Internet are rising. According to figures from the Department of Commerce in the *U.S. Census Bureau News* ("Quarterly Retail E-Commerce Sales," February 15, 2008, http://www.census.gov/mrts/www/data/pdf/07Q4.pdf), U.S. retail e-commerce sales in the last quarter of 2007 were $36.2 billion, an increase of 4.6% over the previous quarter and an increase of 18% from the fourth quarter of 2006. Such figures indicated an area of the American economy that offered favorable opportunities to small business operators working through the Internet.

IMPORTANT NAMES AND ADDRESSES

AFL-CIO (American Federation of Labor–Congress of Industrial Organizations)
815 16th St., NW
Washington, DC 20006
(202) 637-5000
URL: http://www.aflcio.org

American Staffing Association
277 S. Washington St., Ste. 200
Alexandria, VA 22314
(703) 253-2020
FAX: (703) 253-2053
E-mail: asa@americanstaffing.net
URL: http://www.americanstaffing.net

Center for Women's Business Research
1411 K St. NW, Ste. 1350
Washington, DC 20005-3407
(202) 638-3060
FAX: (202) 638-3064
E-mail: info@womensbusinessresearch.org
URL: http://www.nfwbo.org

Employment and Training Administration
U.S. Department of Labor
Frances Perkins Bldg.
200 Constitution Ave. NW
Washington, DC 20210
1-877-US-2JOBS
URL: http://www.doleta.gov

Employment Standards Administration
U.S. Department of Labor
Frances Perkins Bldg.
200 Constitution Ave. NW
Washington, DC 20210
1-866-4-USA-DOL
FAX: (703) 997-4890
URL: http://www.dol.gov/esa

Equal Employment Opportunity Commission
1801 L St. NW
Washington, DC 20507

(202) 663-4900
1-800-669-4000
URL: http://www.eeoc.gov

Families and Work Institute
267 Fifth Ave., Floor 2
New York, NY 10016
(212) 465-2044
FAX: (212) 465-8637
URL: http://www.familiesandwork.org

National Association of Manufacturers
1331 Pennsylvania Ave. NW
Washington, DC 20004-1790
(202) 637-3000
FAX: (202) 637-3182
E-mail: manufacturing@nam.org
URL: http://www.nam.org

National Center for Health Statistics
3311 Toledo Rd.
Hyattsville, MD 20782
(301) 458-4000
1-800-232-4636
URL: http://www.cdc.gov/nchs

National Labor Relations Board
1099 14th St. NW
Washington, DC 20570-0001
(202) 273-1991
1-866-667-NLRB
FAX: (202) 273-1789
URL: http://www.nlrb.gov

National Safety Council
1121 Spring Lake Dr.
Itasca, IL 60143-3201
(630) 285-1121
FAX: (630) 285-1315
E-mail: info@nsc.org
URL: http://www.nsc.org

Occupational Safety and Health Administration (OSHA)
U.S. Department of Labor
200 Constitution Ave. NW
Washington, DC 20210
1-800-321-OSHA
URL: http://www.osha.gov

Society for Human Resource Management
1800 Duke St.
Alexandria, VA 22314
(703) 548-3440
1-800-283-SHRM
FAX: (703) 535-6490
E-mail: shrm@shrm.org
URL: http://www.shrm.org

U.S. Bureau of Labor Statistics
U.S. Department of Labor
Postal Square Building
2 Massachusetts Ave. NE
Washington, DC 20212-0001
(202) 691-5200
FAX: (202) 691-6325
E-mail: blsdata_staff@bls.gov
URL: http://www.bls.gov

U.S. Census Bureau
4600 Silver Hill Rd.
Washington, DC 20233-0001
(301) 763-3030
FAX: (301) 457-3670
E-mail: comments@census.gov
URL: http://www.census.gov

U.S. Chamber of Commerce
1615 H St. NW
Washington, DC 20062-2000
(202) 659-6000
URL: http://www.uschamber.com

U.S. Department of Commerce
1401 Constitution Ave. NW
Washington, DC 20230
(202) 482-2000

FAX: (202) 482-5168
E-mail: webmaster@doc.gov
URL: http://www.commerce.gov

U.S. Department of Education
400 Maryland Ave. SW
Washington, DC 20202
1-800-USA-LEARN

FAX: (202) 401-0689
E-mail: customerservice@inet.ed.gov
URL: http://www.ed.gov

U.S. Department of Labor
Frances Perkins Bldg.
200 Constitution Ave. NW
Washington, DC 20210

(202) 693-4676
1-866-4-USA-DOL
URL: http://www.dol.gov

U.S. Small Business Administration
1-800-U-ASK-SBA
E-mail: answerdesk@sba.gov
URL: http://www.sba.gov/

RESOURCES

The Bureau of Labor Statistics (BLS), a branch of the U.S. Department of Labor, is an important source of information on employment and unemployment in the United States. *Employment and Earnings*, an annual BLS publication, gives complete statistics on employment in the United States. *The Employment Situation* is released monthly to give more current statistics on employment and unemployment. In addition, the BLS publishes the *Monthly Labor Review*, which contains articles on issues relating to jobs and how workers are affected by changes in the labor market. The *Monthly Labor Review* also provides historical data and supplies information on employee benefits, including medical and life insurance, disability insurance, and retirement.

The BLS also publishes periodic reports on special issues in employment. Reports used in this book include *A Profile of the Working Poor, 2005* (September 2007); *National Compensation Survey: Employee Benefits in Private Industry in the United States* (August 2007); and *A Chartbook of International Labor Comparisons: The Americas, Asia-Pacific, Europe* (January 2008). The BLS News Service periodically examines special issues in employment as well. Reports used in this book include *College Enrollment and Work Activity of 2006 High School Graduates* (April 2007); *Employment Characteristics of Families in 2006* (May 2007); *Employee Tenure in 2006* (September 2006); *Union Members in 2007* (January 2008); *Workplace Injuries and Illnesses in 2006* (October 2007); *National Census of Fatal Occupational Injuries in 2006* (August 2007); *Worker Displacement, 2003–2005* (August 2006); *Survey of Workplace Violence Prevention, 2005* (October 2006); *Productivity and Costs* (February 2008); *Regional and State Employment and*

Unemployment: December 2007 (January 2008); *Employment Projections: 2006–16* (December 2007); and *American Time Use Survey—2006 Results* (June 2007).

The BLS biennial *Occupational Outlook Handbook* is one of the most complete sources on jobs available. The 2008–09 edition of the handbook outlines future job projections to 2016. It also provides detailed descriptions of most jobs and directs the reader to further information. The *Occupational Outlook Quarterly*, published by the BLS, contains valuable articles on employment and the labor market.

The U.S. Department of Education also publishes research on education and its relationship to career opportunities and earnings potential. This book particularly relied on *Digest of Education Statistics, 2007* (September 2007). The U.S. Equal Employment Opportunity Commission (EEOC) publishes *Enforcement Statistics and Litigation* on an annual basis, which provides information on cases filed with the EEOC under antidiscrimination and sexual harassment statutes.

The U.S. Census Bureau, a branch of the U.S. Department of Commerce, is a major source of information about the American people. Some of its studies concern employment and employee earnings. Helpful publications from the U.S. Census Bureau include *Income, Poverty, and Health Insurance Coverage in the United States: 2006* (August 2007). The U.S. Small Business Administration offers a library of free publications, including fact sheets and startup guidelines for current and prospective business owners. Especially helpful in preparing this book was *The Small Business Economy 2007* (December 2007).

INDEX

Page references in italics refer to photographs. References with the letter t following them indicate the presence of a table. The letter f indicates a figure. If more than one table or figure appears on a particular page, the exact item number for the table or figure being referenced is provided.

A

ADA (Americans with Disabilities Act), 120, 122t
Adams, Jennifer Ann, 51
Addresses/names of organizations, 135–136
Administrative occupations, 84
Adolescents, unemployment for, 42, 43
AFL-CIO (American Federation of Labor–Congress of Industrial Organizations), 21, 135
African-Americans
    at-home work by, 29
    business ownership, 133
    college enrollment, 52, 57
    degrees awarded to, 57, 59
    earnings of full-time, year-round workers, 89
    education, labor force participation and, 7
    employment by occupation, 11
    families, employment characteristics of, 7
    jobs, number held, 20
    labor force participation by, 1, 59
    labor force participation by, future projections, 69–70
    poverty rates, education and, 64
    self-employment of, 127
    shift schedules and, 34–35
    unemployment for, 42, 43–44, 47
    as union members, 23
    work schedules, flexible, 33
    working poor, 14
AFSCME (American Federation of State, County, and Municipal Employees), 21
AFT (American Federation of Teachers), 21

Age
    college enrollment of older students, 52
    of contingent workers, 13
    discrimination in workplace, 120, 121 (t8.5)
    employee tenure and, 18–19
    employment status of population, by sex, age, race, 4t
    of labor force, future projections, 67
    labor force and, 3–5
    labor force status of persons aged 16 to 24 years old, 5t
    poverty status of people in labor force for 27 weeks or more, by age, sex, race/ethnicity, 15t
    unemployed persons by, 43t, 46t
    unemployment, duration of, 47, 48–49
    unemployment and, 42, 43–44
    of workers with alternative arrangements, 14
    working poor and, 14
Age Discrimination in Employment Act of 1967, 120
Alaska, unemployment rate in, 41
Alcohol testing, 124
Alternative work arrangements
    contingent worker characteristics, 12–13
    reasons for, 11–12
    types of, 13–14
American Federation of Labor–Congress of Industrial Organizations (AFL-CIO), 21, 135
American Federation of State, County, and Municipal Employees (AFSCME), 21
American Federation of Teachers (AFT), 21
American Management Association, 125
American Staffing Association, 135
American Time Use Survey—2006 Results (BLS), 30, 32
Americans with Disabilities Act (ADA), 120, 122t
Application. *See* Job application

Arnold, David W., 125
Asian-Americans
    at-home work by, 29
    business ownership, 133
    college enrollment, 52, 57
    earnings of full-time, year-round workers, 89
    education, labor force participation and, 7
    employment by occupation, 11
    families, employment characteristics of, 7
    labor force participation by, 1, 59
    labor force participation by, future projections, 69, 70
    poverty rates, education and, 64
    self-employment of, 127
    shift schedules and, 35
    unemployment, duration of, 47
    unemployment for, 42, 43, 44
    as union members, 23
    working poor, 14
Associate degrees, 57, 81f
Association of Personnel Test Publishers, 125
At-home work
    employed persons working at home, at workplace, time spent working at each location, 33t
    time spent at work, 30–31
    trends in, 29
    See also Home-based businesses

B

Bachelor's degrees
    conferred by race/ethnicity, sex of student, 58t
    by discipline, 59
    earnings and, 61, 64
    increase in adults with, 52
    number awarded, 57
    occupations with most growth that require, 80f
    projected job growth and, 77

discrimination in workplace, 118–119
displaced workers by, 36
earnings and, 89, 91*t*–97*t*
education, earnings and, 61
education, poverty rate and, 14, 16
employed persons by occupation, race, Hispanic ethnicity, sex, 12*t*–13*t*
employment status of population by, 2 (*t*1.2), 6*t*–7*t*
high school dropouts and, 59
of labor force, future projections, 67–69
labor force and, 1
labor force participation by, 3, 59, 69 (*f*5.2)
multiple jobs by, 35
occupations of working poor and, 16
persons at work by occupation, sex, usual full- or part-time status, 31*t*
poverty status of people in labor force by, 15*t*, 16*t*
shift schedules and, 34
tenure and, 18–19
time spent at work, 30
unemployed persons by age, sex, race/ethnicity, marital status, duration of unemployment, 46*t*
unemployed persons by marital status, race, Hispanic ethnicity, age, sex, 43*t*
unemployed persons by occupation, sex, 45*t*
unemployment and, 42, 43–46, 47–48
union membership and, 23
working poor and, 14
"The Gender Wage Gap and Pay Equity: Is Comparable Worth the Next Step?" (Levine), 61
"The G.I. Bill and the Changing Place of U.S. Higher Education after World War II" (Adams), 51
G.I. Bill of Rights, 51
Goods-producing industries
benefits in, 97
employment projections, 71–72, 74
people employed in, 9
shift to service-producing industries, 27–29
work schedules, flexible, 34
Government employees
AFSCME labor union for, 21
benefits for, 97
jobs in government, 27–28
polygraph testing of, 124
tenure of, 19
work schedules, flexible, 34
Gross domestic product (GDP), 70
Guide to American Directories, 107

H

Harassment, sexual
charges filed with EEOC, state/local Fair Employment Practices agencies, 123*t*
in workplace, 122

Health care
employment projections for, 71
expenditures, projected increase of, 70
projected job growth, education and, 77
small businesses in, 130
Health savings accounts, 98
Health-care benefits
family coverage medical plans in private industry, 101*t*
for government employees, 97
percent of workers in private industry with access to, 102*t*
in private industry, 98–99
single coverage medical plans in private industry, 100*t*
workers in private industry with access to/participation in, 99*t*
Health-care reimbursement accounts, 98
"Help Wanted" advertisements, 108
High school
completion, unemployment and, 59
completion rates, 52
earnings and education, 61
poverty rates and, 64
High school dropouts
earnings of, 61
labor force status of, 59, 62*t*–63*t*
Higher education. *See* College
Highlights of Women's Earnings in 2006 (BLS), 70
Highway incidents, fatal, 115, 117*f*
Hirsch, Barry T., 21
Hispanics
at-home work by, 29
business ownership, 133
college enrollment, 52, 57
degrees awarded to, 57, 59
earnings of full-time, year-round workers, 89
education, labor force participation and, 7
employment by occupation, 11
employment status of Hispanic population, by sex, age, detailed ethnic group, 3*t*
families, employment characteristics of, 7
jobs, number held, 20
labor force, percent growth in, by Hispanic ethnicity, projected 2006–16, 69 (*f*5.4)
labor force participation by, 1, 59
labor force participation by, future projections, 69, 70
poverty rates, education and, 64
self-employment of, 127
shift schedules and, 35
unemployment for, 43, 44, 47
as union members, 23
work schedules, flexible, 33
working poor, 14

Historical Income Tables (U.S. Census Bureau), 89
Holidays, paid, 97–98
Home-Based Business and Government Regulation (Beale), 131–132, 133
Homebased Business: The Hidden Economy (Pratt), 133
Home-based businesses, 131–133
Homicide, 115, 117*f*
Honesty testing, 124–125
"Hostile work environment" sexual harassment, 122
HotJobs Web site, 108
Hours
employed persons working, time spent working on days worked, 32*t*
employed persons working at home, at workplace, time spent working at each location, 33*t*
flexibility of, 35*f*, 111
hours worked per employed person, annual, international comparison of, 30*f*
part-time work, persons at work 1 to 34 hours per week, 37 (*t*2.7)
persons at work by occupation, sex, usual full- or part-time status, 31*t*
time spent at work, 29–32
workers' hours, survey of, 32–33
workers' rights, 113–114
"Hours of Work in U.S. History" (Whaples), 32
Household income
definition of, 89
earnings of full-time, year-round workers, 89
income/earnings by selected characteristics, 90*t*

I

Idaho, unemployment rate in, 42
Ilg, Randy E., 32
Illnesses, occupational
compensation for, 116–117
incidence rates of, 116*f*
statistics on, 115–116
The Impact of Location on Net Income: A Comparison of Homebased and Non-Homebased Sole Proprietors (Pratt), 133
Income, 89
See also Earnings; Wages
Income, Earnings, and Poverty Data from the 2006 American Community Survey (U.S. Census Bureau), 89
"Increase in At-Home Workers Reverses Earlier Trend" (U.S. Census Bureau), 29
Independent contractors (freelancers), 12–14
Individual income, 89
Industry
change in wage/salary employment by industry sector, projected 2006–16, 71 (*f*5.5)

mass layoff activity, measures of extended, 38t

multiple jobholders by selected demographic, economic characteristics, 36t

nonfatal occupational injuries/illnesses, incidence rates of, 116f

occupations, thirty with largest number of job openings, projected 2006–16, 79t

occupations, thirty-fastest growing, 77t

occupations with high fatality rates, 118f

occupations with most growth that require associate degree or postsecondary vocational award, projected 2006–16, 81f

occupations with most growth that require bachelor's degree, projected 2006–16, 80f

occupations with most growth that require short- or moderate-term on-the-job training, projected 2006–16, 83f

occupations with most growth that require work experience or long-term on-the-job training, projected 2006–16, 82f

part-time work, persons at work 1 to 34 hours per week, 37 (t2.7)

persons at work by occupation, sex, usual full- or part-time status, 31t

population/labor force, 1996, 2006, projected 2016, 68f

poverty status of families by presence of related children, work experience of family members, type of family, 18t

poverty status of people in labor force for 27 weeks or more, 15t

poverty status of people in labor force for 27 weeks or more, by educational attainment, race/ethnicity, sex, 16t

poverty status of people in labor force for 27 weeks or more, by occupation of longest job held, race/ethnicity, 17t

poverty status of workers by educational attainment, race/ethnicity, sex, 66t

productivity, annual average changes in, 37 (t2.8)

public opinion on job satisfaction, 111t

public opinion on satisfaction with amount of on-the-job stress in employment, 111f

public opinion on satisfaction with flexibility of hours, 35f

race-based charges filed/resolved under Title VII of Civil Rights Act of 1964, 121 (t8.4)

security, percent of establishments/ employment, by type of security, size of establishment, 120t

self-employed workers, occupations with most, projected 2016, 87f

self-employment demographics, 128 (t9.1)

sexual harassment charges filed with EEOC, state/local Fair Employment Practices agencies, 123t

small business owners' perception of success, 130f

tenure with current employer for employed wage/salary workers, by age/ sex, median years of, 19t

tenure with current employer for employed wage/salary workers, by industry, median years of, 20t–21t

time spent in primary activities, percent of civilian population engaging in each activity, 34t

unemployed jobseekers by sex, reason for unemployment, active job search methods used, 107t

unemployed persons by age, sex, race/ ethnicity, marital status, duration of unemployment, 46t

unemployed persons by marital status, race, Hispanic ethnicity, age, sex, 43t

unemployed persons by occupation, industry, duration of unemployment, 48t

unemployed persons by occupation, sex, 45t

unemployed persons by reason for unemployment, sex, age, 49t

unemployment, persons not in labor force, by desire/availability for work, age, sex, 50t

unemployment, states with rates significantly different from U.S. as a whole, 42t

unemployment in families, by presence/ relationship of employed members, 9t

unemployment rate, seasonally adjusted, 42f

unemployment rate of persons 16 years old and over, by age, sex, race/ ethnicity, educational attainment, 61t

union affiliation of employed wage/ salary workers, 24t

wage/salary employment by detailed industry, decline in, projected 2006–16, 72f

wage/salary employment by detailed industry, numeric growth in, projected 2006–16, 74f

wage/salary employment by industry sector, change in, projected 2006–16, 71 (f5.5)

wage/salary employment by industry sector, percent change in, projected 2006–16, 71 (f5.6)

workplace violence incident, percent of establishments that have experienced, 119t

work-related fatal events, four most frequent, 117f

Stress

career choice and, 106

job satisfaction of workers, 111, 111f

Struck by object incidents, 115, 117f

Structure, of small business, 129

Student financial aid, 105

Student workers, 5

Subchapter S corporations, 127

Success, small business owners' perception of, 130, 130f

T

Taft-Hartley Act, 123

Taxes, 101

Technology

employment by industry and, 70

information technology workers, demand for, 76–78

use of workers and, 75

Teenagers, unemployment for, 42, 43

Telecommuting, 133

Telephone use, monitoring of, 125

Temporary help agency workers

employment for, 70

work of, 13, 14

Tenure

by industry, 19

median years of tenure with current employer for employed wage/salary workers, by age/sex, 19t

median years of tenure with current employer for employed wage/salary workers, by industry, 20t–21t

number of jobs held and, 19–20, 22t–23t

trends in, 17–19

Testing

by employer, 124–125

for job, 110

Thiemann, Alan J., 125

Ticket to Work and Work Incentives Improvement Act (TWWIIA), 122

Time

employed persons working, time spent working on days worked, 32t

employed persons working at home, at workplace, time spent working at each location, 33t

hours worked per employed person, annual, international comparison of, 30f

persons at work by occupation, sex, usual full- or part-time status, 31t

public opinion on satisfaction with flexibility of hours, 35f

schedules, flexible work, 33–34

schedules, shift, 34–35

spent at work, 29–32

spent in primary activities, percent of civilian population engaging in each activity, 34t

unemployed persons by age, sex, race/ ethnicity, marital status, duration of unemployment, 46t